NEWSPAPER
COVERAGE
of
INTERETHNIC
CONFLICT

NEWSPAPER COVERAGE *of* INTERETHNIC CONFLICT

Competing Visions of America

HEMANT SHAH
MICHAEL C. THORNTON

SAGE Publications
International Educational and Professional Publisher
Thousand Oaks ▪ London ▪ New Delhi

For information:

Sage Publications, Inc.
2455 Teller Road
Thousand Oaks, California 91320
E-mail: order@sagepub.com

Sage Publications Ltd.
6 Bonhill Street
London EC2A 4PU
United Kingdom

Sage Publications India Pvt. Ltd.
B-42, Panchsheel Enclave
Post Box 4109
New Delhi 110 017 India

Printed in the United States of America

Library of Congress Cataloging-in-Publication Data

Shah, Hemant, 1957-
Competing visions of America / by Hemant Shah and Michael C. Thornton.
     p. cm.
Includes bibliographical references and index.
ISBN 0-8039-7231-8 (Cloth) — ISBN 0-8039-7232-6 (Paper)
   1. Minorities-Press coverage-United States. 2. Ethnic press-United States.
I. Thornton, Michael Charles. II. Title.
PN4888.M56S48 2003
070.4′4930556—dc211

                                2003009043

Printed on acid-free paper

03   04   05   06   07   08   09   10   9   8   7   6   5   4   3   2   1

Acquiring Editor:	Margaret H. Seawell
Editorial Assistant:	Alicia Carter
Production Editor:	Claudia A. Hoffman
Copy Editor:	Mary L. Tederstrom
Typesetter:	C&M Digitals (P) Ltd.
Indexer:	Molly Hall

Contents

Preface

This book studies how the press depicts tensions among non-White ethnic groups (specifically, Blacks, Latinos, and Asian Americans) in three U.S. cities. This topic has become important for general circulation and ethnic minority newspapers and their audiences as global migration patterns and changing demographics in the United States heighten racially based anxieties for established White and Black communities alike. Not long ago, White racial anxiety in the United States was primarily about Black power—social, political, and cultural. Now, White communities are also anxious about the increasing presence of "strangers" from Asia and Latin America, who are sometimes viewed as threats to core American values—however nebulously defined those might be. In recent years, as new immigrants from Asia and Latin America establish footholds in urban areas, poorer Black communities also are feeling racial anxiety as Asians and Latinos begin competing with Blacks for jobs, bank loans, housing, and other resources. And many people in both Black and White communities feel threatened culturally by an increasingly complex mix of languages, foods, and communication styles that now characterize America's major cities.

Although this cultural turmoil bubbles within and between Black and White communities, the media often ignore the voices of Asian Americans and Latinos, giving the impression that these communities are silent on the subject of cultural anxiety. In reality, these communities too are anxious about how they fit into the predominant racial vision of America, what being American means to their communities, and the fear their presence seems to generate among other ethnic groups. Asians and Latinos in the United States are often taken by surprise when White and Black Americans view them as a threat: for example, the Korean American community's utter disbelief when Blacks attacked their properties in Los Angeles. Often, Asian American and Latino communities are left wondering if and under what conditions they will ever fit in as Americans and with what other communities they could find comfortable alliances.

Recent interethnic conflicts in U.S. cities illustrate these issues in many ways. Given that most people learn about race relations from mass media sources, news coverage of these issues and events has an important impact on the way readers perceive both racial minority groups and Whites, imagine a more diverse America, and understand the complexities of the racial dimension of American life. The representation of interethnic conflict is also important for understanding the role of news media in the process of racial formation—a process at the heart of the interplay between the symbolic and material dimensions of race relations—and, inevitably, the very organization of society. To address these issues and how they are represented in the news media, we examined how newspapers covered interethnic conflicts in Miami in 1989, Washington, D.C., in 1991, and Los Angeles in 1992.

Our interest in this topic was piqued in the wake of the 1990 Black boycotts of Korean-owned businesses in New York. Several subsequent incidents sustained our interest in interethnic conflict. First, there were multiethnic riots in Washington, D.C., in May 1991, involving Blacks and Latinos, and in Los Angeles following the announcement of the not-guilty verdicts in the trial of four Los Angeles police officers who had beaten Rodney King in March 1992. Second, police violence directed specifically at Blacks sparked disturbances in Black communities in Indianapolis in July 1995 and in Cincinnati in April 2001. Then, in summer 2001 there was a series of conflicts in England, where South Asian immigrants clashed with police and local White residents in the cities of Oldham, Birmingham, and Bradford. In each of these cases, a potent mixture of immigrant communities clashing with established ones, tense relations between police and ethnic minority communities, unresponsive or ineffective local government, and domination of key institutions by Whites contributed to the disturbances. In the British cases, another factor was right-wing political parties using racist rhetoric to incite anti-Asian violence during parliamentary elections.

In the case of the U.S.-based incidents, the general circulation press covered the events fairly heavily. Ethnic minority papers, however, reported the events unevenly or sometimes not at all, even when the communities they primarily served were directly affected. For example, some Black and Asian American papers gave virtually no attention to the Black boycott of Korean-owned stores in New York City. Similarly, although the general circulation press covered the Washington, D.C., disturbance, the local Black press gave the events extremely limited coverage. The Black press outside the area often failed to mention the events at all. The only event to receive widespread attention from all news media was the Los Angeles disturbance in spring 1992.

This pattern of coverage highlights the newspapers' tendency to focus on race as conflict. This tendency had an impact on the way we conceptualized the research for this book. Our original intent was to examine everything the press wrote about interethnic relations, but we soon discovered that for the news media this meant relations of conflict and, most commonly, outbreaks of rioting. Ultimately, this pattern of coverage forced us to change the parameters from an effort to investigate news coverage of all interethnic relations to a focus on the coverage of three interethnic conflicts.

We wish to acknowledge several people who helped ensure the completion of this book. James P. Danky, head of the periodicals section of the State Historical Society library on the campus of the University of Wisconsin, is the leading bibliographer of ethnic minority media in the country. In addition, his award-winning work on print culture in the United States has been recognized as an important scholarly contribution. Nevertheless, Danky was more than generous with his time and gave us important advice for obtaining samples of the ethnic minority newspapers that we needed for our project. Ellen Burke, the librarian at the State Historical Society library in charge of interlibrary loans, helped us obtain a number of ethnic minority newspapers from libraries across the country. The Asian American Studies Center library at the University of California, Los Angeles, was a key source for many of the articles from Asian American newspapers. There, especially helpful students and staff photocopied articles that we required for analysis. Carol Hartman, a journalism graduate student, Nayith Pedroza, project assistant in the Chicano Studies program, and Kim Wahlgren, also a journalism student, helped translate Spanish language press accounts. Wahlgren also assisted with the coding of *La Opinión*. We also want to thank Jim Danky and Tess Arenas for reading the manuscript and providing valuable comments. Finally, we thank Margaret Seawell at Sage Publications for her consistent support and encouragement during this book's long gestation period. We also want to thank at Sage Alicia Carter, Claudia Hoffman, and especially Mary Tederstrom for her superb editing.

On a more personal note, we would each like to acknowledge a number of other people important in our lives.

Hemant Shah

I first send my love and thanks to my parents Gamanlal and Usha Shah. They arrived in the United States as immigrants in the early 1960s with a five-year-old in tow (me). The social and cultural adjustments were not always smooth, but they managed to create an environment in which my siblings and I could survive the inevitable crises of cultural identity as first-generation Indian Americans. There were ups and downs, good times and not-so-good times, but my parents' love and support for us was and is unwavering and unconditional. I also want to thank several people who constitute a family of another sort. These friends have been an important part of my network of personal support. They include Tess Arenas, Frank Durham, Jo Ellen Fair, Lew Friedland, Kirin Narayan, Sunita Reddy, Michael Thornton, and Lauren Tucker.

Over the years, I have had the very good fortune to interact with a number of colleagues who have contributed in substantial ways—though some of them may not know it—to my development and growth as a university teacher and researcher. They include Herb Altschull, Jim Baughman, Carl Bybee, Jim Danky, Bob Drechsel, Frank Durham, Jo Ellen Fair, Lew Friedland, Shanti Kumar, Amy Ling, Christine Ogan, Michael Thornton, Joe Turow, and David Weaver.

Finally, I want to dedicate this book to my daughter, Mela Shah. As a mixed-race person, she is bound to experience some of her own internal interethnic conflicts as she grows into young adulthood and beyond. But I am certain that her intelligence, resourcefulness, concern for social justice, sense of humor, generosity of spirit, creativity, charm, effervescence, and love of life will help get her through the toughest of times. My daughter inspires me every day to try to be a better person.

Michael Thornton

I would like to thank several people who have been and remain important in my life: I send thanks to my parents, Nobuko Otsuki Thornton and Charles Robert Thornton, for planting the seed that inspired me to understand the complexities of race and race relations, but also how one crosses racial boundaries. What I do well and any contributions I will make to this world are direct results of their example. To my surviving sisters, Madi Vannaman and June Thornton, I send appreciation for helping me see that political labels are most often incomplete in revealing the complexity lying behind the people those labels are affixed to. I also applaud them for their courage when going through hard times. Although she has been gone from this world for almost 24 years, I also wish to thank my sister Margie, who with her passing made me aware that I must be good to those I care about before it's too late. To my good friends Robert Taylor, Oliver Williams, Marino Bruce, and Hemant Shah, I thank them for sharing themselves and their families, especially at times in my life when I needed it most. Special thanks go to Robert for his kindness, his mentoring, and his concern for my well-being.

Saving the best for last, my wife, Nora Medina, and her son James, have perhaps had the most effect on who I am as an adult, and they are the strength that takes me through times of trouble. James has taught me fundamental things about what it means to be a father, although at times I have not done as well as I might and have not always been a cooperative student. But James shines as an example of what can happen when there are people who care. Nora is my lifeline; her laughter brightens my life, gives me hope for the future. Her concern for others is a guiding light to what the world has to offer. I am lucky to be able to do what I do and to have the support of so many people in my life. I only wish that others were as lucky.

PART I

1

Introduction

Immigration, Racial Anxiety, and Racial Formation

The world has experienced phenomenal political-economic change in recent years. Whether we use as our benchmark the postcolonial era of the 1950s and 1960s, the global economic recession of the 1970s, or the fall of the Berlin wall in 1989, there is little argument that economic, political, and cultural relations among nations have been undergoing an irreversible transformation. The scope, breadth, and depth of these changes have been captured conceptually by the term *globalization,*[1] which is used today in reference to the following aspects of the international political economy (see Gabriel, 1998):

- The liberation and independence of former colonies
- The alienating effects of mass culture, in terms of both bureaucracies over which people have little control and the standardization of consumer goods
- A growing lack of security and powerlessness at work, typified in short-term contracts, fluctuating hours, and redundancies
- The commodification of culture, resulting in the blurring of the distinction between "elitist" and "popular" culture
- Global migrations and diaspora brought about by political and economic pressures with far-reaching cultural consequences
- Spatial compression brought about by more efficient means of distributing media and cultural products

Although the idea of globalization may bring to mind a postnational world of weak states and strong global governance, it is important to note that globalization is centered in many important ways in the still-formidable institutions of Western nations.[2] Nevertheless, globalization also has had a decentering effect on the West. Current conditions have forced the West to confront fears about its own security and privileges, as well as its vulnerability to forces truly global in scope.

For example, global migration patterns have brought Asian and Latin American immigrants to the United States in numbers that have created substantial levels of anxiety over White identity, culture, and privilege. This anxiety in turn has spurred on efforts at important institutional sites such as law enforcement, legislative bodies, courts, and mass media to monitor and control the activities of immigrants. The presence of these new immigrants also has been of concern to established African American communities, which already felt precariously positioned socially, economically, and politically. Taken together, these trends have raised anew a number of anxious questions about the fundamentals of national identity and culture: How will the "new" America—more multiracial and multicultural than ever before—be defined? What will it mean to be "American"? Who should be included and excluded in the "new" America?[3]

As Benedict Anderson (1991) has suggested, answers to these types of questions—questions at the heart of constituting communities—require imagination, which must be mobilized to consider and reconsider new ways to envision the organization of the body politic and who will benefit from the production, accumulation, and distribution of all kinds of resources. To the extent that national identity must be addressed according to the ways it is imagined, we will be concerned in this book with what Arjun Appadurai (1997) has called resources of the imagination. A substantial part of this pool of resources includes the "forms of address, images, texts and performances being produced and used in popular discourse to construct what it means to be American" (Giroux, 1996, p. 190). And, to the extent that White, Black, and recent immigrant communities might imagine America in clashing, opposing, even contradictory ways, we will be concerned with competing visions of America.

The model of competing visions of America that informs this book is akin to recent thinking about civil society and the public sphere. To make a long intellectual history very short, theorizing about the nature of the public sphere within civil society has moved from an assumption that communities strive for consensus through rational public debate to recognition that communities are in fact fractious and comprise multiple, competing public spheres. Further, the competing public spheres are not on equal footing. Those aligned with dominant social groups have more visibility and influence and can more easily define issues, establish terms of debate, and command public attention. Those public spheres comprising less powerful groups must often scramble for resources—including visibility and influence—and much of their activity focuses on monitoring and countering the discourse of the dominant public sphere (see Dahlgren & Sparks, 1991; Hartley, 1996; Jacobs, 2000).

The issue of unequal distribution of power among social groups is of vital importance in understanding the dynamics of civil society and the ways in which communities imagine and reimagine themselves on that terrain. Thus, although the idea of competing public spheres is an important step forward in conceptualizing community interaction, we want to inject into the formulation an even more explicit discussion of power. In other words, we want to recognize that communities are unstable but also insist that their instability is not simply a matter of argument and disagreement over policy and politics but rooted in the exercise of power by the dominant members to keep certain groups in subordinate positions. We believe that the interplay between ideology and hegemony, as described by Gramsci and others, gives us the proper perspective on forms of power to help us understand the issues at hand.

Another concern in this book is immigration to the United States from Asia and Latin America, the resulting interethnic tensions between immigrants and established communities (both White and Black), and how these conflicts are represented in the news. Certainly, we are not the first to take up these questions. In fact, perhaps the most well-known examination of racial conflict and news was the *Report of the National Advisory Commission on Civil Disorders* (1968). President Lyndon Johnson created the Kerner Commission, as the group is more commonly known, in July 1967 after a summer of racial violence involving Blacks in several U.S. cities. One of the issues examined by the commission was "the overall treatment by the media of the Negro ghettos, community relations, racial attitudes and poverty" (*Report of the National Advisory Commission on Civil Disorders,* 1968, p. 20). On this point, the report was clearly critical of what it called the "white press"—referring to dominant news organizations of the nation. For instance, the commission wrote,

> The media failed to report adequately on the causes and consequences of civil disorders and on the underlying problems of race relations. They have not communicated to the majority of their audience—which is white—a sense of the degradation, misery and hopelessness of life in the ghetto. (*Report of the National Advisory Commission on Civil Disorders,* 1968, p. 383)

The report also criticized news coverage for exaggerating Black community involvement in the rioting, relying too heavily on police sources, ignoring Blacks when they assisted in controlling the violence, and ignoring Whites who contributed to the unrest (*Report of the National Advisory Commission on Civil Disorders*, 1968, pp. 374-376).

Given the trends toward globalization described earlier, the events and issues surrounding interethnic conflicts today are more complex than those examined by the Kerner Commission. For example, recent interethnic discord in the United States has involved more than only Black and White communities. In addition, U.S. foreign policy, new immigrant communities, and increasing global economic interdependence also have contributed to an increasingly complex political economy in America's major cities. Yet the problems noted by the commission members in regard to the news coverage of civil disorder in the summer of 1967 still provide a relevant framework for examining news coverage of contemporary interethnic conflict 35 years later.

We will consider some of the issues and relationships surrounding news coverage of contemporary interethnic conflict in the context of a theory of racial formation (Omi & Winant, 1994) and examine three specific instances of interethnic conflict through the lens of news coverage. Competing news images depicting the people and groups involved, conveying explanations of causes and consequences of tensions, and articulating the connections between race and nation provide some of the key resources of the imagination that may be used by news consumers to organize their understanding of a multiracial America and to privately or collectively act on those ideas. Before discussing racial formation and news, we first provide some background on recent immigration to the United States and its impact.

Recent Immigration Patterns

The size, origin, and composition of immigration to the United States changed dramatically as a result of the Hart-Cellar Act of 1965 and recent amendments to it (especially the Immigration Reform and Control Act of 1986 and the Immigration Act of 1990). Yearly legal immigration from 1920 to the passage of the Hart-Cellar bill averaged about 206,000 per year, mostly from northern and western Europe. From the mid-1960s to the 1990s, the annual figure more than doubled to 500,000. Among these more recent arrivals were a large number of refugees, parolees, and asylum seekers.

Although the extent of illegal immigration is less clear, after the 1986 Immigration Reform and Control Act granted amnesty and U.S. citizenship to those without proper documentation, 3 million stepped forward to avail themselves of the opportunity (Johnson, Farrell, & Guinn, 1997). By 1996, there were an estimated 5 million people illegally living in the United States (Center for Immigration Studies, 1997).

During the 1980s and 1990s, half of the world's emigrants made the United States their destination. The 10 million legal immigrants who arrived during the 1980s exceeded the previous high recorded earlier in the 20th century. These immigrants are also notable in that nearly 80% of them came from Asia and Latin America (Thornton, 1995). Among the industrialized countries, the United States takes in the largest number of non-European immigrants, the number increasing from less than 3 million in the 1960s to nearly 4.5 million in the 1970s to more than 7 million in the 1980s. Largely due to immigration from Asia, the number of non-White minorities grew seven times as fast as Whites in the 1980s (Frey, 1993).

In the United States, these new immigrants represent a progressive expansion of ethnic diversity. Among them are substantial proportions of Mexicans and Central Americans (Colombians and Dominicans); Caribbean and African Blacks (Jamaicans, Haitians, and Nigerians); East Asians including Koreans, Iranians, and Chinese (from Hong Kong, Taiwan, and the People's Republic of China); Southeast Asians from Vietnam, Cambodia, and the Philippines; and South Asians from India, Pakistan, Bangladesh, and Sri Lanka. As a consequence of high rates of immigration and natural increase, racial and ethnic minorities will account for the majority of the nation's population increase over the next six decades (Martin, 1995). Predictions about population growth indicate the potential impact of these immigration trends on the future ethnic and racial mix in America. Between 1996 and 2050, the number of Blacks in the United States is predicted to increase by 95%, the number of Native Americans by 209%, the number of Latinos by 238%, the number of Asian/Pacific Islanders by 412%, and the number of Whites by 30% (Johnson et al., 1997).

The immigrants have gravitated to a handful of geographical centers in the United States. Three fourths of post-1980 immigrants settled in just six states, the most popular ones being California (38% of the total), New York (14%), Texas (8%), and Florida (8%; Fix & Passel, 1994; Center for Immigration Studies, 1997). This immigration began to transform the ethnic demographic balance in U.S. cities. Among the immigrants who entered the country after 1980, 50% moved to eight cities, among them, Los Angeles, Miami, Chicago, Washington, D.C., Houston, and San Francisco (Frey & Tilove, 1995). The impact of immigration on some of these cities can also be seen in the proportion of their residents who are foreign born. According to the 1990 census, 93% of the foreign born live in metropolitan areas, in contrast to 73% of native-born Americans. In 1990, Miami was 46% foreign born, and Los Angeles, two-thirds foreign born. Furthermore, different ethnic groups were drawn to varying locations. Latinos settled mainly in California and Texas; Asians in Los Angeles, New York, and San Francisco; whereas European immigrants were more evenly distributed throughout the country (Johnson & Oliver, 1989; Rose, 1989).

Racial Anxiety and Conflict in the "New" America

One result of the geographical concentration of immigrants in major U.S. cities is anxiety among established communities—both White and Black. A number of sources point to strong popular sentiments directed against immigrants from Asia and Latin America in particular. In California, a statewide poll taken in the 1980s found that 66.9% of Blacks and 75.5% of Whites thought that the presence of Asians and Latinos would make it hard to maintain American traditions (Field Institute, 1988). In 1992, the Gallup Poll revealed that Americans believed the presence of immigrants from Vietnam, Mexico, Haiti, and Cuba created more problems than benefits. The polls indicated that Americans predicted that most immigrants from Latin America would end up on welfare and involved in crime. In addition, polls showed that Americans thought immigrants were willing to take low-paying (as opposed to unwanted) jobs from residents and thus hurt the economy by driving down wages (Gallup Poll, 1993, pp. 250-253).

One of the tangible indicators of these views and their attendant anxieties is the phenomenon of White flight. In the last half of the 1980s, for every ten immigrants who arrived in places such as New York, Chicago, Los Angeles, and Houston, nine residents left for other cities, regions, or states (Frey & Tilove, 1995). White anxiety about brown immigrants is responsible not only for White flight but also for political rhetoric and social movements designed to curtail immigration and control immigrants already in the country. For example, many communities are uneasy about the spread of Spanish into educational, business, and governmental agencies. As of 1998, 22 states had passed referendums or laws declaring English as the official language of the state.

Some places enforced the rule with gusto. In Norcross, Georgia, all business signs had to be written in at least 75% English, and local law enforcement officers have been authorized to fine store owners who violate the rule. Sergeant H. Smith, a Norcross marshal, said he has fined Mexican stores, Korean churches, and an "Oriental beauty shop." Justifying his actions,

Smith said, "If an *American* was out there driving by, he wouldn't know what that was" (Branigan, 1999, p. 29, emphasis added). Another example is California's Proposition 187, designed to force school officials and health care providers to police the immigration status of immigrant students and their parents. The measure was the first salvo in more recent rounds of the anti-immigrant backlash in the state. The measure passed in November 1994—garnering 59% of the vote—and almost immediately spawned similar movements in other states. Both houses of the United States Congress also participated in the immigrant backlash. Large numbers of Democrats and Republicans supported bills to slash legal immigration by one third, refugee admissions by one half, and to deny welfare, Medicaid, and food stamps to legal immigrants. The sentiment of many Whites, fearful of a Black and brown and yellow planet, was captured by the comments of Senator Alan Simpson, the principal author of the Senate's anti-immigration bill: "The American people are fed up. When they want the law enforced, they are called racist and xenophobic" (Welcome to America, 1995, p. 13).

With this background of political rhetoric and action from the nation's leaders, it was no surprise when William Masters, a self-appointed vigilante in San Fernando Valley, California, shot two youths whom he called "Mexican skinheads" for spraying graffiti on a highway overpass. Masters killed Rene Arce and wounded David Hilo, but District Attorney Gil Garcetti did not arrest Masters. Instead, Garcetti arrested the wounded Hilo for vandalism. When police released Masters, he said to the press: "Where are you going to find 12 citizens to convict me anyway?" (Davis, 1995). As this example makes clear, when White anger turns into racist political discourse and policies, racist acts are likely to follow.

Another result of recent trends that have brought Asian and Latin American newcomers into urban areas has been the escalation of competition with Blacks over jobs, neighborhoods, political clout, and lifestyle (Booth, 1998). One of the most visible conflicts is one between Blacks and Latinos. As older, established Latinos have made political inroads and as new Latino immigrants have taken low-paying service jobs, Blacks have complained that Latino success has come at their expense. Latinos have countered that Blacks are insensitive to the needs of the Latino community and do not want to share with other minorities the benefits of civil rights victories (Shah & Thornton, 1994). These tensions are reflected in several empirical studies that suggest that Black–Latino discord in U.S. cities can be attributed to competition for scarce resources (Diamond, 1998; Hahn, Klingman, & Pachon, 1976; McClain & Karnig, 1990; Oliver & Johnson, 1984; Shah & Thornton, 1994). For example, Kirschenman and Neckerman (1991) found in a survey of hiring practices among Chicago area employers a strong preference for immigrant over urban workers because employers viewed immigrants as cheaper and less troublesome (Tienda & Stier, 1996; Waldinger, 1986).

The preference for nonunion immigrant labor was dramatized in *Bread and Roses,* a film made in 2001 by Ken Loach about the plight of Los Angeles janitors' union, Local 399 of the Service Employees International. In the 1970s, a small number of large unionized firms, with mostly Black employees, dominated the market for janitorial services in high-rise office buildings. Their competition came generally from midsized firms employing mostly nonunion Latinos. The pay for union workers continued to climb, and by 1982 it was $12 per hour. But the companies they worked for could no longer compete with the nonunion firms who paid their immigrant workers $4 per hour. Over time, the number of Black workers declined markedly (Heer, 1996).

Another highly visible conflict is among Blacks and new Korean immigrants. A common sight in many metropolitan areas is Korean American–owned grocery stores (Thornton & Shah, 1996). Korean American immigrants established businesses in the poorest and toughest neighborhoods, often predominantly Black, where rents were low and com-petition was scarce. Once they succeeded, however, store owners moved to "safer" neighborhoods. Blacks complained about cultural insensitivity on the part of store owners, who rarely made eye contact and avoided touch-ing their customers even to give change, and often claimed that Korean American store owners prejudged them as potential criminals the moment they walked into the stores. For Blacks with limited economic opportunity, there was tremendous resentment toward a new immigrant group perceived to be moving easily up the economic ladder. In addition, many Asian immi-grants brought with them stereotypical understandings of Blacks as crimi-nals, drug addicts, being lazy, and so on, cultivated through U.S. media exports to Asian countries (Johnson & Oliver, 1994; Yoon, 1995). Some Korean Americans admit that they may be prejudiced toward Blacks but claim their fears are justified by high rates of crime in depressed urban areas and personal experience with being victimized by Black thieves or muggers.

Again, these social tensions are reflected in empirical research. For example, surveys in the early 1980s found that Blacks expressed the greatest social dis-tance from Indochinese refugees (Starr & Roberts, 1982; Thornton & Mizuno, 1995; Thornton & Taylor, 1988) and believed that Indochinese refugees strain scarce resources (Donnely, 1982; Fuchs, 1983, 1990; U.S. Commission on Civil Rights, 1987). Generally, Blacks tend to favor immigration restrictions more strongly than Whites because Blacks fear losing their jobs to immigrants (Cain & Kiewiet, 1986; Harwood, 1986). The perceived ability of some middle-class Asian Americans to financially leap over Blacks further heightens economic tensions (Wong, 1986). One study of Black responses to Korean American merchants found that the animosity among Blacks is rooted in economic envy rather than racism (Cheng & Espiritu, 1989).

Whites' cultural anxiety about and Blacks' economic resentment toward immigrants was exacerbated by rapidly changing domestic economic conditions, which are also linked to processes of globalization. For non-White immigrants coming to the United States in record numbers beginning in the 1970s, it was often a dream come true—the best of times (Tienda & Liang, 1994). But by the 1980s, for many immigrants it was also the worst of times, because it was during this decade that an increasing supply of less-skilled workers, the movement of jobs to overseas locations, and technological innovations led to a decreasing demand for their services (Blank, 1994). These effects were magnified in the nation's largest metropolitan areas, which underwent drastic restructuring in both numbers and kinds of jobs available (Scott, 1988a, 1988b). Taken together, these trends led to high rates of unemployment and decreasing rates of labor force participation among the poor, especially in urban Black communities (Kasarda, 1983; Wilson, 1987).

The 1980s was also a time of shifting concentration of wealth. The Congressional Budget Office revealed that between 1977 and 1989 the wealthiest 1% of American families amassed 60% of the growth in income, whereas the bottom 40% experienced a drop in income. During this period, wage inequality increased across the board, but especially for the young, those without college education, and Blacks. Between 1979 and 1988, real earnings of 25- to 34-year-old men with less than a 12th grade education declined dramatically. White males (in 1988 dollars) with less than a high school diploma saw their incomes decline from $19,848 to $16,108, and those with a high school education had salaries that went from $24,889 to $21,776 (Freeman & Holzer, 1991). Black males, starting at lower salaries than Whites, also lost ground. Salaries for Blacks with less than a high school diploma went from $14,596 to $14,594, and those who graduated from high school went from earning $19,449 in 1979 to $16,638 in 1988. Relative to their White male counterparts, between 1973 and 1989 earnings declined for Black men at every educational level (Moss & Tilly, 1991). There is a similar pattern for women: Among White women who had not earned a high school diploma, incomes went from $12,623 in 1979 to $10,853 in 1988; those who graduated held their incomes steady. White female college graduates made the greatest advance of any group: Salaries increased from $20,987 to $23,791. For Black women with a high school education, salaries went from $14,596 to $13,825 (Freeman & Holzer, 1991).

The statistics also indicate that even highly educated ethnic minorities, although experiencing better lives than their less-educated counterparts, became increasingly more likely from 1979 to 1988 to be among low wage earners. Among college-educated men, Blacks were 1.26 times more likely and Latino men .92 times more likely to be in poverty than Whites in 1973. In 1987, Blacks were 1.86 times and Latino men 2 times more likely as Whites to live in poverty. At the same time that the wages of many working-class and middle-class families were dropping during the 1970s and 1980s, the salaries of corporate chief executive officers were increasing at the rate of 35% to 120%.

The foregoing discussion of examples and trends clearly points to a link between globalization, immigration, and the "new" America. White anxiety about immigration is based on the national origin and "strangeness" of potential immigrants, with nations of the "third world" creating more concern than other nations. As Frankenberg (1997) and many others have noted, in the United States, notions of who can legitimately belong to a nation is based on race, because ideas of "Whiteness" and "American-ness" have been closely connected. White fear of being culturally overwhelmed—again, with certain cultures and languages being perceived as more threatening than others—provides the justification for anti-immigration policies, anti-immigrant rhetoric, and actions that help Whites maintain the equation between Whiteness and American-ness. This formulation is the central axis for a peculiar "culture of nationalism" that is xenophobic and authoritarian but, at the same time, steeped in the rhetoric of liberal democracy (Giroux, 1996). For Blacks, anxiety is also based on the presence of "strangers" from Asia and Latin America. However, Black anxiety appears to be limited primarily, but by no means exclusively, to the economic rather than cultural impact of Asian and Latin American immigrants.

The "Cost" of Immigration

A *Time* magazine cover story described the potential impact on White America of recent Latino and Asian immigration. "Someday soon," the magazine noted, "White Americans will become a minority group" (Henry, 1990, p. 28). For some, this future is frightening, and the fear manifests itself in arguments about the loss of American culture (e.g., English-only movements), resurgent nativism (e.g., California's Proposition 187), and a growing number of hate crimes against ethnic minorities. Politicians, law enforcement officials, educators, and the press have expressed concern over these issues—in other words, concern is expressed at almost every institutional site dominated by Whites.

Ostensibly, the concern over immigration revolves around its cost or contribution to American society. In recent years, one emphasis on evaluating the impact of immigrants has evolved into a "more is better" model, in which higher immigrant earnings lead to a more positive economic and social impact. Reitz (1998, p. 14) argues that this belief is based on a series of assumptions. Immigrants with higher incomes are perceived as making a positive net contribution to the government balance sheet because they pay higher taxes. Their financial independence also reduces the potential need for social services and unemployment compensation. Further, because they acquired their skills elsewhere, U.S. institutions incurred no costs for their training. Thus, these "good" immigrants are a source of stronger consumer demand and, through higher rates of self-employment, job creation. These good immigrants also are often held up as examples of successful cultural assimilation because they often attempt to integrate into national life (Tarver, 1994).

On the other hand, less-skilled workers are viewed as costly to society because they undercut the position of domestic labor (although for consumers and businesses they are also a source of cheap labor), pay almost nothing to the tax base, and create a strain on the public education, health care, and correctional systems. In addition, there is the cost related to the often-negative social and political fallout from the perception that immigrants are contributing virtually nothing to society while enjoying the benefits. Culturally they are often viewed as resisting assimilation and perhaps even hostile to American values.

Reitz (1998) also suggests that although the economic calculus of evaluating immigration is a long-standing and routine procedure, its current configuration contains new factors. Earlier immigrant groups were seen as hardy workers making a contribution despite working in low-prestige occupations. The current thinking about immigrant economic viability demands that more attention be paid to the economic bottom line in a way never previously expected. This formula, according to Reitz, is related to three developments. First, a changed labor market has created high demand for highly skilled workers but has not created more high-skill jobs. Second, fewer workers are supporting greater proportions of the social entitlement programs, and immigrants are expected to earn their own entitlements: If they are receiving state aid, then they must earn the right by contributing to public coffers. Finally, higher skill levels and earned entitlements become intertwined with an anxiety about the social, cultural, and racial impact of immigration from non-European countries. Because of the cultural and social distance many "native" Americans feel from newcomers, there may be a stronger demand for social and economic benefits to compensate for anticipated social and cultural costs.

The widespread perception that one of the primary costs of immigration is that immigrants take jobs from and depress the wages of other Americans, particularly Blacks, is not entirely supported by recent empirical work. The situation is much more complex than this perception because immigration has hurt some Blacks in some regions, helped in other regions, and was unrelated to what happened to Blacks in still other regions. Butcher and Card (1991) examined how immigration was related to the decline in real earnings for the least skilled workers during the 1980s. They found a rise in wage inequality in larger cities with relatively little immigration. Immigration was most related to growth in wages at the higher end of the pay scale than to a decline of wages at the lower end. Econometric studies show that this is so because immigrants do not compete with native workers and do not decrease their wages or employment levels (Borjas & Tienda, 1987; LaLonde & Topel, 1991). Borjas (1984, 1986) found no support for the view that Latino male labor, whether immigrant or native, depressed Black male wages. In one study, Borjas (1984) discovered that male immigration increased the earnings of Black males of all ages. He also found that White male immigration and an increase in female labor force participation reduced employment rates among Black males.

These trends are more complicated when specific geographical areas are examined. Stepick and Grenier (1993) found that hiring practices in Miami resulted in displacement of low-skilled Black and White workers, whereas Latino immigrants benefited. Heer (1996), reviewing the social science literature on the impact of Mexican immigration on Los Angeles County, found a range of trends related to unemployment. In the period prior to 1970, an era with relatively little immigration from Mexico, the unemployment rate in the county was higher than the national rate. In the 1980s, a decade with major immigration, unemployment was lower for Blacks in the county than in the United States. Heer suggests that undocumented Mexicans harmed mostly Mexican Americans and other Latinos who were in the United States legally. He found that other ethnic minorities were marginally affected by the presence of large numbers of undocumented Mexicans.

The influx of large numbers of new immigrants and the anxiety and tensions they have created among established White and Black communities are not a temporary aberration. It is a portent of a major point of demarcation in U.S. history, for it is an era in which global migration is commonplace, and questions about race have once again become a major domestic issue. These factors all contribute to a "browning" of America that signals a dramatic change in racial composition and cultural orientation. How the general circulation press and ethnic minority press depict these issues and patterns of interracial interaction is the focus of this book.[4] Suffice it to say at this point that the quantity and quality of the attention and coverage Asian and Latino immigrants draw from news organizations likely has a major impact on how society currently understands race and race relations as well as what it means to be American.

Racial Formation

The concerns and debates over immigration and the increasing tensions among ethnic minorities represent elements of racial formation. With Omi and Winant (1994), we view race as neither an objective essence based on biology and/or classification of phenotypes nor simply an ideological construct or illusion that masks other, and supposedly more significant, material conditions such as class. Rather, race is better understood as conditional upon historical trajectory, political relationships, and global contexts (Winant, 1994, p. 18). This view is embodied in the idea of racial formation, "the sociohistorical process by which racial categories are created, inhabited, transformed, and destroyed" (Omi & Winant, 1994, p. 55). An essential element of racial formation is racial projects, which may be understood as attempts to employ racial categories to mobilize specific meanings and accomplish specific social and political goals. Racial projects link cultural representations that identify and give meaning to race and social structures that organize human bodies and resources along racial lines. On the one hand, cultural representations provide explanations and justifications for racialized structural organization. On the other hand, racialized social structures provide the fodder for cultural representations. Thus, racial projects are "simultaneously interpretation[s], representation[s], or explanation[s] of racial dynamics and . . . efforts to organize and distribute resources along particular racial lines" (Winant, 1994, p. 24). By social structure we are referring to politics (e.g., elections, policy making), distribution of resources, and social movements involved in distributional conflicts. The dimension of cultural representation refers to signifying practices and struggles over meaning, identity formation, and creation of symbolic boundaries around communities. The relationship between culture and structure provides racial projects with an element of coherence. Once a racial project makes a choice about how the link between culture and structure will be represented, a narrative chain follows logically and effortlessly, though it may be somewhat unstable and marked with internal contradiction.

An important dimension of racial projects is that they are public. As Omi and Winant (1994) note, racial projects

> include large-scale public action, state activities, and interpretations of racial conditions in artistic, journalistic, or academic fora, as well as the seemingly infinite number of racial judgments and practices we carry out at the level of individual practices. (pp. 60-61)

The efforts of racial projects to link cultural representation and structural organization typically are acts of public discourse. Certainly matters of private thought and opinion about race may never be articulated publicly. But family socialization patterns, personal economic activity, and other dimensions of private life that are influenced by private thoughts often do feed into the public activities of interpreting, representing, and explaining racial dynamics. Thus, racial projects are an important mechanism by which debate and discussion about race is carried out. But as we suggested earlier, because of unequal distribution of power, the participants in this debate are not necessarily on equal footing. Racial ideology and racial hegemony—key components in differential relations of racial power—inflect discussion of race in the public sphere.

The activities of racial projects are guided, to a large extent, by racial ideology. Ideology refers to a set of beliefs, values, and meanings articulated in texts and everyday practices, perhaps arising from a set of material interests, that reflect and justify the worldview of a given social grouping (Comaroff & Comaroff, 1991, p. 24). According to Hall (1982, p. 35), racial ideology articulates and defines what race is, circumscribes what meanings the imagery of race carries, and suggests ways to classify the world in terms of racial categories. Racial ideology has a life of its own, providing a vocabulary that enables people to interpret and evaluate events, people, and issues within existing racial frameworks. These frameworks are rooted in ideas about intellect, sexuality, emotional disposition, and so forth, and they permeate the processes of cultural presentation and structural organization.

Gandy (1998, p. 82) has noted that racial ideology is evaluative and comparative. The comparative dimension is reflected in the notion of racial hierarchy, one of the core elements in the logic of racial thinking. Within the racial ideology prevalent in Anglo-European nations, Whites are situated at the top of the racial hierarchy, and others are arrayed below. In these nations, features that reinforce the dominant positions of Whites and their privileges characterize racial hierarchy. For example, racial hierarchy tends to classify non-White groups into gradations based on stereotyped characteristics. Racial hierarchy also implies that the culture and sensibilities of non-Whites higher in the hierarchy are superior and more valuable than those viewed as lower in the hierarchy (Shah, 1999; Shah & Thornton, 1994). Because racial ideology and its central elements such as racial hierarchy operate at the level of common sense, its "conceptions, assumptions, and definitions of the normal, even desirable, social and racial order" (Gray, 1987, p. 385) are often uncritically incorporated into the everyday practices of many racial projects.

To clearly understand the role of racial projects and racial ideology in racial formation, we must also consider the idea of racial hegemony. Hegemony refers "to that order of signs and practices, relations and distinctions, images and epistemologies . . . that come to be taken for granted as the natural and received shape of the world and everything that inhabits it" (Comaroff & Comaroff, 1991, p. 23). Hegemony refers to things that go without saying, that are presumptively shared and, therefore, usually not the subject of explication and argument (Bourdieu, 1977). In other words, hegemony refers to ideologies that have attained through systems of cultural and structural practices (such as racial projects) a naturalized, taken-for-granted existence. As De Certeau puts it, "hegemony is silent while ideology babbles on" (quoted in Comaroff & Comaroff, 1991, p. 24).

The ability to silence and prevent people from thinking and saying things by putting certain ideas beyond the bounds of credibility and rationality is the power of hegemony. Because of its stealthy mode of operation, hegemony is difficult, though never impossible, to contest directly. However, under hegemonic systems, opposition and difference are modified, transformed, or recreated and then absorbed by the prevailing social order. Hegemony involves a "doubling of opposition" (Winant, 1994, p. 29) in which it simultaneously wins and loses: Opposition gains entrance into hegemonic discourse, but only after it has been co-opted into the mainstream and deprived of its critical content. Any challenge is energetically resisted, for once the "natural becomes negotiable [and] the ineffable put into words" (Comaroff & Comaroff, 1991, p. 24), hegemony, which is mute, nonnegotiable, and interested in homogenizing thought and practice, can be revealed as an ideology, which is explicit, openly assertive, and subject to dispute.

A system of cultural and structural practices such as racial projects is central to this process. The prevailing racial hegemony in the United States is one based on a racial hierarchy that valorizes Whiteness and masks White privilege. Whiteness, and the qualities thought to be associated with it, is often accepted as the norm against which people are measured and judged. Whiteness as a category of skin hue is arbitrarily associated with positive characteristics and with social, political, and cultural privilege, whereas being non-White is to lack positive characteristics and privilege (Fine, Weiss, Powell, & Wong, 1997; Frankenberg, 1993; Goldberg, 1993; Pieterse, 1992). In this racial logic, Whiteness is, of course, a *symbol* of privilege, not a literal denotation. Whiteness as a symbol is created from an always-moveable set of criteria for inclusion and exclusion. This flexibility is, in part, the basis for the power of Whiteness as a category of racial classification. The elasticity of Whiteness allows relatively easy, indeed natural, policing of who will and who will not be considered White and enjoy the power and privilege associated with being so designated (Dyer, 1997, p. 57). In this sense, Whiteness has the status of hegemony. It is an ideology that has become, through the practices of racial projects such as colonialism, slavery, exploitation, conquest, extermination, and so on, hegemonic. It is precisely the "naturalness" of its existence and operation that masks the economic, social, and cultural power of Whites. Thus, Whites in Anglo-European countries often despise, fear, and subjugate non-White immigrants because their appearance reveals the arbitrary nature of White privilege and threatens the very logic of existing racial order in those places.

In this era of globalization, an array of racial projects that carry forward a range of racial ideologies, including new articulations of White power and privilege, are revealing and even challenging America's racial hegemony (see Winant, 1994). The interaction between the prevailing but perhaps crumbling racial hegemony and the various racial projects, as well as the interactions among the racial projects and the ideologies that animate them, is the current terrain of racial formation. Racial projects are the key component of racial formation because they are the vehicles through which racial ideologies can realize their hegemonic desires and through which racial hegemonies can be challenged.

Racial Formation and the News

To repeat an earlier point, racial projects link the discursive means of identifying race and the institutional and structural forms by which it is organized. Thus, in the United States institutional and structural forms of racial hierarchy and White privilege are linked to news representations of race. The specific form of this mediation forces us to focus on "the 'work' essentialism does for domination, the 'need' domination displays to essentialize the subordinated" (Omi & Winant, 1994, p. 71). To essentialize is to engage in a process by which cultural complexities are distilled into a few supposedly fundamental characteristics of a culture or a people. The key for us here is that the process of asserting that social bodies and cultures have essential qualities unique to each group, by which beliefs in true human essences existing outside of social and historical relations are cultivated, is fundamentally a process of *representation,* of making public the discursive choices for classifying race and constructing narratives of meaning for race. Thus, institutions such as news media play an important role in the racial formation process. On the one hand, the news media provide information, reporting on and representing the activities of racial projects in the public sphere of open discussion on racial issues of the day. On the other hand, the news media themselves function in the public sphere as racial projects in that they provide opinion and editorials presenting their positions on racial issues, often in ways that limit and shape discussion.

News media are an important source of cultural production and information. Their representations of the social world provide explanations, descriptions, and frames for understanding how and why the world works as it does. As with all racial projects, the news media are animated by racial ideology (as well as other ideologies of class, gender, nationality, sexuality, etc.). The perpetuation of racial ideology and the work needed to push it into hegemonic status is not a conscious effort on the part of journalists and their news organizations. In fact, day-to-day journalistic routines often incorporate it as conceptions, assumptions, and definitions of the normal and the desirable. Journalists select certain issues, events, actors, and sources for coverage and emphasis over others and transform their selections into finished news items by identifying and contextualizing them in frames of reference recognizable to their consumers.

One of our assumptions here is that the normal workings of both the general circulation press and the ethnic minority publications reinforce racial ideologies. However, we assert that the racial projects represented by each type of news organization must be understood in different ways, because the arguments they carry into the public sphere may serve to oppose the status quo or to serve its interests. Previous research suggests that the general circulation news media work to enhance social control and preserve the status quo through selective reporting of social conflict. On the other hand, an ethnic minority press may be more likely to reveal problems with existing power relations and present challenges to the racial status quo (see Viswanath & Arora, 2000, for a brief summary).

Thus, for the general circulation news media in the United States, we expect that journalistic routines will result in news content characterized by patterns of reporting and writing that contain elements of the prevailing racial ideology of White power and privilege (an ideology that has attained hegemonic status). Conversely, ethnic minority papers, although they must engage with the prevailing racial hegemony, likely will articulate links between structures of White power and privilege and racial representation in ways that challenge racial hegemony. These links may be thought of as part of racial ideologies that have not attained hegemonic status. We would expect the news content of ethnic minority news organizations to reveal a different set of concerns, values, and assumptions about the social world than the news in the general circulation news media.

Although the racial formation process implies a fluid and historically contingent relationship among racial projects, commercial, organizational, and cultural pressures make the news somewhat consistent in terms of the general categories and narratives through which social relationships are represented. For example, the journalistic practice of reporting on the "who, what, when, where, why, and how" related to events covered by news organizations is likely to be honored by both general circulation and ethnic minority newspapers. In the context of the news about ethnic tensions in the United States in the era of globalization, another similarity is that the pattern of representation is likely to be informed by various understandings of the prevailing racial hegemony, which will then find their way into news texts. Our previous research suggests some of the broad patterns of representation that are likely to organize news coverage of interethnic conflict (Shah, 1994, 1995, 1999; Shah and Thornton, 1994; Thornton and Shah, 1996). Though there are at times considerable variations within the themes, three dominant patterns of representing ethnic minorities in the news involve ethnic minorities as (1) perpetrators and victims of violence, (2) having and causing a variety of social problems, and (3) having a tenuous status in terms of belonging to the body politic of the nation. For both general circulation media and ethnic minority media, the tools of linguistic emphasis such as treatment, intensity, imagery, phrasing, positioning, and placement weave the elements of their animating ideologies into the news narrative.

The current phase of globalization has been complicated by the geography of race and ethnicity, which has become completely internationalized. As Winant (1994) suggests:

> Today we have reached the point where the empire strikes back, as former (neocolonial) subjects, now redefined as "immigrants," challenge the majoritarian status of the formerly metropolitan group (the Whites, the Europeans, the "Americans" or "French"). (p. 19)

In this book we will examine the role of newspaper journalism (in both the general circulation and the ethnic minority media) in the process of racial formation in the United States. Our primary concern is the relationship among Asian and Latin American immigration, White anxiety and fear, and increasing tensions between Blacks and new immigrants. To explore these concerns, we focus our analysis of news coverage on three U.S. "global cities" where during the 1980s and 1990s these issues came to a head (see Sassen, 2001).

One aspect of the term "global cities" refers to the large cities in North America, Europe, and Asia that are central financial nodes of a global economy. Global cities are also places that attract people from all over the world, bringing together a wide variety of nationalities and cultures. Thus, these cities are the embodiment of diversity, complexity, and variety. Lewis Mumford has called global cities "the most complete compendium of the world" (Mumford, 1991, p. 639). This complexity and variety are bounded by local settings that intensify metropolitan life, giving rise to new forms of social interaction. The global city would have excited Robert Park, the Chicago School sociologist, who viewed the city as a laboratory "in which human nature and sociological processes may be most conveniently studied" (quoted in Eade, 1997, p. 58).

In this book, we use Miami, Washington, D.C., and Los Angeles as case studies. All are global financial hubs. Miami is a key point of trade and commerce for Central and South America and the Caribbean; Los Angeles is a commercial center for the Pacific Rim; and Washington, D.C., is the headquarters for many intergovernmental organizations and world aid organizations that are central to the global financial infrastructure. These three cities are also among the top U.S. destinations for immigrants, both skilled and unskilled, from Latin America and Asia. All three cities were sites of interethnic conflicts—Miami in 1989, Washington, D.C., in 1991, and Los Angeles in 1992—brought on by the complex dynamics of immigration and racial anxiety. Though we examine the media coverage of immigration and anxiety in each city thoroughly and carefully, the Los Angeles case occupies a larger proportion of the book than either Miami or Washington, D.C. In part, this imbalance is a result of the greater quantity of materials available for analysis, but it is also a consequence of the unprecedented magnitude and complexity—in terms of the groups involved, injuries, deaths, damage, and consequences—of the conflict in Los Angeles.

Research Methods

We examined general circulation newspapers and leading ethnic minority newspapers in the three cities of interest. To access this diverse set of sources we relied heavily on Nexis, a newspaper database archiving general circulation newspapers, and Ethnic NewsWatch, a database concentrating on ethnic minority publications. When needed, we supplemented this search with hard-copy holdings from libraries around the country. (See Appendix A for details.) Historical and other background information that we provide for each of the newspapers in the analysis chapters was gathered from various sources, including recent books, newspaper Web sites, Ethnic NewsWatch, and personal communication.

We examined news articles, editorials, columns, and letters to the editor that provided accounts of interethnic interaction. We defined interaction as direct or indirect contact between and among Black, Latino, or Asian American individuals or groups. We also examined articles that discussed implications of the interethnic interaction for social, political, economic, and other impact (e.g., population growth, school integration) in and between the ethnic minority communities. The following chart shows the number of items from the general circulation and ethnic minority publications in each city included in our analysis.

	General Circulation	Black Press	Latino Press	Asian American Press
Miami	55	24	38	—
Washington, D.C.	51	7	12	—
Los Angeles	83	43	127	135

Coding Process

First, some aspects of the articles were quantitatively assessed using a coding scheme based on one we developed in previous work (following Shah & Thornton, 1994). That process involved reading articles and enumerating themes, frames, the race of various types of actors and victims, and a number of other categories. (See Figure 1.1 for basic coding scheme and definition of categories.) After several practice runs, discussion, and adjustments to the coding scheme, independent coding by the authors and other coders consistently resulted in about 90% agreement over all coding decisions. Tabulation of the newspaper articles according to this protocol revealed the people, issues, and themes that were most and least frequently covered and guided our textual analysis, the second level of our empirical investigation of news coverage of interethnic conflict.

Textual analysis is the close examination "of language and rhetoric, of style and presentation," supported by and linked to the social, political, and cultural context in which the texts are produced (Hall, 1975, p. 15). The

Figure 1.1   Coding Protocol

I. Actors and Victims

Actors		Victims	
Actual	Potential	Actual	Potential

Types
Government
Society
Blacks
Whites
Asian Americans
Latino
Jews
Definitions:
Actors: individuals, institutions, or society at large depicted as actually or
    potentially taking action or causing effects on other individuals or institutions.
Victims: individuals, institutions, or society at large that is affected by the actions
    of actors.
Government: includes government officials and representatives, law enforcement
    personnel, judiciary personnel, etc.
Society: societal culture, social relations, the social fabric, etc.
Blacks: including African American, West Indians, and Africans.
Whites: Anglos, European, etc.
Asian American: including Japanese, Chinese, Korean, and Indian Americans.
Latino: Mexican Americans, Cubans, those from Central and South America.

Note: Some tables report specific ethnic categories when specificity is relevant. Most tables
report only general categories.

II. Themes

1. Pathology: perceived cultural or social shortcomings of individuals and
    groups explained with reference to inherent or innate inferior culture, social
    inabilities, mental instability, etc.
2. Invasion/Immigration: immigration represented as dangerous or as a threat
    to the status quo.
3. Fear: fear of actions, attitudes, or behavior directed at specific individuals or
    groups (direct fear); fear of any spillover effect from direct action, attitudes,
    or behavior directed at specific individuals or groups (indirect fear).
4. Racism: discrimination of any kind by individuals, groups, or institutions.
5. Culture/Values: individual or group traditions, worldviews, assumptions.
6. Violence: verbal (involving no physical contact), personal (physical contact
    or use of weapons against people), or property (destruction of property).

(Continued)

Figure 1.1, Continued

---

7. Cause of conflicts: individual-, institutional-, or structural-level causes of conflict.
8. Reassurance: expressions of hope, positive spin
9. Discontent: expressions of remorse, sadness, skepticism, disillusionment, etc.
10. Conflict: physical or verbal antagonism.
11. Cooperation: expressed sentiments for or actual efforts to establish harmony among minority groups.
12. Pluralism: sentiment in favor of or examples of multiculturalism, "tossed salad" metaphor, respect for all cultures, etc.
13. Assimilation: examples, evidence, or discussion of individuals or groups trying to "fit in" with society's mainstream.
14. Attitudes: when individual or group attitudes are themselves the issue.
15. Minority intersection: examples, evidence, or discussion of the common interests, problems, shared future of minority groups.
16. Role of race: determination of whether race played a primary, secondary, or nonexistent role in the conflicts.

Note: We do not mean these categories to be mutually exclusive, as in traditional content analyses, because articles may have multiple interpretations and represent a convergence of several themes. For each article, therefore, we recorded all relevant themes.

textual analysis used in this study is open to the possibility that the "really significant item may not be the one that continually recurs, but the one which stands out as the exception from the general pattern—but which is also given, in its exceptional context, the greatest weight" (Hall, 1975, p. 15). This method provides strategies that allow researchers to examine the main organizing ideas that suggest why given events are important and how they are to be understood (Gamson, 1989; Gitlin, 1980). It is then possible to ascertain the specific ways certain aspects of issues are highlighted and given prominence, whereas others aspects are downplayed, de-legitimized, or ignored.

In this analysis, we noted any underlying sentiments or themes about the groups involved revealed by words and phrases used to describe people, places, or processes; by juxtapositions or contrasting imagery conveyed by language use; and so on. Using these techniques, we try to make explicit the latent meanings about groups involved in interethnic conflict contained in the articles and show how those meanings are connected to the process of racial formation.

Significance of the Book

Our project is unique on several counts. First, in the now fairly extensive literature on mass media representation of racial minorities, there is almost no attention given to the depictions of interethnic relations. Most studies examine how the mass media represents a single minority group, and if there is any comparison at all it is with the White majority. In this book, we focus on the relations among racial minorities in conflict situations. Although our focus is interethnic conflict, our theoretical framework includes and our analysis is, to some extent, informed by a critical view of the role of whiteness both in the way these conflicts originate and in the way the conflicts are represented. Thus, even though our study moves beyond the Black–White paradigm that underpins most research on media and racial minorities, we retain whiteness as an important concept because it provides a powerful analytical tool for understanding the nature and implications of media representations.

Second, most media studies in the United States have focused on general-circulation media, or those that are owned and staffed primarily by Whites, thought to have no particular orientation toward any one racial or ethnic group and who produce news they deem to be of interest to a general readership. Our study expands the focus to include ethnic minority papers, or those that are owned and staffed primarily by members of one ethnic or racial group, have an explicit orientation toward members of that group, and produce news items of particular interest to members of that group. By including both categories of news coverage in our analysis, we believe we will develop a more comprehensive understanding of the range of discourse about interethnic conflict potentially available to all members of a community. Further, by expanding the focus of analysis in this way, we are able to consider the role of news in the racial formation process from a more comprehensive perspective because we are examining a wider range of groups and a wider range of news media than typically examined.

Third, many (if not most) studies of race and media in the United States are descriptive and lack an organizing conceptual or theoretical framework. Significant exceptions to this trend are the bodies of work (in the United States) by Robert Entman, John Fiske, Oscar Gandy, and Herman Gray. In this book, we bring to the study a set of conceptual and theoretical tools that are in some respects unique to the study of race and media. Our study is framed by a theory of racial formation that allows us to consider the reciprocal relationships between structure and culture as it applies to news coverage of racial minority groups. For instance, the racial formation approach helps us interpret our empirical analysis in terms of the relations between cultural representations of ethnic groups and their use in structures of racial domination. Racial formation also allows us to bring the concepts of ideology and hegemony into play to help us demonstrate the importance of the press as a key producer of cultural symbols that can either buttress the racial status quo or offer alternative visions of how the world operates. This part of our analysis leads us to a critique of press performance and recommendations for improvement.

Finally, our approach allows us to grapple with issues that most existing media research on race does not address. For example, we are able to consider the analytical usefulness of media research informed by Black–White models of race relations in a multiethnic America. Our analysis may help us better understand the demographic complexity of the United States in the 21st century. Specifically, our study may contribute to an understanding of ethnic minority press and the role it assumes in the creation of the "new" America. Do these newspapers take on a counterhegemonic role that challenges racial hegemony, thus contributing to competing visions of interethnic relations? How is racial ideology played out in the racial projects of the general circulation and ethnic minority press? What are the implications for racial hegemony and racial formation, generally? In the following chapters we will take on these and other questions by analyzing the press coverage of interethnic tensions in three U.S. cities.

Organization of the Book

We have divided the book into two main parts. The chapters in these parts represent the empirical analysis of the news coverage of interethnic conflict in the three cities. Part I contains Chapter 2 on news coverage of events in Miami, in 1989, and Chapter 3 on news coverage of disturbances in Washington, D.C., in 1991. Each chapter begins with an overview of the city's political economy and ethnic relations at the time the disturbances broke out.

Part II is devoted entirely to Los Angeles, in 1992. The scope, scale, and significance of the disturbances there were unprecedented. The now-famous videotape of Los Angeles police officers vigorously beating a Black motorist was viewed around the world and drew condemnation from human rights groups and concerned citizens from around the globe. The four officers involved in the beating were indicted and put on trial for assault. For several weeks, the case was a constant feature in news and popular culture in the United States and, to a lesser extent than the videotape of the beating, globally. When the verdicts exonerating the police were announced, much of the world's attention was focused on Los Angeles. Thus, the aftermath of verdicts—the outbreak of violence, looting, and arson—drew more extensive news coverage than did the Miami and Washington, D.C., conflicts and gave us a unique opportunity to examine Los Angeles in a way not available for the other two cities. As a result, we could not contain a comparative analysis of the news coverage of Los Angeles in the same manner as the chapters on Miami and Washington, D.C. Chapter 4 is an introduction to the political economy and ethnic relations in Los Angeles in the spring of 1992. The next four chapters report analyses of news coverage of the disturbances: Chapter 5 is on the city's general circulation newspaper; Chapter 6 covers the city's leading Spanish-language newspaper; Chapter 7 is on Black press coverage; and Chapter 8 presents coverage by the Asian American press.

Chapter 9, the last chapter, presents our conclusions regarding lessons learned about the role of news in racial formation, the place of ethnic minority media in the public sphere, and the importance of "competing visions" in imagining America.

2

Miami, 1989

In this chapter, we focus primarily on the ways three Miami newspapers
depicted and discussed Latino–Black interaction during an episode of
race-related violence in the Overtown and Liberty City sections of Miami
in early 1989. The three local newspapers we examined are the *Miami
Herald,* the city's general circulation daily newspaper, the *Miami Times,* a
weekly serving Miami's Black community, and *El Nuevo Herald,* a daily
that serves the Latino community. After describing these newspapers, we
present an overview of the political economy of Miami at the time of the
local disturbances. Then we begin our analysis of the news coverage.

John and James Knight bought the *Miami Herald* from Frank Shutts in
1937. Although there were other competing newspapers in the city at the time,
the *Herald* was the leading newspaper in terms of both circulation and influence (Smiley, 1974, p. 19). The Knight brothers were interested in creating a
highly profitable newspaper, but they also were determined to publish a paper
connected to the community (Smiley, 1974, p. 330). Thus, the *Herald,* with a
circulation of about 340,000, has always been a key player in the civic life of
the city and one of the primary elements of the local power structure. This role
meant, on the one hand, that the *Herald* was central to the growth and development of the city. But, on the other hand, sections of the community that did
not always benefit from the paper's positions resented its influence. For example, during the 1980s, when major changes in the composition of the city's
population were taking place, the relationship between the *Herald* and the
Cuban community was strained at best (Croucher, 1997, p. 48).

Perhaps in an effort to improve relations, the *Miami Herald* launched a
Spanish-language newspaper called *El Herald* in 1976. It was the country's

first Spanish-language paper attached to a major U.S. daily newspaper. The first issue of *El Herald* was distributed as an insert in the *Miami Herald*. The *Miami Herald* delivered it to all subscribers with a Spanish surname. *El Herald*'s content was mainly translations of articles in the *Miami Herald* with some emphasis on news from Latin America. Initially, the Latino community criticized *El Herald* for its lack of editorial independence. In 1987, the Spanish-language paper's name was changed to *El Nuevo Herald*, its offices were moved to a section of Miami where other Spanish-language media made their home, and it was published as a separate newspaper with complete editorial independence (Rodriguez, 1999, p. 125). Miami's Latino community received the move with favor, although some still resent the lingering influence of the *Miami Herald* in local politics. Nevertheless, at the time of the 1989 disturbances, *El Nuevo Herald*, with an estimated circulation of 70,000, was perhaps the most influential Spanish-language medium in Miami, establishing the agenda for other Spanish-language media in the area (Veciana-Suarez, 1990, p. 50).

The *Miami Times* is the city's Black-owned and -operated weekly. Henry E. S. Reeves, who emigrated from the Bahamas in 1919, founded the newspaper in 1923. Reeves also owned a printing business, the profits from which were used to keep the *Miami Times* afloat. The newspaper struggled to survive. Reeves printed the paper himself, and his children often sat around the kitchen table folding the papers before delivering them. Reeves was dedicated to providing, through the newspaper, a forum for the voice of Miami's Black community. The newspaper has won several awards for its reporting on issues of concern to the Black community such as lynching, the Ku Klux Klan, segregation, political power, and so on (Dunn, 1997, p. 90). The newspaper continues, under the leadership of Reeves's son Garth and Garth's daughter Rachel, to actively speak out for Miami's Black community. The *Times* has a circulation of about 24,000.

The Political and Economic Context in Miami, 1989

Long known as a popular tourist attraction and a major financial hub for Latin America and the Caribbean, Miami is one of the most cosmopolitan cities in the United States. Drawn by warm temperatures, beaches, and exotic Latin culture, millions of tourists every year from around the nation and the world are attracted to Miami. As people from all across Latin American and the Caribbean began immigrating to Miami, the city quickly established itself as the economic center of the region and, in some ways, its social and political center as well. Just below the surface in Miami, however, there are long-standing racial anxieties borne of ethnic diversity and political battles over control of resources.

To understand the political economy of racial tension in Miami, we must first review some of the basic demographic changes in the area since 1960. Simply put, Miami is one of the most internationalized cities in the United States. The city has the highest proportion of foreign-born population among all major U.S. cities. Latinos, who made up 63% of the city's population, dominated Miami's 1990 population of about 358,000. Blacks made up 25%, "non-Hispanic Whites" accounted for 11%, and others accounted for the remaining 1% (Miami Department of Planning and Zoning, 2001).[5] Among the Latino population, the dominant group was Cubans, with smaller communities of Colombians, Nicaraguans, Salvadorans, and others. Jamaicans, Haitians, and other West Indians accounted for most of the population that was not Latino, White, or U.S.-born Blacks.[6] This demographic trend has affected Miami's neighborhood settlement patterns, political struggles, employment patterns, and even U.S. foreign policy. And all these issues relate to the city's race relations.

Miami has experienced interethnic tensions since the early 1960s when upper- and middle-class, almost exclusively White Cubans, displaced by Fidel Castro's revolution, immigrated there. The U.S. government immediately classified the Cubans newcomers as "friends." The émigrés served a useful symbolic function: the U.S. government portrayed their journey as a flight to freedom, which legitimized Cold War foreign policy. The U.S. government soon provided these Cubans with a wide range of public-assistance programs under the legislation of the Civil Rights Act of 1964. The Cuban expatriate community rapidly prospered and used its economic might as leverage to consolidate and maintain political power, which translated into gains in other areas (Dunn & Stepick, 1992). For example, public schools created classes to accommodate Spanish-speaking Cubans, whereas American-born Blacks remained segregated. The area's business owners hired Cuban workers, which displaced many Black workers (although large numbers of Whites also were displaced, according to Stepick & Grenier, 1993). Also, lending practices increasingly favored White Cuban entrepreneurs and led to a slow death for the American-born Black business community (Harris, 1994).

Blacks were embittered and felt isolated by a sense that they had been abandoned by liberal native-born Whites and the local, state, and federal institutions they dominated, just as the Black community felt it was about to make political and economic gains against entrenched racism and discrimination. Resentment among Blacks grew as another wave of immigrants from Cuba in 1980 (that brought many Black Cubans to Miami) and Nicaraguans in

1989 were welcomed and given asylum. Miami's Blacks resented the quick acceptance of Latino immigrants, especially because Black Haitians trying to flee the Duvalier regime were turned away despite the objections of Miami's Black community. Eventually, the U.S. government allowed Haitian immigration, but because of cultural differences and a perception that the Haitians were also economically outpacing native Blacks, a strong Haitian–Black alliance never materialized (Stepick, 1992, pp. 62-63). Meanwhile, Latinos— especially "White" Cubans—rejected accusations that they were responsible for Black unemployment and poverty, claiming that the problems existed even before they arrived. These racial dynamics also show the almost inevitable rift that developed between Cubans with African lineage and Cubans with European lineage. As highlighted in a recent *New York Times* series on race relations, White Cubans gravitated toward the power and privilege afforded by their light complexion, whereas Black Cubans eventually realized that in the United States they would be forced to take a place alongside Black Americans on the lowest rungs of racial hierarchy (see Ojito, 2000).

As immigration from the Caribbean, Central America, and South America continued, an unusual housing pattern emerged in Dade County. Most Latinos settled in Miami or established contiguous municipalities around Miami, concentrating their political base. A vast majority of Haitians settled in Little Haiti, a few blocks north of downtown Miami. Native Blacks continued to live in physically unconnected neighborhoods, which undermined their influence in local and city politics and made organizing difficult. In combination with native White flight and the growing economic clout of Latinos, these settlement patterns helped Latinos gain and maintain a measure of political power in the form of seats on city and county commissions, school boards, and other municipal agencies (Warren, Corbett, & Stack, 1990). The increasing political influence enjoyed by Latinos was illustrated in 1984, when the Puerto Rican-born mayor of Miami and two Cuban City Commission members ousted a popular Black city manager and replaced him with a Cuban American. Later, the city elected a White Cuban American, Xavier Suarez, to serve as mayor for the following term. Despite growing economic and political power of White Cubans, native Whites remained the most powerful group in Miami, controlling most of the capital and almost all of the media and dominating the many important political bodies (Harris, 1994, p. 86; Perez, 1992, p. 104; Warren et al., 1990, pp. 158-164).

As a result of these and other similar trends, Black Miamians grew disillusioned with what they perceived as gains among the Latino community, which came at the expense of the continuing impoverishment of Miami's Black community. Adding to the resentment was the fact that White Cubans and other Latinos (and to a small extent, Haitians) continued to benefit, with the support of White-controlled government institutions, from policies enacted as a result of pressure from Black leaders of the civil rights movement. Blacks were, as Harris (1994, p. 81) points out, in "the unenviable position of watching newcomers being granted precisely what they had been attempting to secure for themselves: the uninterrupted opportunity to develop viable, life-sustaining institutions."

The racial tension between the Latino and Black communities in Miami burst into violence four times in the 1980s, each time the shooting, looting, and arson taking place in the predominantly Black communities of Overtown and Liberty City.[7] In May 1980, an all-White jury acquitted five Metro-Dade police officers in the beating death of a Black motorcyclist named Arthur McDuffie in December 1979. Violence broke out in the Liberty City, Overtown, and Coconut Grove areas of Miami as Blacks reacted to the jury decision. In December 1982, Luis Alvarez, a Latino police officer with the Miami police department, shot and killed Nevell Johnson Jr. while trying to arrest him in an Overtown video arcade. The subsequent violence was limited to the Overtown area. Alvarez was tried on manslaughter charges. When an all-White jury acquitted Alvarez in March 1984, violence broke out in Liberty City.

Finally, on January 16, 1989, William Lozano, a Colombian American police officer, shot and killed motorcyclist Clement Anthony Lloyd as he was apparently fleeing an off-duty police officer. Lloyd's passenger, Allan Blanchard, died the following day from massive head injuries sustained when the motorcycle crashed into an oncoming car. Shortly after the shooting, Mayor Xavier Suarez was alerted of the incident and rushed to the scene to help avert racial violence that had occurred three times already in the 1980s. When Suarez arrived, paramedics had already covered Lloyd's body and a crowd of angry local residents, mainly Black, was gathering and growing rapidly. The crowd began to throw sticks, bottles, and bricks, and assistants quickly took Suarez away. Three days of violence and arson followed, mainly in the Overtown and Liberty City areas. In contrast to the earlier outbreaks of racial violence in Miami, the 1989 incident received wide national coverage because the country's news organizations had sent a total of about 1,500 reporters to Miami to cover the Super Bowl scheduled for January 22. The incident gained further attention because the shooting occurred a few hours after the city's Martin Luther King holiday parade.

The Coverage

Over the time period analyzed, the *Miami Herald* published a total of 55 items, the *Miami Times* published 24 items, and *El Nuevo Herald*

Table 2.1   Number and Percentage of Articles in Miami Newspapers Mentioning Various Groups

	MH (n = 55)		MT (n = 24)		ENH (n = 38)	
	#	%	#	%	#	%
Blacks	49	89.0	23	95.8	28	73.7
Latinos	31	56.0	19	79.0	33	86.8
Whites	20	36.6	10	41.6	5	13.2
Cubans	3	5.5	3	12.5	7	18.4
Haitians	3	5.5	3	12.5	0	0
Nicaraguans	3	5.5	1	4.2	2	8.3
Colombians	2	3.6	0	0	11	45.8
West Indians	1	1.8	0	0	2	8.3

MH = *Miami Herald*
MT = *Miami Times*
ENH = *El Nuevo Herald*

published 38 items. *El Nuevo Herald* reprinted 25 news articles from the *Miami Herald*. Only *El Nuevo Herald* published the remaining 13 articles, mainly columns and editorials. We examine all 38 *El Nuevo Herald* articles as a group, however, because the editors selected all of them to appear in the paper.

Ethnic Groups in Miami

The *Miami Herald* and the *Miami Times* mentioned Blacks in the news stories more than any other group. (See Table 2.1.) In the *Miami Herald* and the *Miami Times,* at least 85% of the articles mentioned Blacks, with the *Miami Times* mentioning Blacks in nearly 96% of their articles. In *El Nuevo Herald,* Latinos were mentioned more than any other group (in nearly 87% of the stories), although Blacks appeared in a large proportion of the stories as well (nearly 74%). However, if we look at the 13 articles appearing only in *El Nuevo Herald*, Blacks are the most frequently mentioned group.

The *Miami Herald* and the *Miami Times* mentioned West Indians as distinct from Blacks three times each, and always in reference to Haitians. Even though Clement Lloyd was a native of the Caribbean island of St. Thomas, and Allan Blanchard was a native of the Virgin Islands, the *Miami Herald* and the *Miami Times* articles referred to Lloyd and Blanchard as Blacks. *El Nuevo Herald* distinctly mentioned West Indians twice but not in reference to Clement Lloyd or Allan Blanchard.

In the *Miami Herald* and the *Miami Times,* the second most frequently mentioned group was "Hispanic," which was used as an umbrella term that referred most commonly to Cubans, Nicaraguans, and Colombians (the home country of William Lozano), although these and other nationalities from the Latin American region were rarely named. For example, although it was clear from the context of certain news articles that the term "Hispanic" was meant to refer to Cubans in Miami, the *Miami Herald* and the *Miami Times* only mentioned Cubans explicitly three times each. In the case of Lozano's nationality, the *Miami Herald* explicitly mentioned it twice, and the *Miami Times* never mentioned it.

As indicated earlier, Latinos were the most frequently appearing group in *El Nuevo Herald.* The newspaper more frequently used specific nationalities when referring to people of Latin cultures (although the umbrella term "Hispanic" was still the most frequently used label) than the *Miami Herald* and the *Miami Times.* For example, there are many references to William Lozano and his Colombian supporters in Miami, recent Nicaraguan immigrants, and Cubans who dominated city politics and business.

The use of ethnic labels can gloss over the cultural complexity of these groups and their interactions. By almost always using the categories "Black" and "Hispanic," newspaper articles potentially ignore the within-group diversity among these groups and may present the nature of the race-related problems in an oversimplified manner. One instance in which the erasure of complexity and cultural uses of ethnic labeling became clear was in the way the *Miami Herald* referred to Lozano. In most cases, the *Miami Herald* referred to him either by name or as a Miami police officer. But when it attached an ethnic label, an interesting transformation took place. Initially, Lozano was referred to as a White police officer ("Police Chase Sparks Violence," *Miami Herald,* January 17, 1989, p. 1A; "Rage Spreads From Overtown," *Miami Herald,* January 18, 1989, p. 1A). Then, he was referred to as a "Hispanic officer" ("Violence Ebbs; City Sets Probe," *Miami Herald,* January 19, 1989, p. 1A; "Calm Prevails in Black Community," *Miami Herald,* January 20, 1989, p. 1A). Next, he was a "White Hispanic officer" ("3 Days of Anguish in Miami," *Miami Herald,* January 22, 1989, p. 1A; "Policeman Arrested in Cycle Deaths," *Miami Herald,* January 24, 1989, p. 1A). Finally, he became a "Hispanic officer" again ("The Lozano Charges," *Miami Herald,* January 25, 1989, p. 12A; "Congressman Hears Anger of Overtown," *Miami Herald,* January 28, 1989, p. 1D; "Blacks Need Tough Love of Middle Class," *Miami Herald,* February 2, 1989, p. 19A).

The *Miami Times,* on the other hand, identified Lozano as Anglo from the very beginning of its coverage whenever it used an ethnic identifier

("Motive of Officer Unclear to Police," *Miami Times,* January 18, 1989, p. 1A; "New Police Review Panel Questions Powers to Act," *Miami Times,* January 26, 1989, p. 2A; "Sharpton Visits Miami," *Miami Times,* February 2, 1989, p. 3A; "Miami Race Relations," *Miami Times,* March 2, 1989, p. 4A). This labeling decision may indicate a different cultural (or political) perspective on race relations than the *Miami Herald* and suggests the basis for articulating racial ideology that may expose White privilege.

Although the focus of the news coverage was Black–Latino interaction, Whites were mentioned in roughly 40% of the *Miami Herald*'s and the *Miami Times*'s coverage. *El Nuevo Herald* mentioned Whites in about 13% of its coverage. But in all papers, Whites were the racial group least frequently mentioned. The *Miami Times* printed the greatest proportion of stories mentioning Whites, followed by the *Miami Herald* and *El Nuevo Herald,* which means that the *Miami Times* published proportionately more stories about Whites, Blacks, and Latinos than the *Miami Herald* and a greater proportion of stories about Blacks and Whites than *El Nuevo Herald.* The *Miami Herald* also published a greater percentage of its stories about Blacks and Whites than *El Nuevo Herald.*

Actors and Victims

Table 2.2 shows that news coverage in all publications examined focused mainly on actual rather than potential actors and victims. News coverage mentioned Blacks as actual actors in a greater proportion of *Miami Herald* articles (39.5%) than either the *Miami Times* articles (29%) or the *El Nuevo Herald* articles (20%). In almost each case, Blacks as actual actors in the *Miami Herald* and *El Nuevo Herald* were framed as enthusiastic participants in the rioting and as angry complainers about a history of police brutality in Miami. For example, the news article about the events in Overtown immediately following the shooting portrayed a crowd of Blacks in Overtown as angry and out of control:

> Police were randomly fired on. At least two buildings and several vehicles were set on fire. An auto parts store was set ablaze and fire trucks were unable to get near the cause of gunfire. Several police officers, reporters and passersby were hit by rocks and bottles. ("Authorities Cordon off Parts of City," *Miami Herald,* January 17, 1989, p. 1A)

Although the *Miami Times* also made reference to Blacks as actors participating in the disturbances, there were also stories about Blacks as actors in other contexts. For example, the paper reported on calls for calm

Table 2.2 Number and Percentage of Articles in Miami Newspapers Discussing Various Actors and Victims

	Number (Percent)											
	Actors						Victims					
	Actual			Potential			Actual			Potential		
	MH	MT	ENH	MH	MT	ENH	MH	MT	ENH	MH	MT	ENH
Blacks	16 (29)	5 (20)	15 (39.5)	2 (3.6)	1 (4.2)	1 (2.6)	36 (65.5)	20 (83.3)	24 (65.8)	3 (5.5)	0 (0)	1 (2.6)
Latino	14 (25.5)	15 (62.5)	18 (47.7)	0 (0)	1 (4.2)	1 (4.2)	0 (0)	0 (0)	2 (5.3)	4 (7.2)	0 (0)	1 (2.6)
Whites	11 (20)	8 (33.3)	3 (7.9)	0 (0)	0 (0)	0 (0)	1 (1.8)	1 (1.8)	0 (0)	0 (0)	0 (0)	0 (0)
Gov't.	13 (23.6)	6 (24.9)	7 (18.4)	0 (0)	0 (0)	0 (0)	3 (4.4)	0 (0)	1 (2.6)	0 (0)	0 (0)	0 (0)
Police	5 (9.0)	1 (4.1)	3 (7.9)	1 (1.8)	0 (0)	0 (0)	1 (1.8)	0 (0)	1 (2.6)	1 (1.8)	0 (0)	0 (0)
Society	3 (5.5)	0 (0)	0 (0)	0 (0)	0 (0)	0 (0)	0 (0)	0 (0)	0 (0)	0 (0)	0 (0)	0 (0)

MH = Miami Herald
MT = Miami Times
ENH = El Nuevo Herald

issued by Black leaders such as Yolanda King ("Yolanda King Calls for Commitment to Father's Dream," *Miami Times,* January 26, 1989, p. 1A) and Congressman John Conyers ("Cop Speaks of Racism in Miami Force," *Miami Times,* February 2, 1989, p. 3A).

Latinos were mentioned as actors in the greatest proportion of stories in the *El Nuevo Herald* (62.5%), followed by *Miami Herald* (47.4%) and the *Miami Times* (25.5%). Most of the *Miami Times* references to Latinos as actors were to Lozano shooting Lloyd and to leaders such as Mayor Xavier Suarez and city manager Cesar Odio defending their actions in the aftermath of the shooting. In *El Nuevo Herald,* mentions of the activities of Lozano's family and supporters and the actions of Latino leaders accounted for the bulk of the references to Latinos. Only three stories actually reported Lozano as the man who did the shooting, a contrast to the *Miami Times's* emphasis on Lozano as the shooter.

The *Miami Herald* mentioned Blacks as actors more often than it did Latinos, perhaps because its focus was on the riots. On the other hand, the *Miami Times* mentioned Latinos as actors three times as often as Blacks as actors, perhaps because it wanted to focus more on the causes of the riots. Clearly, the *Miami Times* views Latinos as the primary actors, whereas the *Miami Herald* views both Blacks and Latinos as significant actors. *El Nuevo Herald* views Latinos and Blacks as the main actors.

White actors are the least frequently coded group for all newspapers. The *Miami Times* mentions Whites as actors in about one third of its stories, the *Miami Herald* in about one fifth of its stories, and *El Nuevo Herald* in about 8% of its stories. The overall pattern of reporting suggests that the *Miami Herald* coverage pays little attention to the role of White-dominated centers of economic and business power and emphasizes the actual violence and looting by paying more attention to Blacks and Latinos and government as actors. Meanwhile, the *Miami Times* emphasized that Latino actors (not Whites alone) also created conditions that led to violence. *El Nuevo Herald* de-emphasizes White action, downplays Lozano's role, and plays up the "problems" of Black actors.

The *Miami Herald* and the *Miami Times* mentioned government leaders as actors in about one quarter of the articles, almost always in reference to police action (such as shootings, patrolling, and investigations) or Mayor Suarez announcing new initiatives. In *El Nuevo Herald,* government leaders are actors in about 18% of the stories, perhaps indicating reluctance to discuss the role and actions of the Latino-dominated Miami government in creating conditions that led to the violence.

All publications clearly depicted actual victims mainly as Blacks. (See Table 2.2.) Blacks were the targets in almost all the coding of personal violence, in relation to the shootings of Lloyd and of a Black teen shot by a White motorist during the disturbances in Liberty City. The *Miami Times* brings this out a bit more as a proportion of their total coverage than either the *Miami Herald* or *El Nuevo Herald*. The *Miami Herald* and *El Nuevo Herald* mention Blacks as victims in a smaller proportion of their articles than the *Miami Times*.

El Nuevo Herald mentioned Blacks as victims in a bit more than 65% of the articles, in reference to the deaths of Lloyd and Blanchard or more generally to high rates of unemployment and poverty among Blacks in Miami. In two items (the only two with Latinos as victims), recent Nicaraguan immigrants are referred to as victims because they are refugees of war and forced temporarily to live in an outdoor stadium ("Who Should We Help," *El Nuevo Herald*, January, 22, 1989, p. 6).

Conflict, Fear, and Outrage

In the *Miami Herald*, the *Miami Times*, and *El Nuevo Herald*, the conflict theme was coded more than any other, indicating that a focus on the tension between Blacks and Latinos often was the "hook" used to organize coverage of the events. (See Table 2.3.) The recurrence of conflict in Miami for the fourth time in the 1980s led to much sadness and disillusionment on the part of both journalists and the sources they consulted. But the tone and context of the reporting is quite different among the *Miami Herald*, the *Miami Times*, and *El Nuevo Herald*.

The *Miami Herald* presented the sadness and disillusionment in a context of fear of Blacks. Although the reporting in the *Miami Herald* seems to be detached, analytical discussion of the issues, there is also fear about the implications of the conflict. Fifteen articles were coded as containing the fear theme. Fear is reported in the stories that mention police working to cordon off and seal the violence in Liberty City and Overtown so that it didn't spill over into other areas. For example, the first report of the disturbance was headlined "Police Chase Sparks Violence; Overtown Melee Erupts After Motorcyclist Dies; Authorities Cordon off Parts of the City" (*Miami Herald*, January 17, 1989, p. 1A). The latter subhead referred to police roadblocks to keep the violence from spreading into upscale sections of Miami to the south (in Coconut Grove) and east (in Coral Gables).

The *Miami Times* reported sadness and disillusionment about the conflict in what could be described as outrage using the voice of people who have seen and lived the pattern of perceived abuses of the Black community by the Latino-dominated Miami city government. These stories contain

Table 2.3   Number and Percentage of Articles in Miami Newspapers
Discussing Various Content Themes

	MH (n = 55)		MT (n = 24)		ENH (n = 38)	
	#	%	#	%	#	%
Immigration	6	10.9	7	24.2	3	10.5
Fear	15	27.3	1	4.2	8	21.0
Racism	19	34.3	16	66.7	10	24.3
Culture/Values	9	16.4	1	4.2	5	13.1
Violence						
Verbal	0	0	0	0	0	0
Personal	35	63.6	19	79.2	22	57.9
Property	27	49.0	12	50.0	17	44.7
Causes						
Individual	21	43.1	10	42.7	14	36.8
Institutional	22	38.2	13	54.3	14	36.8
Structural	17	31.0	9	37.5	5	13.2
Reassurance	6	10.9	2	8.3	2	5.3
Discontent	35	63.6	19	79.2	20	57.1
Conflict	40	72.7	19	79.2	28	73.7
Cooperation	4	16.7	2	3.7	2	3.6
Pluralism	3	5.5	0	0	0	0
Assimilation	2	3.6	0	0	1	2.6
Attitudes	5	9.1	12	50.0	1	2.6
Minority	4	7.3	1	4.2	4	10.5
Intersection						
Role of Race						
Primary	25	45.5	15	62.5	15	39.5
Secondary	7	12.7	2	8.3	2	5.3
None	1	1.8	1	4.2	1	2.6
No Mention	22	40.0	6	25.0	20	52.6

MH = *Miami Herald*
MT = *Miami Times*
ENH = *El Nuero Herald*

fragments of racial ideology that challenge racial hegemony by exposing
forms of structural domination of racial bodies. The paper quotes Black
community residents to emphasize the point:

> "Being a Black man in the city of Miami is a dangerous occupation," said
> Overtown resident Ronnie Hardman. ("Black Miamians Question Use of
> Lethal Force by Police," *Miami Times*, January 26, 1989, p. 3A)

A similar sentiment is expressed in an editorial:

Our people are pushed to the limit by police violence and a background of neglect and discrimination. ("Pushed to the Limit," *Miami Times*, January 26, 1989, p. 4A)

Unlike the *Miami Herald*, there is hardly any mention of fear in the *Miami Times*. There is, in fact, only one story that was coded as containing fear. In the story, a Black resident who is tired of violence in Black suburbs fears the eventual breakdown of the Black community ("Blacks Need to Let Go of Scapegoats," *Miami Times*, January 26, 1989, p. 3).

In *El Nuevo Herald*, the sadness and disillusionment appeared to be about continuing racial friction between Black community leaders and the Latino-dominated city government. Conflict was clearly a central theme in stories published in the days immediately following the shooting of Lloyd (January 17 to January 20). These stories were hard news stories with headlines such as "Riots in Overtown" (January 17); "The Violence Has Spread" (January 18); "Armed Employees Take Care of Store" (January 19); and "The Miami Riots" (January 20). In the coverage between January 17 and January 20, all stories but one (14 of 15) were direct translations of the *Miami Herald* articles. Conflict also was mentioned as a theme in coverage between January 21 and March 3 but was not as central to the story. Of the 23 items appearing between these dates, many were analytical and explanatory columns written by *El Nuevo Herald* staff, not *Miami Herald* staff. Thirteen of these 23 items appeared only in *El Nuevo Herald*. In these pieces, more often than not, conflict appeared as background for discussion of other issues.

Despite the conflict frame, *El Nuevo Herald* writers expressed some sympathy for Blacks on some items. There is acknowledgment in some items that Blacks and Latinos face similar problems. For example, in one signed column, the writer asks rhetorically: "Aren't the rights of the Black minority being stepped on daily? Don't we see opportunities closed to our own citizens?" ("The Veins of Hatred," *El Nuevo Herald*, January 20, 1989, p. 6A). In another column, the writer suggests that "Black, Hispanic and White construction workers can work together" to rebuild damaged buildings ("In Search of Solutions," *El Nuevo Herald*, January 27, 1989, p. 6A). Perhaps as a result of this empathy for the condition of the Black community, *El Nuevo Herald* writers encouraged Latinos to help Blacks. In a one item, the writer declared,

The Hispanics of Miami have a duty. As victims of political and economic oppression, we should take responsibility toward respecting universal human rights. ("The Veins of Hatred," *El Nuevo Herald*, January 20, 1989, p. 6A)

The other papers also published only a small number of articles about cooperation.

Heroes

Mayor Suarez

One of the first heroes in the *Miami Herald* coverage of the disturbances was Mayor Suarez. On the night of the shooting, Suarez went to the site of the incident to talk with residents and relatives of Lloyd. The lead paragraph of the lead article about the disturbances was

> Miami Mayor Xavier Suarez became the target of rocks and bottles as he walked alone down a street trying to calm the neighborhood. ("Police Chase Sparks Violence," *Miami Herald,* January 17, 1989, p. 1A)

The paper also emphasized Suarez's actions as he comforted Lloyd's mother and sister even though he was in such a precarious position.

Police

Despite the heroic mayor image, without question, the biggest heroes in the disturbances were the police, according to the *Miami Herald* and *El Nuevo Herald*. Police were depicted as carrying out an extremely difficult task under potentially deadly circumstances:

> An officer took a bullet in his protective vest in a pitched gun battle between riot police and angry youths about 9:30 p.m. in Liberty City. He wasn't badly hurt. ("Rage Spreads From Overtown," *Miami Herald,* January 18, 1989, p. 1A)

Later, in another article, readers learn that this officer had been shot before while chasing fleeing suspects. "After each of the episodes," the article reports, "Butler [the officer] went back to the streets, where he wanted to be" ("Officer Survives a Bullet—For a Second Time," *Miami Herald,* January 18, 1989, p. 13A).

Another dimension of the heroic image of police created by the *Miami Herald* was that despite the very real dangers the police faced during the disturbances, they did not overreact. The *Miami Herald* prominently quotes the police chief Perry Anderson as he explained his strategy to deal with the disturbances:

His first priority was to "make sure all the areas were blocked off" he said Wednesday. Anderson immediately ordered every available car and body into the streets. But Anderson said he counseled moderation, telling officers to avoid brandishing shotguns "like we were going into Vietnam"—and to avoid police dogs because residents could see them as agitators. ("Lesson of Past Is Contain, Control, Police Say," *Miami Herald,* January 19, 1989, p. 21A)

In this passage, the article depicts police as working to make sure the violence does not spread to other parts of the city and making sure that police do not upset people in the neighborhood with shotguns and police dogs. The *Miami Herald* adds to the police-as-hero image by including Anderson's reference to another tense Third World context, which implies the danger in Liberty City and Overtown faced by police.

Not only were police in the streets heroic but also police working indoors contributed to defuse the tense situation. The *Miami Herald* reported that the Dade County Jail started using a shorter arrest form to "expedite the flow of prisoners" ("Rage Spreads From Overtown," *Miami Herald,* January 18, 1989, p. 1A).

Latino Businessmen

Another set of heroes, depicted only in *El Nuevo Herald,* were local Latino businessmen and civic leaders who were making plans to rebuild Overtown and Liberty City even as the disturbances were ongoing. These *El Nuevo Herald* articles emphasize that Latino organizations and individuals, who are depicted as going out of their way to strengthen the Black community in Miami, are heroic (almost saintly) because they are helping the ones who hurt them. For example, prominent attention is given to Latino financial leaders in the area organizing an "aggressive campaign to attract money back into the Black neighborhoods" ("Is There a Solution for Overtown?" *El Nuevo Herald,* January 22, 1989, p. 3B).

Blacks

The depiction of heroes in the *Miami Times* is almost literally 180 degrees different from both the *Miami Herald* and *El Nuevo Herald.* First, there were few discussions of heroes. Only two articles contained references to heroes. Second, the discussion of heroes focused on Blacks. In one article, the paper reported on the efforts of an elderly Overtown resident who tried to stop the destruction of a store he helped found and who eventually died from inhaling tear gas ("Man Dies From Tear Gas,"

Miami Times, January 26, p. 2A). In a second item ("Riot or Tea Party," *Miami Times,* January 26, p. 4A), a writer claims that the "acceptability [of rioting] is influenced by the ethnicity of the rioter." The writer claims that the Boston Tea Party was a riot that a majority of colonists found acceptable. He argues that the Overtown disturbances were a riot that the majority of Miami residents (particularly Whites and Latinos) found unacceptable. He then argues that both the Boston Tea Party and the Overtown disturbances were heroic acts of "human beings behav[ing] humanly" ("Riot or Tea Party," *Miami Times,* January 26, 1989, p. 4A). The writer gives the disturbances legitimacy by interpreting them as political action. And by framing the events as political acts, the people involved are given agency, an important basis for nonessentialized cultural representation.

Villains

Blacks

In the *Miami Herald* and *El Nuevo Herald,* the villains of the disturbances are Blacks. For example, Blacks were singled out for their destruction of property in the Overtown neighborhood. A *Miami Herald* article reported,

> [The] racial violence began Monday night, escalated Tuesday and diminished Wednesday. There remained after effects of frustration, tension and the daunting results of burning and looting sprees that ruined many non-Black businesses in Black neighborhoods. ("Calm Prevails As City Looks for Solutions," *Miami Herald,* May 20, 1989, p. 1B)

The construction of this paragraph codes "racial violence" as Black and depicts the "non-Black businesses" as the target of Black violence. The extent of Black violence and villainy is represented graphically in the form of a map that indicated the location of 38 various incidents of shootings, clashes, looting, vandalism, and fires ("A Night of Violence," *Miami Herald,* May 19, 1989, p. 11A).

The Blacks-as-villain image was magnified by personalized accounts of the impact of Black violence. For example, several stories report about specific store owners whose merchandise was stolen and whose property was destroyed. One typical story detailed the store owners' backgrounds, reported the damage to their property, and discussed how the people planned to survive.

Homer and Comer Stembridge have been in this life together since the day they were born 65 years ago. They were raised on a cotton farm in Alabama, joined the Army then went into business in Miami. This week they are facing adversity together. Homer figures he and his brother lost $75,000 worth of merchandise and they have no insurance. They employ seven people from the neighborhood and charge no interest when people buy on credit. "You can do a good business here," said Homer, "but with a loss like this." ("Looters Hit Twins Who Stayed," *Miami Herald,* January 20, 1989, p. 2D)

This story villainizes Blacks by humanizing their victims. The article reports the twin store owners' life circumstances and the fact that they have been responsible community citizens. But they are also the innocent victims of "racial violence," the code for Black rioters.

Other innocent victims of Black violence were children who were frightened by the events going on outside their houses. A story with interviews of a number of schoolchildren painted a sad picture of third graders' reactions to the disturbances:

Tuesday night Yolanda did not sleep because of all the gunfire. Neither did Chartevia. She was afraid someone would burn her house down. "The people next door were shooting a lot of guns and I was afraid that a bullet might come through my window," said Yolanda. ("Kids Learn Lesson in Fear," *Miami Herald,* May 19, 1989, p. 20A)

These descriptions depict the acts of Black rioters as particularly treacherous because the victims are children. Having created the cultural representation of the Black villains, in part by emphasizing their innocent victims, the villains can then be legitimately disciplined through structural domination.

El Nuevo Herald also portrayed Blacks as villains in ways similar to those found in the *Miami Herald.* One article reported that a Latino man was stoned by a group of Black men ("Riot in Overtown," *El Nuevo Herald,* January 17, 1989, p. 1A). Another reported that Blacks were involved in "seven gun shot injuries, 1 death, 321 arrests, and the robbing or looting of 22 stores" ("Panel to Investigate Police," *El Nuevo Herald,* January 19, 1989, p. 1A). A third article takes Blacks to task for causing the cancellation of a Miami Heat professional basketball game ("The Violence Has Spread," *El Nuevo Herald,* January 18, 1989, p. 1A).

Police and Latino City Leaders

In the *Miami Times,* villains are almost exclusively police and Latino city officials. The first article calls the Lozano–Lloyd incident an "unwarranted shooting of an unarmed motorcyclist by a non-Black Miami police officer" that was "just one of a series of instances of unnecessary police violence against Blacks." A page 1 editorial decried "the unconscionable acts of police brutality [against Blacks]" ("A Harsh Lesson," *Miami Times,* January 19, 1989, p. 1A). The city and its leaders also were depicted as villains. The paper quoted a lawyer for Lloyd's pregnant girlfriend who said,

> We intend to sue the City of Miami on behalf of the unborn child. This is a senseless act [by a city police officer] that has robbed a child of its father and the city should pay for this mess. ("Black Miami Erupts in Another Angry Revolt," *Miami Times,* 1989, January 19, p. 1A)

As in the *Miami Herald* reports that used children to depict Blacks as villains, this *Miami Times* report uses an unborn child as a symbol of the villainy of an agent of the city's police force.

Countertrends

The depiction of villains and heroes was a fairly stable rhetorical construction in the newspapers. There were a handful of exceptions to the general trends, however. In the *Miami Herald,* where the heroes were the police, the mayor, and Latinos, and the villains were mainly Blacks, a few articles disrupted these classifications. For example, the newspaper depicted the police "heroes" as out of control. In one article, a community resident is quoted saying, "We've been victimized all our lives [by police] and now they're treating us like animals" ("Authorities Cordon off Parts of City," *Miami Herald,* January 17, 1989, p. 1A). In another article, the image of the Black "villains" was countered by a well-publicized report of three Black men escorting Mayor Suarez from the danger of the Black crowd hurling bottles at him ("Holiday Honoring King Turned to Night of Anger," *Miami Herald,* January 18, 1989, p. 1A).

El Nuevo Herald, in which the "heroes" were Latino organizations and the mayor, and the "villains" were Blacks, also published the article about the Black men who came to the aid of the mayor as he tried to calm Blacks in Overtown ("King Celebration Turns Into Night of Violence," *El Nuevo Herald,* January 18, 1989, p. 1A). An *El Nuevo Herald* article that counters the Latino hero image is one that reports that some Latino employers discriminate against Blacks. The article reports that "construction contractors, many of whom who are Cuban Americans, agree that knowledge of Spanish and hate for communism makes Nicaraguans more attractive employees," and "many employers say [Blacks] are victims of racism"

("Nicaraguans Take Day Labor Away From Blacks," *El Nuevo Herald,*
January 20, 1989, p. 1A).

In the *Miami Times,* in which Blacks were the "heroes," and police were
the "villains," one article depicted Blacks as the villains. The story quoted
a community resident:

> The police killing the man was wrong but the violence and the stealing were
> wrong, too. Those type things put a bad mark on all Black people. ("What the
> People of Miami Are Saying," *Miami Times,* January 26, 1989, p. 6A)

There were no stories in the *Miami Times* that countered the police as
"villains" image, however.

Causes of Conflict

The *Miami Herald* pinned the blame for the Liberty City/Overtown
disturbances on a wide range of problems, people, institutions, and social
structures.

Individual-level Causes

Among the individuals noted as causes are Nicaraguan refugees
("Overtown Feels Pain, Frustration," *Miami Herald,* January 18, 1989,
p. 1A; "For Poorest, Life Only Gets Worse," *Miami Herald,* January 18,
1989, p. 1B; "Violence Ebbs, City Sets Probe," *Miami Herald,* January 19,
1989, p. 1A), Latino business owners who discriminate against Blacks
("Blacks Feel Left Out As Refugees Get Jobs," *Miami Herald,* January 20,
1989, p. 10A), White police officers for brutality against Blacks ("Promises
to Public Haven't All Been Kept," *Miami Herald,* January 18, 1989, p. 13A;
"A Painful Cry: What Does It Take to Be Heard?" *Miami Herald,* January 19,
1989, p. 1B; "Prominent Blacks Feel Frustration," *Miami Herald,* January 19,
1989, p. 1C; "Congressman Hears Anger of Overtown," *Miami Herald,*
January 28, 1989, p. 1D), and Lozano for the deaths of Lloyd and
Blanchard ("Calm Prevails in Black Community," *Miami Herald,* January 20,
1989, p. 1A).

Although the *Miami Herald* never directly blames Blacks for the conflict
in Liberty City and Overtown, the paper does print quotes from sources
and guest columns that suggest Black culture and values may be linked to
the conflicts. In one article, a Black resident says that looting and violence
made Blacks look "primitive and destructive" ("A Dream in Ashes," *Miami
Herald,* January 19, 1989, p. 1C). In another article, a Black resident says,

"they [the rioters] think it's a manly thing to do" ("Black-Oriented Radio Stations Try to Calm Listeners," *Miami Herald,* January 19, 1989, p. 2C). A guest column suggests that the most serious problems are endemic to the Black community: "the problems would not be solved if all Anglos and Latinos left tomorrow" ("Our Black Ghettos Need Bold Action," *Miami Herald,* January 29, 1989, p. 1C). Another column says that Blacks need self-discipline and stronger community values ("Blacks Need Tough Love of Middle Class," *Miami Herald,* February 2, 1989, p. 19A).

In contrast, only one of the nine *Miami Herald* articles containing discussions of Latino culture and values was about the superior work ethic and willingness to work at almost any job on the part of recent Nicaraguan immigrants. Although only one article offers this perspective on a Latino group, in relation to the image of Black culture and values depicted, the coverage suggests that the *Miami Herald* places Blacks and Latinos at different places on the racial hierarchy.

Discussions of individual-level causes of the conflict frequently discussed the role race played in the conflict. The *Miami Herald* depicted the issue in terms of Latino racism against Blacks, a Latino police "vendetta" against Blacks, and White police racism against Blacks. For example, a high-school student is quoted as saying, "White cops, Black victims. It happens so many times in the past and justice hasn't been found" ("A Painful Cry: What Does It Take to be Heard?" *Miami Herald,* January 20, 1989, p. 1B). Significantly, none of the items mentioned racism by Whites generally, only by White police officers. Nor is racism by White-dominated institutions in Miami, such as mass media or corporations, mentioned.

In the *Miami Herald,* stories about immigration also seemed to suggest individual-level causes of conflict. The newspaper depicts Blacks as complaining and avoiding their own responsibilities by diverting blame to others for problems in the Black community. For example, one *Miami Herald* article about a meeting between government officials and Overtown residents is characterized as "one citizen after another complain[ing] of a Latino police 'vendetta' against Black men" with little explanation of the history of Latino–Black tensions in Miami. Later in the same article, the reporter writes, "Besides the complaints of racism on the part of Latino officers, many Overtown residents pointed a finger at the recent wave of Nicaraguans arriving in Miami [who are] getting preferential treatment over native Blacks" ("Rage Spreads From Overtown," *Miami Herald,* January 18, 1989, p. 1A).

Among the individual-level causes mentioned by the *Miami Times* were Cubans in power in city government ("Leaders Say Rebellion Could Have Been Avoided," *Miami Times,* January 19, 1989, p. 2A; see also "Suarez

Unveils 'Comeback Plan' Following Uprising," *Miami Times,* January 26, 1989, p. 3A). Other people blamed included Whites ("A Harsh Lesson," *Miami Times,* January 19, 1989, p. 1A; "Miami Not Only City With Potential for Riot," *Miami Times,* February 9, 1989, p. 5A; "Miami Race Relations," *Miami Times,* March 2, 1989, p. 4A), Latinos ("Things Just Don't Happen: A History of the Cuban Problem," *Miami Times,* February 16, 1989, p. 5A; "Miami Uprising: A Time When Our Dreams Turn Into Nightmares," *Miami Times,* February 16, 1989, p. 5A; "Miami Race Relations," *Miami Times,* March 2, 1989, p. 4A), irresponsible Black parents who "allowed and, in some cases, encouraged their children to [participate in the violence]" ("Overtown: In Black Perspective," *Miami Times,* February 2, 1989, p. 5A), Blacks who patronize Cuban-owned businesses ("Pushed to the Limit," *Miami Times,* January 26, 1989, p. 4A), and middle-class Blacks who have turned their backs on poor Blacks ("Middle Class Needs to Return to Overtown," *Miami Times,* January 26, 1989, p. 6A).

The *Miami Times* published only one item that made reference to a cultural shortcoming of Blacks: that parents were not taking responsibility over their children. But the column was quite clear that the reference was to parents of Black youths involved in the violence—the statement was not a blanket condemnation of the culture and values of an entire group. The writer states: "A lot of the people out there were kids who had their parents with them, stealing stuff. . . . There is no point in having kids and having no control over them" ("Blacks Need to Let Go of Scapegoats," *Miami Times,* January 26, 1989, p. 6C).

In *El Nuevo Herald,* the most frequently mentioned individual-level cause of the disturbances is Blacks. These items suggest that one of the explanations for deteriorating conditions in Black communities is Blacks shooting each other: "The Black community has adopted, ironically, the beliefs of their former oppressors. They [Blacks] blow themselves up" ("The Veins of Hatred," *El Nuevo Herald,* January 20, 1989, p. 6A).

Other explanations in *El Nuevo Herald* blaming Blacks for the poor conditions in Black communities were the Black middle class ignoring poor Blacks ("The Other Help for Blacks," *El Nuevo Herald,* February 3, 1989, p. 1B) and Blacks taking shortcuts to success ("No That Is Not the Way," *El Nuevo Herald,* January 22, 1989, p. 1B). Taken together, articles such as these blame the victims for their own conditions. Even if this assertion were accurate, the explanations provided are at best incomplete, at worst willfully ignorant of the history and political economy of Miami's Black community.

The *El Nuevo Herald* coverage, like the *Miami Herald* coverage, contained some unflattering images and statements about Blacks, despite some empathy with the concerns of the Black community. These came through in a number of articles that revealed the Latino view of Black life in Miami. For example, one suggests that Blacks made civil rights gains through force. The problem for Blacks now, according to the writer, is that "Blacks [are] killing one another" ("No, That Is Not the Way," *El Nuevo Herald*, January 22, 1989, p. 1B). A similar view is taken in another item in which the writer suggests that Blacks prefer to take the easiest route to success: "The short cut is to squat in the shade of color, blaming society."

Another article reveals the stereotypes that fuel attitudes toward Blacks: "What can we do for the Black community? Children of 14 and 15 [years of age] are already mothers and, of course, they seek welfare. Are there more children than there is social assistance?" ("Miami For All," *El Nuevo Herald*, February 13, 1989, p. 6A). This statement clearly shows a prejudiced view that Black girls tend to become teen-aged mothers, immediately get on and stay on welfare, and are a drain on the social services resources.

In *El Nuevo Herald*, 40% of the items mentioned that the role of race was an individual-level factor in the incidents (an additional 5% mentioned race as a secondary factor), and about 25% of the items mentioned racism as a theme. For example, one of the articles quoted a resident expressing the sentiments of his acquaintances: "I think they have not given this community an answer about the racial problems between the Latino officers and Black youths. Nobody is willing to admit that a problem exists" ("The Violence Has Spread," *El Nuevo Herald*, January 18, 1989, p. 1A).

Institutional-level Causes

Among the institutions blamed for the disturbances were mass media, the police department, and the courts. A *Miami Times* article, quoting Miami NAACP president Johnnie McMillan, blamed the general circulation mass media institutions and their negative depictions of the Black community:

> "Most Black Miamians were glad to see the media descending on Overtown during the disturbances," McMillan said. "But will they be there tomorrow when there is no disturbance to cover? And if the media forget about Overtown as long as it isn't burning, isn't the message being given to Overtown citizens one of 'burn and we'll listen, obey the law and we'll ignore you'?" ("NAACP Blasts Coverage of Disturbance," *Miami Times*, February 2, 1989, p. 3A)

Other institutions noted as causes of the disturbances include the Miami police department for its inadequate policing ("Promises to Public Haven't All Been Kept," *Miami Times*, January 18, 1989, p. 13A; "Rebuilt Liberty City Tries to Protect Its Progress," *Miami Times*, January 20, 1989,

p. 10A); city, state, and federal government for neglect of Black poverty; unemployment ("For Poorest, Life Only Gets Worse," *Miami Times,* January 18, 1989, p. 1B; "Promises to Public Haven't All Been Kept," *Miami Times,* January 18, 1989, p. 13A; "U.S. Orders FBI Probe of Shooting," *Miami Times,* January 18, 1989, p. 1A); and the judicial system for not enforcing civil rights laws ("A Call for Renewed Federal Enforcement," *Miami Times,* January 22, 1989, p. 1C).

But the *Miami Times* also noted institutional racism and White racism as problems for the Black community that contributed to the outbreak of violence in Liberty City and Overtown. The *Miami Times* depicted these views by including quotes from residents about the incidents. For example, one Liberty City resident said the "police department in this area shoots first and asks questions later when it comes to Blacks" ("Black Miamians Question Use of Lethal Force by Police," *Miami Times,* January 26, 1989, p. 3A). A unique aspect of the coverage of racism by the *Miami Times* is that it provided a forum for the "voice" of Black residents. The experiences and perspectives on racism and its relation to the disturbances are amply covered. For example:

> "Here we are once again," said Willie Sims, who serves on the Dade County Community Relations Board. "The Black community takes all these negatives and they store them up and you've got a powder keg. It's just a question of who would detonate it." ("Miami's Blacks Have Been Kept Out," *Miami Times,* January 26, 1989, p. 1A)

> "Look, I don't want [to] talk about the Super Bowl," said Jerome Baskins. "That's all these White folks' minds is on—money, money and money." ("What People of Miami Are Saying," *Miami Times,* January 26, 1989, p. 6A)

> A Miami police officer has spoken out on racism within the department and has lashed out at her superiors, who, she says, continue to harbor bigoted attitudes towards Blacks. . . . "Around the office, you get to hear all kinds of racist comments being made by Latin and White officers, and that's a shame, since we are all sworn to protect all the people." ("Cop Speaks of Racism in Miami Force," *Miami Times,* February 2, 1989, p. 3A)

Miami Herald coverage provided few instances of reporting the opinions and views on racism from Black residents ("A Painful Cry: What Does It Take to Be Heard," *Miami Times,* January 19, 1989, p. 1B; "Congressman Hears Anger of Overtown," *Miami Times,* January 28, 1989, 1D; "Our Black Ghettos Need Bold Action," *Miami Times,* January 29, 1989. p. 1C). Thus, although the *Miami Herald* acknowledges that racism is an important institutional factor in explaining causes of the disturbances, the paper's readers do not "hear" the voices of those most affected by racism.

Some *El Nuevo Herald* items also discussed institutional problems contributing to Blacks' anger and disillusionment, which led to the conflicts. For example, there is recognition that "the rights of the Black minority are stepped on daily" ("The Veins of Hatred," *El Nuevo Herald*, January 20, 1989, p. 6A). A second item gives prominence to a list of complaints from the Black community: police brutality against Blacks and general insensitivity toward Black concerns and needs by the city government ("Miami Puts Voting by Districts on the Ballot," *El Nuevo Herald*, February 10, 1989, p. 1B).

But *El Nuevo Herald* also gave prominence to an article about a Reagan administration representative who visited Miami and said that institutional issues are relatively unimportant, and residents "should focus on the specific incident that caused the disturbance" and "incarcerate the officers who kill." The official continues with his analysis:

> "I'm under the impression that this [rioting] has resulted in a lot of bloodshed. . . . Periodically, we have to shed the blood of a few Black citizens" he said. "Then, the whole world comes to demand more money. One begins to ask oneself what the connection is between the death of Lloyd and the Black businessman who receives a loan from the Small Business Association." ("Federal Leader: Miami Needs to Resolve Its Racial Conflict," *El Nuevo Herald*, February 24, 1989, p. 1B)

The official seems to imply that Blacks engage in violence so that they can take advantage of federal programs. The official is close to suggesting that the Black business community may find the periodic violence by the Black poor functional for their economic interests.

El Nuevo Herald, like the *Miami Times* and unlike the *Miami Herald*, provided some other Black perspectives on various issues. Two articles dealt with the Black complaints that the city is obsessed with sports activities rather than the problems faced by the Black community ("Miami Heat Game Suspended," *El Nuevo Herald*, January 18, 1989, p. 1A; "Peace in Miami Favors Super Bowl," *El Nuevo Herald*, January 20, 1989, p. 1A). Another item published Blacks' belief that immigrants were taking jobs from them ("Nicaraguans Take Day Labor Away From Blacks," *El Nuevo Herald*, January 20, 1989, p. 3A). Two other articles reported frustration and skepticism among Blacks about panels established to investigate the shootings and the conditions in Overtown and Liberty City ("Panel to Investigate Police," *El Nuevo Herald*, January 24, 1989, p. 1B). One article reported Black demands for political changes that would give them more representation in government ("Miami Puts District Voting on Ballot," *El Nuevo Herald,* February 10, 1989, p. 1B).

Structural-level Causes

Structural-level explanations of the disturbances explicitly highlighted societal distribution of resources and how it related to race and class relationships. In the *Miami Times,* these included joblessness, housing shortages ("Leaders Say Rebellion Could Have Been Avoided," *Miami Times,* January 19, 1989, p. 2A; "What People of Miami Are Saying," *Miami Times,* January 26, 1989, p. 6A), and slavery ("Miami Still in Mourning After Yet Another Civil Disturbance," *Miami Times,* February 9, 1989, p. 5A). In the *Miami Times,* the articles on immigration serve to help legitimize the complaints among the Black community about structural conditions. For example, one of the articles outlining the economic deterioration for the Black community summarizes the dilemma in the following way:

A "Cubanization" of Miami has transformed it from a southern, tourism-based resort to a thriving center for Latin commerce, as refugees from Fidel Castro's revolution stopped being exiles and exerted financial, social and political influence. ("Blacks Have Been Kept out of City's Success," *Miami Times,* January 26, 1989, p. 2A)

The *Miami Herald* mentioned several structural-level causes of the disturbances, including deterioration of intergroup relations ("For Poorest, Life Only Gets Worse," *Miami Herald,* January 18, 1989, p. 1B), increasing poverty in Black communities ("Civil Rights and Wrongs," *Miami Herald,* January 22, 1989, p. 1C), and corruption in city government ("U.S. Orders FBI Probe of Shooting," *Miami Herald,* January 18, 1989, p. 1A). One of the articles about the effects of poverty, written by a White columnist, depicts Blacks in timeworn stereotypes:

What surprises me is the [White] community's surprise. Violence, ugly, relentless, bloody, is a way of life in the urban slums of Miami, spilling into other areas as well. It has dogged the city's heart, shut down once-flourishing businesses on the fringes and made life difficult for those who remain.

Mindless violence, spawn of ghetto life, hasn't changed since 1968. If anything it's worse in this age of crack cocaine. And impoverished young women are still producing broods of children by successions of men, none of whom assumes responsibility of fatherhood; kids who grow up in the street, abandoned, unloved, tomorrow's rioters. ("Root Causes of Unrest Unchanged in 20 Years," *Miami Herald,* January 24, 1989, p. 1B)

Although recognizing the structural conditions that may have contributed to the outbreak of the disturbances, this column also epitomizes some of the worst coverage of the Miami riots of 1989. The column suggests that Whites should have expected violence from the "urban ghetto," clearly a coded reference to Blacks, where promiscuous Black women, irresponsible Black men, and children being readied for life as criminals characterized a certain "way of life."

El Nuevo Herald printed three stories about immigration. One revealed Black demands for fairer treatment in employment as legitimate ("Nicaraguans Take Day Labor Away From Blacks," *El Nuevo Herald,* January 20, 1989, p. 1A), one presented the situation of Black unemployment as not the fault of refugees or those hiring the refugees over Blacks ("A Welcome Help," *El Nuevo Herald,* March 3, 1989, p. 8A), and the third simply concluded that Miami has a serious problem ("Who Should We Help?" *El Nuevo Herald,* January 22, 1989, p. 8A). Overall, *El Nuevo Herald* seems to acknowledge that there is a problem of unemployment among Blacks but that it (and, therefore, the violence in Overtown and Liberty City) is not the fault of the Latino community. In fact, in *El Nuevo Herald* there were a total of 11 items that placed the blame for the rioting on poor economic or structural conditions, such as poverty and unemployment, in the Overtown and Liberty City areas.

Implications of the Conflict

The reporting of conflict in Liberty City and Overtown, and the fear and remorse it created, required a certain amount of follow-up reporting on the reactions of the different communities. For the *Miami Herald,* much of the follow-up coverage aimed at reassuring Miami residents that despite the disturbance, social order would soon be restored. Two kinds of reassurance discussed in the *Miami Herald* seemed directed toward calming Miami's Black community. One type of reassurance story was about city and federal officials promising an investigation into the shooting that served as the catalyst to the subsequent disturbances ("Rocks, Bottles Fly As Mayor Tries to Calm Residents," *Miami Herald,* January 17, 1989, p. 1A; "Calm Prevails As City Looks for Solutions," *Miami Herald,* January 21, 1989, p. 1B). Another kind of reassurance story highlighted police doing their work to restore order. One story reported that a "Crisis Response Team" of 13 community leaders formed by the police chief was going into Overtown to "talk some sense into these people [the Overtown residents]" ("Violence Ebbs, But Anger Builds," *Miami Herald,* January 19, 1989, p. 20A). Another story outlined how police have "avoid[ed] the deadly errors of 1980, [and] moved swiftly this week to take back control of Overtown's streets with a carefully planned display of force and guerrilla-like strikes into trouble spots" ("Lesson of Past Is Contain, Control Police Say," *Miami Herald,* January 19, 1989, p. 21A).

In the *Miami Times,* only two articles contained reassurance. One of these articles was a report of the mayor's "comeback plan" ("Suarez Unveils Comeback Plan," *Miami Times,* January 26, 1989, p. 3A), and the other was in support of an investigation into the shooting ("Rights Groups Rap Police Brutality Against Blacks," *Miami Herald,* January 26, 1989, p. 3A). *El Nuevo Herald* also printed only two articles about reassurance. One of these was about Overtown efforts to rebuild ("Rebuilding Efforts Ongoing," *El Nuevo Herald,* January 20, 1989, p. 4A), and the other was a brief mention of the panel established to investigate the shooting ("Police Cordon Is Loosened in 2 Districts," *El Nuevo Herald,* January 21, 1989, p. 1B).

Aside from the immediate reassurances offered, newspapers also printed items that discussed longer-term solutions to the problems causing the conflicts. The primary solution for the *Miami Herald* is enhanced interethnic cooperation. In one story about a post-disturbance meeting of Blacks and Latinos, one participant says: "We are here and Blacks are here and we have to work together. We have to do whatever it takes" ("Whites Recommit to Aiding Blacks," *Miami Herald,* February 5, 1989, p. 1B). This solution is not mentioned at all in the *Miami Times* (and mentioned only once in *El Nuevo Herald*). In fact, the *Miami Times* articles suggest that there is no interest on the part of the Black community to deal with powerful Cubans from a position of weakness. Instead the *Miami Times* suggests that solutions should include holding Cubans more accountable to Equal Employment Opportunity guidelines and to federal tax laws, because Cuban businesses are not hiring Blacks and may not be paying taxes that would trickle into Black communities ("Things Don't Just Happen: A History of the Cuban Problem," *Miami Times,* February 6, 1989, p. 5A).

A solution that receives frequent mention in both the *Miami Herald* and the *Miami Times* articles is Black self-help—it is the most frequently mentioned solution in the *Miami Times* and is second most frequently mentioned in the *Miami Herald.* There is, however, a significant difference in how each newspaper presents how Black self-help ought to proceed. The *Miami Times* says Black self-help is a necessity because "no one else will help" ("Blacks Need to Let Go of Scapegoats," *Miami Times,* January 26, 1989, p. 6A). The *Miami*

Times also says Black self-help needs to be supported by addressing structural problems related to neglect, poverty, and unemployment in the Black community ("Pushed to the Limit," *Miami Times,* January 26, 1989, p. 4A).

For the *Miami Times,* Black self-help should also be accompanied by improvements in the police department and in policing methods, which also is mentioned by the *Miami Herald,* but less frequently. Overall, it seems that the *Miami Times* has little desire to enact interethnic cooperation as a means to address problems, perhaps because of their experience with powerlessness first with the Anglo community then with the Latino community.

For the *Miami Herald,* Black self-help should take the form of the Black community working harder to solve their own problems (presented in three articles), but with the aid of other ethnic groups and institutions. For example, a *Miami Herald* columnist suggests that

> in concentrating on the wrongs of discrimination and poverty, we may have neglected the fact that there is [a] lot we can do about our own problems ourselves. Government and private sector action is necessary, but so too are the services and concerns that Black organizations can provide. ("Blacks Need Tough Love of Middle Class," *Miami Herald,* February 3, 1989, p. 19A)

The *Miami Herald* also suggested, as did the *Miami Times,* that addressing structural problems was a part of the solution to the problems in the Black community but presented the idea in only two articles.

In *El Nuevo Herald,* the most commonly mentioned solutions were those addressing structural problems in the Black community. The most frequently proposed (appearing in nine items) were for the city government (either with or without help from the state and federal governments) to take steps to provide services and resources that alleviate poverty, provide food aid, and increase the number of Black police officers ("In Search of Solutions," *El Nuevo Herald,* January 27, 1989, p. 6A). *El Nuevo Herald* said the city also needs to reduce its bureaucratic nature, engage in better communication, and do more to investigate and better assess the level of need among the poor ("Who Should We Help," *El Nuevo Herald,* January 22, 1989, p. 8A). Another solution is for Miami's Latino community to come to the defense of Black civil rights ("The Veil of Hatred," *El Nuevo Herald,* January 20, 1989, p. 6A).

Race and Nation

Finally, although the newspapers' coverage is about conflict over jobs and equal treatment at one level, it also is about something much more fundamental. The coverage is also about who is and who is not American. Miami Blacks were upset about the policy that granted Cuban immigrants political asylum, whereas Haitians who asked for the same status were turned away. This was on top of Black perceptions that the newly arrived Nicaraguans were getting preferential treatment. A Black community leader said that "explaining this to Afro-Americans is hard" ("Leaders Say Rebellion Could Have Been Avoided," *Miami Times,* January 19, 1989, p. 2A). The preference for Cuban and Nicaraguan exiles is explained in the *Miami Herald* by each group's supposed hatred for communism, which also made these groups more acceptable to the U.S. government in January 1989 (George H. W. Bush had just been inaugurated), to Miami's Cuban establishment, and perhaps to Miami's White population. In contrast, the general circulation press historically has made much of prominent Black leaders' real or imagined communist ties: Paul Robeson had always been treated with suspicion and contempt for his support of Communism and the Soviet Union (Murray, 1990), Martin Luther King was branded a communist by J. Edgar Hoover's FBI, and Jesse Jackson was heavily criticized for his July 1984 visit to Cuba (Jesse Jackson Goes to Cuba, 1984).[8] With this history, the issue of who is American may have taken on added significance in the context of Black–Latino relations in Miami.

A *Miami Times* column states, "We are run by a Cuban government in exile," and they don't know how to run cities in "the American way" ("Leaders Say Rebellion Could Have Been Avoided," *Miami Times,* January 19, 1989, p. 2A). Another states, "Black people also love America" ("Overtown in Black Perspective," *Miami Times,* February 9, 1989, p. 5A). On the other hand, the message of the *Miami Herald* seems to be that Nicaraguans and Cubans are closer to being real Americans because of their anticommunism (which was, in the height of the Cold War, a valuable coin in the realm), their willingness to work harder, and so on. The paper depicted Blacks as less American because of the lingering residue of allusions of communism made against King and Jackson and because they were depicted as complaining about the success of others. Nevertheless, in the *Miami Times* Blacks claim that they are American, that they love America, and that it is Cubans who do not know the American way.

A number of items in *El Nuevo Herald,* especially some that were coded in the immigration category, contain a subtext about "nation"—about what constitutes a real American, about how to achieve the American Dream. *El Nuevo Herald* items imply that Blacks do not know how to be American. For example, an *El Nuevo Herald* article reports without comment that American employers prefer Nicaraguans partly because of their hate for communism. The item also reports that Nicaraguans are "more inclined to take tough jobs" ("Nicaraguans Take Day Labor Away From Blacks," *El Nuevo Herald,* January 20, 1989, p. 1). Together these sentiments suggest that Blacks do not hate communism and do not work hard and therefore are not good Americans. Further, in an item about how one should succeed in America, a columnist suggests that Blacks have taken the easy road to success ("No That Is Not the Way," *El Nuevo Herald,* January 22, 1989, p. 6). A third item raised the question about which people are worthy of receiving help from the state ("Who Should We Help?" *Miami Herald,* January 22, 1989, p. 4). The column asks whether or not "Nicaraguans . . . have rights in Miami along with other poor Americans and the millions of Haitians and others." The structure of this sentence suggests that Nicaraguans belong to the category of "other poor Americans"—but clearly American in spirit if not by citizenship. The column does not explicitly mention the status of Blacks. In Miami, the writer suggests, the situation is that for a resident "there can be racial links with the victims of chaos in Central America, but not with those in the ghettos of the United States who are literally foreign to him." These items provide an important clue about how *El Nuevo Herald* views Blacks: They are "foreign," not true Americans.

Summary and Discussion

In general, all newspapers tended to use the labels "Blacks" and "Hispanics," despite the fact that these labels obfuscated the diversity of Miami residents with these ethnic backgrounds. This trend held true even though the main participants in the events that sparked the rioting and looting were definitively of specific "Black" and "Hispanic" backgrounds: Lloyd and Blanchard were West Indian, not just "Black," and Lozano was Colombian, not just "Hispanic." Erasing important differences through homogenizing is an important aspect of racial ideology. It is part of a process that helps perpetuate a racial hierarchy in which non-White ethnic minorities suffer constant material and symbolic segregation and degradation (Shah & Thornton, 1994).

The papers depicted Blacks and Latinos as the main actors in the disturbances. There was different emphasis, however, on which of the groups bore the primary responsibility for the incidents. The *Miami Times* depicted Latinos as the main actors, whereas the *Miami Herald* and *El Nuevo Herald* portrayed the main actors as both Latinos and Blacks. Whites are the least mentioned actors in all the papers; they are effectively invisible from the representation of the disturbances, even though Whites dominated many centers of economic, social, and cultural power. The invisibility of Whites suggests that the newspapers all share a shortsighted view of the disturbances and, more broadly, race relations in Miami. By not examining the role of White power holding in the allocation and resources in Miami, the newspapers are unable to reveal root causes of inequality and discontent in the Black community. By not "seeing" the role of White privilege in Miami, the newspapers are forced to explain the disturbances in terms of Black pathology and/or Latino discrimination.

In all papers, victims were mainly Blacks. The *Miami Times* emphasized Blacks as victims more than the other papers. The *Miami Herald* and *El Nuevo Herald* reported Lloyd's previous police record even though it had nothing to do with the shooting and the subsequent disturbances. Whether or not these papers intended to, the reporting of this fact may have provided arguments to help justify Lozano's actions.

Although conflict was the main theme of coverage in all newspapers, the context of reporting was different. The *Miami Herald* presented the conflict in the context of fear for the city, fear of violence spilling into suburbs, and fear that the Super Bowl would be canceled. In the *Miami Times,* the context was outrage at another killing of a Black resident by the Miami police. In *El Nuevo Herald,* the context was disillusionment with the situation, sympathy for Blacks, and calls for cooperation (although other stories in this newspaper were full of negative stereotypes of Blacks that often undermined these themes).

All papers mention a variety of causes of the conflict, ranging from individual to institutional to structural. All papers mention Latinos, Blacks, White police, and immigrants as contributing to the causes of the disturbance. However, the *Miami Herald* hardly mentions Blacks as causing the disturbance, whereas *El Nuevo Herald* mentions Blacks frequently as cause of the conflict, although both papers link Black culture to violence and violent behavior. The *Miami Times* also mentions Blacks as a cause of the disturbances, but the depiction is more carefully handled in that only certain Blacks—irresponsible parents—are depicted as the problem.

All newspapers discussed the role race played in the disturbances. The *Miami Herald* emphasized Latino and police racism against Blacks. The *Miami Herald* never mentioned racism by Whites (except police officers). *El Nuevo Herald* acknowledged racism by Latinos against Blacks but gave more emphasis to racism by police. The *Miami Times* also mentioned racism by the police force and Latinos. In addition, however, the *Miami Times* discussed White racism and institutional racism. The *Miami Times* presented the perspectives on and experiences with racism in the "voice" of Black residents. The *Miami Herald* and *El Nuevo Herald* only rarely provided this type of reporting.

Immigration was one of the key issues within the larger context of Miami's political economy at the time of the disturbances. The *Miami Herald* discussed the Black community's concerns about increased immigration from Central America and the impact on Black employment patterns but de-legitimized the reportorial framing. In contrast, the *Miami Times* presented Black concerns about immigration and employment in a way that legitimized the issues. *El Nuevo Herald* reported Black demands for fairer treatment as legitimate but reported Black unemployment as unrelated to Nicaraguan immigration.

The *Miami Herald,* much more than any other paper, printed stories providing reassurance to its readers. For readers, reassurance came in the form of stories about police doing heroic work to contain the problems and restore order. For various reasons, the *Miami Times* and *El Nuevo Herald* presented little in the way of stories that may have provided reassurance to readers.

In terms of solutions proposed, *El Nuevo Herald* pushed certain structural solutions, whereas the *Miami Herald* favored attempts to foster interethnic cooperation. Of course, this approach is quite functional for maintaining the status quo in terms of power relations. Pushing a liberal "we can get along" solution that emphasizes action at the individual level avoids consideration of resource reallocation policies that would require changes in power relations. The *Miami Times* made no mention of this approach while advocating holding Cuban leaders of Miami responsible for the many years of neglect of the Black community. Both the *Miami Herald* and the *Miami Times* suggested Black self-help as appropriate solutions, but the *Miami Herald* viewed this individual approach in isolation from structural solutions, whereas the *Miami Times* viewed Black self-help in connection with structural change.

According to the *Miami Herald* and *El Nuevo Herald,* Cubans, and even recently arrived Nicaraguans, because of their anti-communist credentials and willingness to take any job they can find and work hard at it, are more American than Miami's Blacks. But the *Miami Times* argues that, in fact, Blacks are real Americans by virtue of their long residence in the United States and their fight for civil rights and that Cubans are the outsiders. This discussion of "who is an American" indicates another aspect of racial ideology. The general-circulation *Miami Herald* and *El Nuevo Herald,* which caters to the powerful Cuban community, both suggest that Latinos have cultural features and sensibilities that are closer to those of Whites and closer, therefore, to being American. Blacks, on the other hand, do not share the traits and temperament required to be American.

3

Washington, D.C., 1991

The main focus of this chapter is to explore how the general-circulation and ethnic press in Washington, D.C., covered Latino–Black relations during and after three days of interethnic violence in May 1991. We will examine the *Washington Post,* the primary general-circulation newspaper in the city; the *Washington Informer* and the *Washington Afro American,* two leading Black newspapers in the city; and *El Tiempo Latino,* a Spanish-language newspaper in the city. After an overview of these newspapers, we provide a brief review of Latino–Black relations in Washington, D.C., before delving into the analysis.

The *Washington Post* was started by Stilson Hutchins in 1877 as a party paper for the Democrats. Much of the local political news was partisan, but there was editorial independence in news of other matters. The newspaper was often racist toward Blacks, Native Americans, and most immigrants; it was progressive in other ways, calling for spending on civic improvements, hiring one of the first women reporters in the country, and uncovering unethical business deals in the capital. Hutchins sold the paper in 1889 to Frank Hatton and Beriah Wilkins, who generally carried on Hutchins's policies. In 1905, John McLean, who was a newspaper owner in the mold of his friend William Randolph Hearst, purchased the paper.

McLean turned the *Post* into a gossipy, sensational replica of Hearst newspapers. By 1933, McLean was deeply in debt and sold the paper to Eugene Meyer, who vowed to make the *Post* an independent and serious paper. To help him run the paper, Meyer brought in son-in-law Philip Graham. Graham was a Harvard-trained lawyer with no newspaper experience, but he was named publisher in 1946 when Meyer took a government assignment with the World Bank (Felsenthal, 1993). Two years later, Meyer transferred his interest in the *Post* to Philip and Katherine Graham (Merrill & Fischer, p. 346). In 1963, Katherine Graham become publisher after her husband committed suicide. In 1979, Donald Graham became publisher. Under the leadership of the three Grahams, the *Post* supported Democratic candidates for political office, made efforts to hire minority journalists, reported more regularly on the city's Black population, and emphasized investigative reporting that culminated in the Watergate story. The *Post* has a circulation of about 700,000 and is owned by the Washington Post Company, which owns newspapers and magazines, radio and television stations, and a book publishing company (Emery & Emery, 1996, p. 555).

The *Washington Afro American* originated in 1932 as the *Afro American and Tribune*. When the American society of Journalism School Administrators issued its annual award to the *Afro American* in 1969, it went for the first time in the award's 23 years to a Black publication (Wolseley, 1990, p. 100). The newspaper gives special coverage to foreign, especially African, news. Along with regional news, there is correspondence from cities with large Black populations. For most of its history, the paper has been family operated. Circulation is estimated at 40,000.

The *Washington Informer* was first published in 1964. Its mission was to report "positive and provocative" news affecting the Washington, D.C., area's Black community. The *Informer* is involved in the communities it serves, and staff members are encouraged to volunteer their time for local institutions. The newspaper covers the typical range of issues, such as politics, education, sports, religion, and entertainment. However, publisher Calvin W. Rolark has directed the staff to avoid crime news. Circulation is about 27,000.

Founded in 1991 by Armando Chapelli, the weekly *El Tiempo Latino* serves the Latino community in the District, Northern Virginia, and Southern Maryland. Chapelli, a Cuban American, started the paper to satisfy unmet information needs of the fast-growing Latino population. Because the Latino population in the D.C. area originates from a number of Latin American countries, *El Tiempo Latino* emphasizes local *and* international news. At times, reporters have been sent abroad to cover events firsthand. Circulation stands at about 34,000.

The Political and Economic Context in Washington, D.C., 1991

In many ways, Washington, D.C., is two cities in one. It is an international center of policy making, diplomacy, and cultural exchange. It is home to some of the country's most fascinating monuments and world-class architecture. However, the city also jails more African Americans than it graduates from high school, has the highest Black infant mortality rate in the nation, and has one of the highest murder rates in the country. Washington, D.C., also is, whether in myth or reality, a symbol of freedom and democracy that attracts immigrants from around the world. Although the parts of the city that are viewed as the global capital are relatively immune from the ethnic tensions wrought by immigration (especially from the countries of the South), the working class and traditional African American areas of the city, especially since the 1980s, are often on edge because of ethnic tensions.

As in Miami, immigration from Central America, the domination of local politics by a single racial group, and changes in the local economy were among the key ingredients leading to the eruption of racial violence in the Mount Pleasant and Adams-Morgan areas of Washington, D.C., in May 1991. As in Miami, the increase in the Latino population in Washington, D.C., can be partially attributed to Reagan-era policies to destabilize certain Central American nations. Although an earlier genera-tion of Latino immigrants in Washington, D.C., was from South America and tended to be well-off, educated, and middle-to-upper class, the recent immigrants were from rural areas of Nicaragua, Honduras, El Salvador, and Guatemala and were mainly poor with little formal education. They streamed north by the thousands during the Reagan years trying to escape war, death squads, and general oppression in Central America. In Washington, D.C., the Latino population grew by 85% between 1980 and 1990 (United States Commission on Civil Rights, 1993, p. 3).

Despite the tremendous growth in the Latino population in the District, they officially comprised only 5.4% of the total population of 606,900 res-idents in 1990, although this figure is disputed by Latino leaders who claim the true proportion of Latinos in Washington, D.C., may be as high as 12%. Nevertheless, Blacks were the clear numerical majority in the city, accounting for about 65% of the population in 1990. Whites accounted for about 27%, and Asian Americans accounted for about 2% of the 1990 population (see United States Commission on Civil Rights, 1993).[9]

In the boom years of the 1980s, Latino immigrants found work in the construction industry and then in the restaurant, hotel, and janitorial ser-vice industries. Blacks were increasingly disinclined, according to Jennings and Lusane (1994), to pursue employment in these sectors for two reasons. First, many Blacks increasingly felt these jobs were unattractive and found certain illegal activities more profitable. Second, Blacks were weary of fac-ing discrimination from the mainly White and Latino employers in these sectors who preferred to hire Latinos. As a result, Black resentment of Latinos grew, and poor Blacks in the city generally had little sympathy for the plight of Latinos when, in 1989, large numbers of Latinos joined the ranks of the unemployed as recession took hold of the nation's economy.

Unlike the case in Miami, Latino immigration has not resulted in segregated housing patterns among Latinos and Blacks. In fact, these groups lived side by side in a number of neighborhoods in Washington, D.C., including Mount Pleasant and Adams Morgan, though not always in the best of conditions and not always by choice. For example, many of the recent Latino immigrants lived in overcrowded, poorly maintained, but affordable housing in Mount Pleasant and Adams Morgan. Latino activists claimed that the poor conditions existed in these areas because developers were using the immigrants as "temporary wedges for taking over poor Black communities only to be cast aside themselves for gentrification" (Jennings & Lusane, 1994, p. 62). In 1980, 70% of these two neighborhoods were Black. By 1990, they were 40% Black, as Latinos moved into the less expensive housing, and mainly Whites moved into gentrified dwellings. Poor Blacks moved to other (predominantly Black and poor) areas of the city. Substandard housing and "ghettoization" has been a part of the experience of Blacks in Washington, D.C., since the city was built (Gillette, 1995), so the pattern of the 1980s was not new. But the trend did not quell Black resentment of Latinos or increase Black sympathy for Latino grievances.

Though Blacks have been a majority in Washington, D.C., since the 1950s, it was not until 1971 that city residents elected a Black mayor and majority Black city council. In 1978, newly elected mayor, Marion Barry, consolidated control of the city government by hiring thousands of Blacks into city government. Latinos were left out of this bonanza: Despite accounting for anywhere between 5% and 12% of the District's population, they represented 1% of city workers in 1992. The city's police force of 4,900 employed about 140 Latinos. Of the 323 elected advisory neighborhood commissioners, only two were Latino at the time of the unrest. A critical problem for Latinos, according to Jennings and Lusane (1994), was that they lacked political representation in the District, where less than 1% of registered voters were Latinos. Barry tried to address Latino concerns about their lack of political voice by creating an Office of Latino Affairs (OLA) and a Commission on Latino Business Development. The commission consisted of 15 voting members appointed by the mayor (subject to the approval of the city council) along with eight nonvoting members. One of the commission's responsibilities was to develop a list of three names from which the mayor appoints a director of the OLA.

Along with the massive hiring of Blacks into city government, Barry also awarded millions of dollars worth of government contracts to Blacks and expanded services for the poor and the working class. But Barry did not face the city's political and economic realities, and by the time he left office in 1990, the District was facing a large debt and about to impose massive cuts in social services. Barry apparently had chosen to ignore the District's "colonial" relationship with the federal government, which denies the District the right to make its own laws and determine how and who to tax. He also seemed to ignore the trends toward cuts in federal aid to cities, private sector abandonment of cities, and White flight to the suburbs.

The growth in the Latino population took place precisely at a time when Washington, D.C., was facing this crisis. Poor and working-class Latinos and Blacks were disproportionately affected because of their status as the most urbanized minority groups in the United States (Jennings & Lusane, 1994, p. 63). An already depressed economic situation magnified the impact of these trends in Washington, D.C. In 1990, 50% of all District households had incomes of less than $20,000, and 20% had incomes less than $10,000 (Jennings & Lusane, 1994, p. 63). As an increasingly diverse population demanded more social services and employment opportunities in the face of decreasing revenues, tensions among Latinos and Blacks grew.

The rapid growth of the Latino population in the 1980s had taken the Black leadership of the District by surprise, and they were ineffective at addressing Latinos' concerns. Although Barry had created the OLA as an advocacy group within the District government and the Commission on Latino Business Development to advise the mayor and the city council on the needs and views of the Latino community, Latinos claimed (as Blacks had about the Cuban ruling elite in Miami in 1989), that issues such as police harassment against Latinos, lack of jobs for teens, disrespect from Black government officials, and so on, remained largely unaddressed by the ruling Black political elite in Washington, D.C. On the other hand, many Washington, D.C., Blacks (like Miami Blacks) felt that Latinos did not respect the civil rights battles Blacks had fought.

Barry was defeated in the 1990 mayoral election by Sharon Pratt Dixon, the first African American woman to be mayor of the city. There was a general attitude in her administration that anything done by the Barry administration should be "discarded, dismantled, or held in suspicion" (Jennings & Lusane, 1994, p. 69). For example, when Dixon took office, OLA had not had a permanent director since April 1990, even though the commission had developed a list of three candidates for the job. The appointment of a permanent OLA director stalled because Dixon mistrusted the commission, whose members were all Barry appointees. Dixon refused to choose any of the three recommended people and did not appoint a permanent OLA director until after the disturbances of May 1991 (see United States Commission on Civil Rights, 1993, pp. 6-7). Thus, two institutional sites for the airing of Latino grievances against the Black city government that could have played a vital role in preventing and responding to the disturbances were without effective leadership as a result of Dixon's inaction.

Latino immigration and lack of political power, working-class Blacks' resentment of Latinos, Black political leaders' unresponsiveness to Latino grievances, and economic decline of the city were among the key ingredients in the political economic brew in Washington, D.C., in May 1991. In addition, there was a history of tense relations between Washington, D.C., police and the Latino community, especially in the Mount Pleasant neighborhood. In 1985, Latinos had expressed their concerns about police treatment of members of their community. Latinos regularly filed complaints against District police with the Civilian Complaint review board about police misconduct, use of demeaning language, excessive use of force, and general harassment (United States Commission on Civil Rights, 1993, pp. 20-22). On the other hand, Whites and many Blacks had repeatedly complained to police about the nuisance created by public urination, drunkenness, and loitering by Latinos hanging out on neighborhood street corners and parks. All of these factors were at work when, on May 5, 1991, a Black rookie Washington, D.C., police officer named Angela Jewell shot Daniel Enrique Gomez, a Salvadoran immigrant who had resided in the city for two years. Gomez survived.

During a Cinco de Mayo celebration in a small park in the Mount Pleasant neighborhood, Gomez and some of his friends were drinking beer and talking. Jewell and another officer tried to arrest Gomez on charges of being drunk and disorderly. According to police, Gomez resisted arrest. A struggle ensued during which Gomez allegedly pulled out a knife and lunged at Jewell, who then shot him in the chest. Immediately, the Latino community presented another version of the events. Latinos agreed that Gomez did resist arrest but claimed Gomez was unarmed and Jewell shot him after he was already in handcuffs. As word quickly spread in the neighborhood that an unarmed, handcuffed Latino was shot by a member of the Washington, D.C., police, Latino youths began to break windows, loot stores, and burn buildings to protest not only the Gomez shooting but also what they perceived to be a history of police harassment and the city's neglect of Latino concerns (Jennings & Lusane, 1994, p. 65). Three days of violence followed the shooting. Anger among Latinos grew on the second day when Mayor Dixon made no effort to visit the area and calm residents.

On the second and third days of violence, significant numbers of Black and White youths participated in the rioting. Peace returned to the area only after a strict curfew and massive show of police force compelled the crowds to stay home.

The Coverage

The *Washington Post* covered the Mount Pleasant incident much more than the District's Black and Latino newspapers examined in this study. Over the time period examined, the *Washington Post* published 51 articles, the *Informer* and the *Afro American* combined published only 7 articles, and *El Tiempo Latino* published 12 articles.

Ethnic Groups in Washington, D.C.

Latinos were mentioned more than any other ethnic group in all publication categories. (See Table 3.1.) The *Washington Post* mentioned Latinos in about 55% of all its articles, *El Tiempo Latino* mentioned them in 92% of its stories, and the Black newspapers mentioned them in all of their stories. Despite frequent mention of Latinos in news stories, the fact that the victim of the shooting was Salvadoran and that there are thousands of people from other Central American nations living in the Mount Pleasant and Adams-Morgan area, the general circulation and Black press presented little in the way of even cursory discussion of specific Latino groups and their individual histories and contemporary position within the local political economy. In *El Tiempo Latino*, two articles mention some of the different Latin American nationalities represented in the area, but they provide little in-depth background or context to explain the disturbances ("Tripled Presence of Police in the Suburb While Latin Problems Continue," *El Tiempo Latino*, May 17, 1991, p. 1; "For a Few Days, Mount Pleasant Opened a Window to the World" *El Tiempo Latino*, May 10, 1991, p. 16). In the *Washington Post*, the only mention of a specific Latino identity is in several references to Gomez's Salvadoran nationality. In the Black papers, one article refers to "Hispanics of color"—those who look Black but are actually Latinos—as participants in the rioting ("TV on Riot," *Washington Afro American*, June 15, 1991, p. A4).

The only other group receiving significant mention was Blacks. The *Washington Post* mentioned them in 10% of all its stories, Black papers mentioned them in 86% of their stories, and *El Tiempo Latino* mentioned them in 17% of its stories. Certainly it is not surprising that the Black press

Table 3.1   Number and Percentage of Articles in Washington, D.C.,
Newspapers Mentioning Various Groups

	WP (n = 51)		AA (n = 7)		ETL (n = 12)	
	#	%	#	%	#	%
Blacks	5	9.8	6	85.7	2	16.6
Whites	1	1.9	0	0	0	0
Korean	1	1.9	0	0	0	0
Latinos	28	54.9	7	100.0	5	41.6
Salvadoran	6	11.7	0	0	2	16.6
Central American	0	0	0	0	1	8.3
Venezuelan	0	0	0	0	1	8.3
"Hispanics of Color"	0	0	1	14.2	0	0

WP = *Washington Post*
AA = *Washington Afro American + Washington Informer*
ETL = *El Tiempo Latino*

mentioned Blacks in almost all stories, but the low proportion of stories mentioning Blacks in the general circulation press is unexpected, given that Blacks played a significant role in the disturbance, especially on the second and third days. Many White youths also participated in the rioting, but the publications rarely mentioned them. In fact, the diversity of the rioters was mentioned in only three items, all in the *Washington Post* ("Police, Hispanics Youths Clash in 2d Night of Violence," *Washington Post,* May 7, 1991, p. A1; "Leaderless Groups Look for Trouble," May 7, 1991, p. A1; "We're Angry 'Cause of Being Hassled," *Washington Post,* May 8, 1991, p. B1). Whites also are not mentioned despite their dominant role in the area of local business and finance. In fact, White economic power is mentioned only in "Roots of a Riot" (*Washington Post,* May 12, 1991, p. C8) and "Black Power's New Dilemma" (*Washington Post,* May 12, 1991, p. C1), which effectively removes White privilege from the mix of contextual factors within which the disturbances occurred.

Actors and Victims

In all the newspapers, the ethnic group that figures most prominently as actors and victims is Latinos. (See Table 3.2.) The *Washington Post* mentions Latinos as actual actors in nearly 40% of its stories, the Black press mentions them in five out of seven stories (71%), and *El Tiempo Latino*

Table 3.2 Number and Percentage of Articles in Washington, D.C., Newspapers Discussing Various Actors and Victims

Number (Percent)

	Actors						Victims					
	Actual			Potential			Actual			Potential		
	WP	AA	ETL	WP	AA	ETL	WP	AA	ETL	WP	AA	ETL
Gov	28 (54.9)	5 (71.4)	7 (58.3)	0 (0)	0 (0)	0 (0)	21 (3.9)	0 (14.2)	13 (0)	0 (0)	0 (0)	0 (0)
Police	13 (25.4)	5 (71.4)	2 (28.5)	0 (0)	0 (0)	0 (0)	8 (15.7)	2 (28.5)	3 (25.0)	4 (25.4)	0 (0)	0 (0)
Blacks	4 (7.8)	1 (14.2)	1 (8.3)	0 (0)	0 (0)	1 (0)	0 (0)	1 (0)	0 (14.2)	1 (7.8)	1 (1.9)	0 (0)
Whites	1 (1.9)	0 (0)	0 (0)	0 (0)	0 (0)	0 (0)	0 (0)	0 (0)	0 (0)	1 (1.9)	0 (0)	0 (0)
Korean Americans	0 (0)	0 (0)	0 (0)	0 (0)	0 (0)	0 (0)	1 (1.9)	0 (0)	0 (0)	0 (0)	0 (0)	0 (0)
Latinos	20 (39.2)	5 (71.4)	3 (25.0)	0 (0)	0 (0)	0 (0)	25 (49.0)	3 (42.8)	5 (41.6)	1 (1.9)	0 (0)	0 (0)

WP = *Washington Post*
AA = *Washington Afro American* + *Washington Informer*
ETL = *El Tiempo Latino*

mentions them in one quarter of its stories. Nearly all of these mentions of Latinos as actors are in reference to Gomez allegedly lunging at the arresting officers with a knife, Latino residents participating in the rioting, Latino leaders taking action to quell the disturbances, and Latino leaders forming an ad hoc group to pressure Mayor Dixon into taking action.

The *Washington Post* identified Latinos as victims in nearly half of its stories, the Black newspapers in three of seven stories (43%), and *El Tiempo Latino* in 42% of its stories. Discussion of the D.C. police officer shooting Gomez and discussion of Latinos as victims of discrimination and bias account for almost all of these references. But when we examined reports of who was doing the actual victimizing, the *Washington Post,* the Black newspapers, and *El Tiempo Latino* infrequently explicitly mentioned that it was (according to Latinos) specific Black persons or groups. Instead, all newspapers conducted most of the discussions of who victimized Latinos in terms of government representatives doing the victimizing. The police as victim category is accounted for by the arresting officer as a potential target of Gomez's knife and by the actual shooting of Washington, D.C., police during the three nights of violence.

To summarize, the newspapers present the issue as one concerning mainly the city government and Latino residents of Mount Pleasant and Adams Morgan. The main actors are the government and Latinos, whereas the main actual victims are Latinos, and the main potential victims are the police. Blacks and Whites are essentially out of the picture as victims, whereas Blacks are mentioned a handful of times as actors. The lack of attention to Whites, despite their prominent role in local business and finance (e.g., the gentrification movement) diminishes their historical role as economic and political power holders in increasingly multiethnic race relations in the District.

Conflict and Anger

As in Miami, all newspapers organized most coverage around the theme of conflict. The conflict theme was coded in all articles in the Black newspapers. In *El Tiempo Latino,* 92% of the articles were coded as containing the conflict theme. Of the *Washington Post* articles, about 77% contained the conflict theme. In the coverage, conflict primarily involved three categories or groups—Latinos, Blacks, and city-government officials. Whites were mentioned infrequently as part of the conflict. See Table 3.3 for a summary of main themes in the coverage.

The main dimensions of the conflict were as follows: Latino residents and community leaders were angry with the Black-dominated city government for ignoring the concerns of the Latino community. Latino community

Table 3.3   Number and Percentage of Articles in Washington, D.C., Newspapers Discussing Various Themes

	WP (n = 51)		AA (n = 7)		ETL (n = 12)	
	#	%	#	%	#	%
Immigration	14	27.0	1	14.3	2	17.7
Fear	13	25.4	3	42.9	2	17.7
Racism	11	21.6	0	0	6	50.0
Culture/Values	8	15.7	1	14.3	1	8.3
Violence						
Verbal	5	9.8	0	0	0	0
Personal	34	66.7	4	57.1	10	83.3
Property	32	62.7	6	85.7	9	75.0
Causes						
Individual	30	59.0	0	0	0	0
Institutional	25	49.0	6	85.7	8	66.7
Structural	13	25.5	0	0	2	17.7
Reassurance	11	21.6	1	14.3	1	8.3
Discontent	29	56.9	5	71.4	8	66.7
Conflict	39	76.5	7	100.0	11	91.7
Cooperation	6	17.6	1	14.3	0	0
Pluralism	3	5.9	0	0	0	0
Assimilation	5	9.8	0	0	0	0
Attitudes	0	0	0	0	0	0
Minority	6	11.6	1	14.3	1	8.3
Intersection						
Role of Race						
Primary	11	21.6	3	42.9	6	50.0
Secondary	2	3.9	1	14.3	0	0
None	4	7.8	0	0	0	0
No Mention	34	66.7	3	2.9	6	50.0

WP = *Washington Post*
AA = *Washington Afro American* + *Washington Informer*
ETL = *El Tiempo Latino*

members were angry about harassment and abuse by White and Black D.C. police officers. Blacks and Whites were angry with Latinos. Black, Latino, and White merchants were angry with police. These conflicts were reported in contexts ranging from the cultural to the personal. These discussions were found mainly in the articles coded in the remorse, skepticism, disillusionment, anger, and blame categories.

Conflict between Latinos and the city government and Mayor Dixon was a commonly reported issue in the *Washington Post* and *El Tiempo Latino*. For example, in a prominently placed *Washington Post* story titled "Dixon's Longest Darkest Day As Mayor" described the long-standing conflict in the context of meetings about the disturbances:

> She had met with religious leaders in the Latino community and sat for an hour as Hispanic community leaders derided her as a leader whose administration was out of touch with even their most urgent concerns. . . . Many Hispanic leaders described the violence partly as a reflection of the deep frustration many have with the D.C. police and the city government. The leaders angrily told Dixon advisers that her absence was proof of their "second-class citizenship." ("Dixon's Longest Darkest Day," *Washington Post,* May 7, 1991, p. A1)

The deep-rooted Latino antipathy for the Washington, D.C., city government is a result of not only a generalized frustration with city authorities but specific encounters with those representing the city power structures.

Although the reports in the *Post* provide a fairly good basic picture of the dimensions of conflict, *El Tiempo Latino* provided some additional information about the general friction between Blacks and Latinos in D.C., as well as some details about the incident not reported in the *Post* or the Black newspapers. *El Tiempo Latino* was the only paper to report the accounts of witnesses who said police had beaten Latinos other than Gomez at the scene of the confrontation. *El Tiempo Latino* also reported that many onlookers indicated that the ambulance had taken an inordinate amount of time before arriving on the scene ("Witnesses Verify That Daniel Gomez Was Handcuffed," *El Tiempo Latino,* May 10, 1991, p. 1). In addition to the details surrounding the confrontation between Jewell and Gomez, *El Tiempo Latino* also discussed what the Latino community perceived to be cultural insensitivity on the part of city government and police. The community complained that few D.C. police are Latino, and almost none of the others speak Spanish. One specific point of contention highlighted by *El Tiempo Latino* (mentioned also by the general circulation papers) was that drinking in public is accepted cultural practice in much of Latin America, so Latinos in D.C. do not view gathering in a park to drink beer with their friends as a problem. Police, on the other hand, view this practice as a violation of city ordinances and, more often than not, arrest offenders ("Peace Returns to the Area," *El Tiempo Latino,* May 10, 1991, p. 1). Thus, although Latinos see cultural insensitivity in the way the police behave toward them, police view the issue as one of law and order.

The coverage also depicted anger directed toward Latino rioters. A typical report indicating anger at rioters was one providing an account of the second day of disturbances. After a description of the various events, the story reports the views of some local residents:

> As several men ran west on Park Road, a woman sitting on her porch nearby reflected the anger of some residents toward the crowds: "Now we have to breathe this [tear gas] in our homes. They ought to bring out the machine guns and start shooting them." ("Leaderless Group Looks for Trouble," *Washington Post,* May 7, 1991, p. A1)

A column by an African American writer that appeared in The *Washington Informer* shows the anger some Blacks felt toward Latino rioters:

> What happened in the Adams Morgan section of town was inexcusable. There was no reason for [the Latinos] to riot, throw rocks and with intent to do bodily harm to officers and to loot and burn police vehicles. Some of the excuses given for their actions just make me sick. ("The Riot in Adams Morgan," The *Washington Informer,* May 9-15, 1991, p. 18)

Villains

Among the clearest images organizing the early coverage of the disturbances, the general circulation and Black press cast Latinos as villains. In the terms of racial formation, Latinos were culturally represented in essentialized ways. These images often, at least implicitly, provided a rationale for imposing structural forms of domination on Latino communities. Much of this coverage was coded as containing the themes of fear, violence, and conflict.

The Latino community is depicted as marked by a lack of discipline and propensity toward violence. Reinforcing this image is the reporting of the weapon allegedly used by Gomez to attack Officer Powell. Although the *Washington Post* consistently refers to the weapon as a "knife," other papers gave varying accounts of the weapon. In an article in the Black press, Gomez is said to have "pulled a gun" and threatened to shoot Powell ("Putting the Blame in the Right Place," *Washington Afro American,* May 11, 1991, p. A4).

The fact that the Black press magnified the threat Gomez represented to the African American police officer by reporting Gomez used a gun rather than a knife may be a reflection of Black resentment and fear of the city's

Latinos. In fact, some of the most disturbing depictions of Latinos as villains were printed in the Black press. In the Black newspapers, the image of Latinos hinged upon an interesting articulation between behavior and place of origin. For example:

> Things escalated harrowingly close to total anarchy as the predominantly Hispanic rioters continued their rampage, employing what some observers described as tactics some of them possibly perfected as guerillas in the jungles of Central America. ("Law and Order Returns to Adams Morgan," *Washington Informer,* May 9-15, 1991, p. 1)

> With the rioting and barbaric action of some of the Hispanics involved . . . I thought I was in some third world country where residents, on a daily basis, did battle with the police. ("The Riot in Adams Morgan," *Washington Informer,* May 9-15, 1991, p. 18)

> I have covered a lot of stories in this town, but I have never seen and experienced the hell which transpired in the Mt. Pleasant community this week. Police clashed with Hispanics who waged Guerilla warfare in the heart of Washington. ("Hamil's Personal Account of the Riot," *Washington Afro American,* May 11, 1991, p. A7)

As these excerpts make clear, the Black press views Latinos as guerillas on a rampage out to destroy Washington, D.C., through the use of tactics they learned in Central America where clashes with police were a way of life. There is no discussion of the U.S. foreign policy that contributed to the civil wars in Central America and that forced millions to flee their countries. The writers express a certain outrage that Latinos are bringing one kind of "place"—the barbaric, violent "third world"—to the heart of another kind of place—Washington, D.C., by implication, the civilized center of the "first world."

Wherever there are villains, there are often innocent victims. All newspapers examined constructed sympathetic images of the victims of Latino violence. A first-person account by a reporter for the *Washington Afro American* wrote,

> I was scared to death . . . for a moment it felt like I was in the middle of the battlefield about to be massacred. The young Latino crowd behind me decided to challenge the police with rocks. They responded with tear gas and guess who was in the middle. Keep breathing . . . it will only last for a few minutes . . . don't wipe your eyes . . . I felt like I was going to die. I pleaded with anybody to call an ambulance. ("Hamil's Personal Account of Riot," *Washington Afro American,* May 11, 1991, p. A1)

Later in the same article, the writer reports: "Babies were screaming through the streets and forced to drink tear gas. They did much worse than the hooded mobsters who seemed to be experienced rioters" ("Hamil's Personal Account of Riot," *Washington Afro American*, May 11, 1991, p. A1).

Another set of innocent victims depicted by the press was the merchants in the Adams-Morgan and Mount Pleasant areas. Articles such as the following were common in the aftermath of the disturbances:

> While no overall estimate of damage was available, several merchants said they lost thousands of dollars worth of goods, some of which will be covered by insurance. Some stayed to sweep away the broken glass that littered the sidewalk, while others simply hung out hand-lettered signs announcing they were closed and left. ("Amid the Ruin, Merchants Decry Police Response," *Washington Post*, May 8, 1991, p. A1)

El Tiempo Latino also printed stories about the impact of the disturbances on local merchants:

> The merchants of Adams Morgan have been affected in the two days of the violent disturbances. Being closed for two days as a result of the curfew has meant a loss of business for the merchants. ("Deep Preoccupation of the Merchants in the Area," *El Tiempo Latino*, May 10, 1991, p. 1)

None of the articles that contain these kinds of innocent-victim images contain substantial discussions contrasting the different victims in a way that reveals the broader historical, political, and social context of disturbances.

Heroes

To some extent, all newspapers depicted police and other agents of city government as heroes, in contrast to Latinos, whom they cast largely as villains. As in the Miami case, the construction of the police-as-hero image begins with reports of police facing dangerous situations. These stories included, among others, articles about police in riot gear and gas masks ready to face down the threat from Latino rioters and accounts of encounters with rock-throwing youths ("Simmering Tension Between Police, Hispanics Fed Clash," *Washington Post*, May 6, 1991, p. A1; "3rd Night of Curfew Quiet but Uneasy in Mt. Pleasant Area," *Washington Post*,

May 9, 1991, p. A1). Building on the image of police in danger is one of police restraint despite the threat. One article reported that police were cautious in their actions:

> "Our whole idea from Day One was to use a minimum of force. That's why we haven't had any persons killed in this community," [said Police Chief Isaac Fulwood]. ("Dixon Moved Cautiously in Effort to Restore Calm," *Washington Post,* May 8, 1991, p. A1)

Another article, without irony, presented police restraint (while reinforcing Latino stereotypes) this way:

> Even with the rioting and barbaric actions of some of the Hispanics involved, you did not see any excessive beatings or kicking of human beings from police officers. ("The Riot in Adams Morgan," *Washington Informer,* May 9-15, 1991, p. 18)

El Tiempo Latino also published two long articles reporting the police perspective of events and police action to contain the disturbance ("Police Version of Incident," *El Tiempo Latino,* May 10, 1991, p. 1; "It Is Not In Our Hands," *El Tiempo Latino,* May 10, 1991, p. 3).

A final element of the heroic police image is the "thin blue line" of officers protecting society from violence. For the general circulation papers, police on the front lines who contained the spreading violence, looting, and arson in the Adams- Morgan and Mount Pleasant areas were heroes. The Black press justified the police action on the grounds that control of the Latino community was necessary to prevent destruction of the neighborhood. Referring to the disturbances, a *Washington Afro American* editorial said, "These are the type of problems that arise when you have a large number of illegal immigrants in a community" ("Putting the Blame in the Right Place," *Washington Afro American,* May 11, 1991, p. A4). The editorial continued to say that police are right to take action against the Latino community and that they should not have been so restrained.

Countertrends

As the coverage continued, the relatively simple dichotomy of heroes and villains began to erode somewhat. Later in the news coverage cycle, as the newspapers began to print analyses of the disturbances, some depictions of police and Latinos did not neatly fit into the categories. For example, police were shown as unfair rather than heroic in their dealings with Latinos. In one article, a resident is quoted as saying, "We are oppressed by the police. . . . If you look Spanish or speak Spanish, they're suspicious of you" ("Simmering Tensions Between Police, Hispanics Fed Clash," *Washington Post*, May 6, 1991, p. A1). In a letter to the editor of *El Tiempo Latino*, one resident wrote:

> The police are not only arrogant, oppressive, and violent, they also ignore the community. What the policewoman did with the shooting, the department is doing daily with their indifference toward the community problems and discrimination. (Letter to the Editor, *El Tiempo Latino*, May 10, 1991, p. 5)

The leader of a Latino youth club succinctly summed up what seemed to be a common view among Latino residents regarding their personal encounters with police in the press reports: "The police treat us like animals" ("After the Violence, Young Voices Unite," *Washington Post*, May 16, 1991, p. J5).

Another set of stories that did not fit the hero–villain dichotomy included some that made distinctions among Latinos. In one column, the writer said,

> I am certain that the looters are [an] infinitesimal part of the Hispanic population in Mount Pleasant and Adams Morgan. They are bad apples who use the legitimate concerns of the Hispanic population as an excuse for criminal behavior. ("Roots of the Riot," *Washington Post*, May 12, 1991, p. C8)

An article that provides the most compelling challenge to the police hero–Latino villain dichotomy humanizes Enrique Gomez, the man who attacked the police officer in the confrontation that precipitated the disturbances. After being demonized as an out-of-control drunk who threatened a police officer trying to do her job, readers learn in one article that Gomez is a legal resident who is devoted to his sister and her family and sends home cash to his ailing father in El Salvador ("The Man in the Eye of the Storm," *Washington Post*, May 13, 1991, p. D6).

Although most of the coverage depicts the disturbances as criminal activity carried out by Latino residents of the Adams-Morgan and Mount Pleasant areas, a handful of articles reveal alternative interpretations of the events. Some articles suggested that the disturbances were not primarily criminal activity. Two of these articles referred to the disturbances as a "rebellion," a term normally used to refer to resistance against authority, which may or may not be criminal in nature ("Dixon Imposes Curfew on Mt. Pleasant Area," *Washington Post*, May 7, 1991, p. A1; "D.C.

Hispanics Find Voice, But Power Is Elusive," *Washington Post,* May 11, 1991, p. A1). Other articles revealed a view held by some that the "rebellion" was justified. The disturbances were presented for some as a logical outcome of the long history of being mistreated by police. For example:

> "They're standing up for their rights," Bea Rodriguez, a Mount Pleasant resident, said of the youths. "This explosion has been brewing in the community for a long time. If you live here, you see a lot of abuse by the police." ("Dixon Imposes Curfew," *Washington Post,* May 7, 1991, p. A1)

In another paper, a letter to the editor stamps the Mount Pleasant disturbances as legitimate political activity by comparing it to other rebellions in history:

> The probing for an explanation for what caused the explosion in Adams Morgan is a search that can go far back as the rebellions of Denmark Vessey and Nat Turner. Quite simply, when people have had enough of the oppression they will respond and react to that oppression. Although this response can take any form, one thing is assured [*sic*] and that is that there will be a response. ("Adams Morgan," *Washington Afro American,* June 22, 1991, p. A4)

Overall, this last set of articles provides readers a peek at what might be considered more complex answers to the question of why the disturbances took place as compared to the predominant image in the general circulation and Black press that the disturbances were solely criminal activity. Although U.S. law considers the activities criminal behavior, a larger social, political, and economic context provided by this relatively small number of articles suggests a broader explanation for the behaviors. These articles challenge the image of Latinos as inherently violent and criminally inclined and thereby eliminate the potential rationale for racial domination.

Causes of the Conflicts

As in the Miami case, after the initial reports describing the disturbances, Washington, D.C., coverage gave much attention to analyzing the causes of the conflicts that led to the disturbances. Many of these articles were coded as containing the themes related to blame, values and culture, assimilation, immigration, and race. In general, the newspapers agreed about the overarching causes of the conflicts: tensions among community residents and between Latinos and police. As in the Miami case, the specific discussions about these tensions and how they emerged can be understood as offering individual-, institutional-, and structural-level explanations for the disturbances.

Individual-level Causes

The individual-level explanations focused on the skirmish between Jewell and Gomez immediately preceding the disturbances. For example, one article claimed that the "disorder was touched off by a shooting by a police officer" ("D.C. Neighborhood Erupts After Officer Shoots Suspect," *Washington Post,* May 6, 1991, p. A1). Another article provided a more detailed account:

> It had begun—on Sunday night—after a Hispanic man, who had allegedly lunged at a police officer with a knife, was critically wounded by a police gunshot. ("Events in Mount Pleasant," *Washington Post,* May 7, 1991, p. A20)

This example shows how the newspaper implies that the immediate and direct cause of the disturbances was a conflict between individuals. A more complex explanation, even at this individual level, could have been formulated by examining the race and gender dynamic of the tussle between Jewell, a Black woman police officer, and Gomez, a young Salvadoran man. However, in all the coverage, the newspapers mention Jewell's gender only five times, and they refer to her race three times. Gomez is referred to consistently as a Latino man or Salvadoran man.

Another set of discussions of individual-level causes of the disturbances is organized around the idea that many Latino residents behaved in ways that aroused the resentment of other community members and suspicion of police who patrol the area. These behaviors were depicted in columns written by residents of the community and by using quotes from community residents as part of news articles. A Black resident of Mount Pleasant wrote about his frustration with his Latino neighbors:

> What do you do when your neighbors get drunk in public and urinate on your building's walls? From the windows of their apartments, some of my neighbors toss beer cans and wine bottles along with the ripped-out pages of pornographic magazines onto the courtyard. ("A Collision of Cultures," *Washington Post,* May 7, 1991, p. E3)

Heavy drinking and drunken behavior by Latinos was a common image portrayed in the general circulation press but was much less frequent in the Black press and in *El Tiempo Latino.*

Three stories in *El Tiempo Latino* mentioned alcohol use among Latinos, but all of these articles mentioned the issue only in passing. For example, a typical sentence from the coverage was "Gomez was arrested for public drinking" ("The Neighborhood Returns to Peace," *El Tiempo Latino,* May 10, 1991, p. 1).

Another individual-level explanation also discussed behaviors but did so in a more general fashion by raising the issue of culture. Articles containing the assimilation and culture and values themes in the local newspapers constructed the issue as one of a cultural clash between Latinos and other residents as the cause of the disturbances. *El Tiempo Latino* described the problem simply:

> There are Hispanics who do not understand the system and there are policemen who do not understand the Hispanic culture and do not speak the language. ("The Neighborhood Returns to Peace," *El Tiempo Latino,* May 10, 1991, p.1)

In reference to the fact that many of the community residents were immigrants, a *Washington Post* column described the problem this way:

> [Latinos] do not assimilate. Perhaps they were ill prepared to abandon their social and family structure; perhaps they are victims of a sort of cultural schizopherenia [*sic*]. ("How to Kill a Neighborhood," *Washington Post,* May 12, 1991, p. C4)

Aside from suggesting that Latinos must change their social and family structure if they are to fit in, the article implies that a failure to assimilate is some sort of cultural pathology, typically associated with groups depicted as occupying the lower rungs of racial hierarchy. Several articles then imply what those pathologies are:

> As we ate, we marveled at the total absence of car horns being used as doorbells, and of the super-amplified music roaring out of cruising cars. ("How to Kill a Neighborhood," *Washington Post,* May 12, 1991, p. C4)

> [Latinos] are demanding that . . . we learn their language instead of them learning English. ("Immigration Problems," *Washington Afro American,* May 25, 1991, p. A4)

Combined with earlier descriptions of how the Latino villain was constructed, these examples help create a menu of "Latino pathologies": prone to violence, inconsiderate of others, refusing to communicate with non-Latinos, intent on destruction of property, and so on. The coverage suggests that these are inherent characteristics of Latinos and that they contributed to sparking the disturbances.

Institutional-level Causes

Institutional-level causes of the disturbances focused on the actions of agents and agencies of the city and federal governments, as well as government policies. A history of being ignored by the city was one of the reasons the Latino community erupted, according to the general circulation papers and *El Tiempo Latino*. Latino community leaders as well as average citizens expressed this view:

> Dixon had met with religious leaders in the Hispanic community, and sat for an hour as the leaders derided her as a leader whose administration is out of touch with even their most urgent concern. ("Dixon's Longest, Darkest Day As Mayor," *Washington Post*, May 7, 1991, p. A1)

El Tiempo Latino presented a specific problem that was depicted as a lack of respect for the Latino community on the part of city police, an important city agency.

> "We recognize the lack of respect that the police give Hispanics. We have asked the city leaders to show cultural sensitivity, to create more jobs, and to double the efforts to promote social programs," said Margarita Roque. ("The Neighborhood Returns to Peace," *El Tiempo Latino*, May 10, 1991, p. 1)

One government agency that did not ignore the Latino community in Washington was the Immigration and Naturalization Service (INS). For a decade before the disturbances, the INS had been interpreting immigration laws in a manner least favorable to Latino refugees in Washington. It was in this context that the INS began to assist local courts to process Latinos arrested during the disturbances, according to the *Washington Post* ("Roots of a Riot," *Washington Post*, May 12, 1991, p. C8). This INS decision further angered the Latino community and may have contributed to a prolongation of the disturbances, reported the *Washington Post*:

> INS and District officials acknowledged that the presence of federal agents during the Mount Pleasant disturbances "could have been incendiary" to the community during the worst hours of the unrest. ("Mount Pleasant Anger Stirred by Distrust of INS," *Washington Post*, May 18, 1991, p. B5)

Another institutional-level factor contributing to the conflict that led to the disturbances was U.S. foreign policy toward Central American nations.

Most discussions rarely explicitly mentioned this factor, but many discussions implicated it when they portrayed immigration as a problem related to the disturbances. Thus, we consider immigration an institutional factor because the heavy exodus of Central Americans to Washington, D.C., during this time period was partly a result of the U.S. government's foreign policy decisions that led to deteriorating conditions in Central America, which forced people to flee their homes.

In the Black press, one argument was that immigrants brought with them a temperament that was bound to create tensions between themselves and police. A columnist for the *Washington Informer*, for example, pointed out that Central American immigrants had anxieties about police that compelled them to participate in the disturbances. The columnist wrote that

> [some] blamed the rioting on the fact that these people were afraid of police; that in their country the police represented repression. ("The Riot in Adams Morgan," The *Washington Informer*, May 9-15, 1991, p. 18)

Though this part of the argument sounds as though the writer is trying to provide some legitimacy to the disturbances, the columnist goes on to write that even though many of the immigrants face poverty in addition to fear of police, immigrants have no "right to riot." As she put it, "What does repression in El Salvador have to do with the price of bread in Washington, D.C.?" ("The Riot in Adams Morgan," The *Washington Informer*, May 9-15, 1991, p. 18).

Another piece in the Black press, an editorial in the *Afro American*, made the argument that the disturbances could be traced to the presence of too many immigrants in the city, which created a strain on city resources:

> [Central American immigrants] are demanding homeless shelters, jobs, expanded social services. This is to be expected but can struggling governments like the District of Columbia be expected to foot the bill? ("Immigration Problems," *Washington Afro American*, May 25, 1991, p. A4)

Thus, arguments in the Black press tried to explain one side of the disturbances: Latinos as the targets of abuse and anger by community residents and police. But the Black press also suggests that the mere presence of Central American immigrants created a number of problems that contributed to the disturbances and that the immigrants brought the problems on themselves.

Structural-level Causes

Structural-level explanations were the least frequently offered in all the newspapers. The articles presenting explanations from this perspective

generally assumed an unequal access to employment, housing, social services, and so on for Latinos. For example, some articles discussed the "recent layoffs [of Latino workers] from restaurant, carpentry and construction jobs" ("Residents Differ on Where to Focus Their Anger," *Washington Post*, May 7, 1991, p. A27), the feeling among Latinos that "they do not get a fair share of [affirmative action] spending and programs" ("Black Power's New Dilemma," *Washington Post*, May 12, 1991, p. C1), and a "series of recent evictions of Hispanic families from their apartments" ("After the Violence, Young Voices Unite," *Washington Post*, May 16, 1991, p. J5).

The issue of resource inequities is revealed also in a number of other stories about structural conditions in the city. A handful of *Washington Post* stories raised class differences as one of the factors contributing to the disturbances. The Mount Pleasant area "has become a border," one story reported ("Mt. Pleasant: A Melting Pot Feels the Heat," *Washington Post*, May 9, 1991, p. C1). The border depicted is one standing between

poor residents—largely Hispanic and Black people—who live in apartments from the more affluent homeowners, mostly White and Black residents who occupy the gentrified row houses to the west. ("Mt. Pleasant: A Melting Pot Feels the Heat," *Washington Post*, May 9, 1991, p. C1)

This excerpt reveals the inequities in housing between rich and poor, but it also reveals the contested access to the spaces around Mount Pleasant. Developers who want to upgrade and sell the housing to wealthy residents desire the older homes in the area. This gentrification process raised prices of surrounding property, including the cheaper housing where Latinos lived. As a result, the space available for affordable housing decreased, and the poor were forced to either share accommodations or move away altogether.

In addition, as the wealthy moved in, police took seriously the new residents' desire for control of the public spaces in the neighborhood where Latinos gathered to socialize. A quote from a 24-year Mount Pleasant resident confirmed that police took heed of the complaints from the wealthy and took action. The resident said that police harassment had always been a problem, but that "when Whites started moving in, the police started getting on people. We used to sit in the park and drink and it wasn't a problem. Now it is." ("Miles Apart in Mount Pleasant," *Washington Post*, May 19, 1991, p. A1)

One other structural issue that received some attention as a factor contributing to the disturbances was the Latino lack of access to political power. The *Post* reported that part of the reason for the lack of political power for Latinos is because only 1% of the city's Latino population is registered to vote ("D.C. Hispanics Find Voice, But Power Is Elusive," *Washington Post*, May 11, 1991, p. A1). Thus, the paper acknowledged, "[Hispanics] cannot vote and so [have] scarcely attracted the attention of politicians, other than in a negative way" ("Roots of Riot," *Washington Post*, May 12, 1991, p. C8). As a contrast, the *Post* portrayed Black political power as the result of visible and effective "representation both in city hall and nationally, as well as well-established network of colleges, civic and professional groups and churches" ("Black Power's New Dilemma," *Washington Post*, May 12, 1991, p. C1). *El Tiempo Latino* also acknowledged the lack of political power for Latinos and calls for a leader to emerge:

> The Hispanics need a leader. A person who knows our problems thoroughly and knows the best ways to let the public know about us so we can look for solutions to our problems. ("We Need a Leader in the Hispanic Community," *El Tiempo Latino*, May 10, 1991, p. 4)

The picture of unequal political power in the local newspapers suggests that without political networking and more registered voters, Latinos may be constrained in changing structural conditions in the city, limited to occasional confrontations with city authorities.

The coverage of the causes of the disturbances indicates a fairly clear pattern. Individual-level factors place the blame for starting the disturbances on Latino residents of the community. Institutional-level explanations seem to place the blame on several agencies and policies. The structural-level explanations are least frequently discussed and provide broad economic and political contexts that explain the disturbances in which Latinos are not implicated as responsible for the disturbances.

Implications of the Conflicts

In all the papers, consequences and effects of the conflict receive relatively less attention than discussion of the causes. In part, this may be because discussing the consequences takes reporters into the area of speculation and conjecture, a territory they are normally reluctant to enter in any explicit way. Projecting into the future is most safely done in columns and editorials, where opinion can be expressed officially. Nevertheless, we do find numerous examples of reporters writing more implicitly about implications in straight news stories as well.

One major focus of discussion in terms of the implications of the disturbances was the costs incurred by the city, the police department, and area merchants. By and large, these discussions focused on immediate economic costs, as opposed to long-term economic costs or, more generally, human costs. The general circulation papers covered costs incurred by city, police, and merchants in the Mount Pleasant and Adams-Morgan areas. In a typical article about costs borne by the city, the *Washington Post* cataloged some of the costs to the city:

> Twenty Metro buses were damaged. . . . At least 31 stores were looted. . . . Eighteen people were taken by ambulance to local hospitals for minor injuries. Since Sunday about 20 police vehicles have been destroyed or damaged, destruction estimated to cost $600,000 to $700,000. ("Curfew Leaves Mount Pleasant Area Quieter," *Washington Post,* May 8, 1991, p. A1)

El Tiempo Latino also discussed costs to police and merchants ("Area Merchants Are Deeply Worried," *El Tiempo Latino,* May 10, 1991, p. 1; "Police Version of the Incident," *El Tiempo Latino,* May 10, 1991, p. 3; "The Solution Is Not in Our Hands," *El Tiempo Latino,* May 10, 1991, p. 3) but reported little about general damage to city property such as buses. The Black press discussed costs in terms of the danger to police and damage to city property but said nothing about costs of the disturbances to merchants.

Although the cost to Latino (and other) merchants was given attention in some of the newspapers, economic costs incurred by the Latino community residents was mentioned in only one article. The *Washington Post* article, which also discussed costs to the city and merchants, devoted its last two paragraphs to describing the economic impact of the disturbances on two Latino workers:

> Two Hispanic men standing outside their apartment building on Mount Pleasant Street late yesterday said they had skipped work yesterday and forfeited a day's pay in fear of being arrested heading to their jobs.
> "It's bad," [s]aid Luis Martinez. "If someone's doing something wrong, they should be punished, but with this, we are not able to work." ("3rd Night of Curfew Quiet but Uneasy in Mount Pleasant Area," *Washington Post,* May 9, 1991, p. A1)

Not only are economic costs to rank-and-file Latino community members ignored, but discussion of social and political costs for the Latino community (whether short-term or long-term), such as a hardening of anti-Latino sentiment in the police department or more difficulty getting residents to vote for Latino candidates for political office, is also largely missing.

Another consequence of the conflicts was that all the newspapers, to some extent, tried to provide reassurance to their readers that conditions would return to normal and maybe even improve. All the stories that contained this theme based these reassurances on restoring law and order. In the Black press, law and order was the only basis presented for reassuring readers. The single story containing a reassurance theme in the Black press was headlined "Law and Order Restored in Adams Morgan Area" (*Washington Informer*, May 9-15, 1991, p. 1). In the *Washington Post* and in *El Tiempo Latino* there was reassurance based on addressing Latino grievances about police and city government (e.g., "Events in Mount Pleasant," *Washington Post*, May 7, 1991, p. A20; "Area Merchants Are Deeply Worried," *El Tiempo Latino*, May 10, 1991, p. 1). In the *Washington Post*, the primary basis for this reassurance was reporting on Dixon's attempts to foster Black–Latino cooperation and the creation of commissions to investigate race relations in the city (e.g., "Dixon Imposes Curfew on the Mount Pleasant Area," *Washington Post*, May 7, 1991, p. A1; "Curfew Leaves Mount Pleasant Area Quieter," *Washington Post*, May 8, 1991, p. A1).

As the previous discussion about reassurance suggests, one of the consequences of the disturbances was that a number of solutions to the conflicts were proposed and then reported in the newspapers. The primary solutions reported in the general circulation press were Black–Latino cooperation such as dialogue between Blacks and Latinos, improved policing, and political solutions such as undertaking an investigation into the shooting. Dialogue between Blacks and Latinos is possible and vital, according to some reports, because these groups share a common plight (minority intersection category). In the weeks following the disturbances, some of the newspapers published articles reporting that leaders of the Black and Latino communities were trying to cooperate to solve the city's racial tensions. Four other articles in the *Washington Post* reported post-disturbance dialogue between Blacks and Latinos.

El Tiempo Latino printed no articles about potential solutions but published one article about minority intersection, which reported the similarities between the living conditions for Blacks in the city in the 1960s and the conditions for Latinos in the early 1990s. Although the article does not call for cooperation explicitly, it is one of the few in all the coverage that makes a historical link between the city's Black and Latino communities.

The Black press printed two items about cooperative solutions, including one letter to the editor that provided a compelling argument for cooperation that emphasized unity, not just dialogue:

African Americans should be the first to identify and unite not necessarily with the actions of the Hispanics but with the sentiment of having had enough. . . . If we are to truly make this nation respond to poverty and seriously grapple with eliminating unemployment, which serve as the match that lights the fire of the riots, then we must form a coalition of oppressed nationalities that can demand a redress of our legitimate grievances. ("Adams Morgan," *Washington Afro American*, June 22, 1991, p. A4)

Whatever validity there might be in the idea that class could bind Blacks and Latinos together, whereas race would perpetuate tensions, the newspapers, in general, do not give much attention to stories about general cooperation (see Table 3.3) and almost none to issues of class unity among Blacks and Latinos.

The solution printed in the general circulation papers and *El Tiempo Latino* calling for better policing primarily was a call for more Spanish-speaking officers on the city police force. (The Black press published no stories reporting a call for better policing.) But there was also some demand for more vigorous policing, as implied in this column from the *Washington Post*:

No matter how victimized a person may be, he or she is not entitled to destroy property and endanger lives. The surest way to drive that message home is to make arrests, make them swiftly, and make them stick. ("No Excuse to Riot," *Washington Post*, May 9, 1991, p. A21)

Assuming that it was Latinos who were most directly involved in the disturbances, the column ignores important contextual factors while constructing Latino culpability around the threat they pose to property and the lives of others. There is no denying that rioters destroyed property and endangered lives and that they wantonly broke the law. However, the column creates a narrow law and order frame for understanding the issue. The view ignores high poverty and unemployment rates that prevent most Latinos from owning property and that constantly endanger their lives.

Political solutions to the conflicts such as forming a panel to investigate the police shooting of Gomez were mentioned mainly in the general circulation newspapers. The *Washington Post* mentioned three other solutions: lobbying the government for more resources to help the city's poor ("Culture Clash in Mount Pleasant," *Washington Post*, May 9, 1991, p. A1; "Community Leaders Assess Mount Pleasant," *Washington Post*, May 15, 1991, p. J5); appointing a leader to OLA ("Mount Pleasant Case Sent to Grand Jury," *Washington Post*, May 21, 1991, p. B3); and revising the immigration laws ("Illegal Aliens," *Washington Post,* May 8, 1991, p. A30). The *Washington Afro American,* in an editorial, advocated revising the immigration laws to restrict Latino immigration ("Immigration Problem," May 25, 1991, p. A4). *El Tiempo Latino* printed a letter to the editor that insisted the disturbances were a political statement and that the solution to the underlying problems in the city was more protests. The letter, worth quoting at length, argued,

> The Hispanic leadership worries more about the carnival than about racism, exploitation, and discrimination. If leaders are organizing more festivals and no protests, the revolt of "la Mara" [the crowd] was a completely logical action. The street fights were what got the attention over the problems of the African-Americans and thanks to these fights important victories were obtained in the fight for civil rights. Now the leaders of the Hispanic community wrongly call for peace to appease the system one more time, but will not call for a protest to obtain by screaming what we cannot obtain by being silent. (Letter to the Editor, *El Tiempo Latino,* May 10, 1991, p. 5)

This was the only item in all the coverage analyzed that called for more protests in the streets as a solution to the problems underscored by the disturbances.

Race and Nation

Although the coverage discusses conflict between Blacks and Latinos, issues related to community and belonging also appear just below the surface. Specifically, the coverage depicted Latinos as unfit to be Americans. The *Washington Post* and the Black press contributed to this construction most obviously. The first step in this articulation of race and nation was the claim to the territory through the use of possessive pronouns. The *Washington Post* gave prominence to a quote from an African American member of the D.C. city council, H. R. Crawford, who said of Latinos: "If they don't appreciate our country, get out" ("Life Gets Back to Normal," *Washington Post,* May 10, 1991, p. A1). In one of the Black newspapers, an editorial complained about Latinos "invading our country" ("Immigration Problems," *Washington Afro American,* May 25, 1991, p. A4). In both of these phrases, not only is a possessive claim made to the United States, but also, in the first example, the speaker was affronted by the presence of "strangers" and saw them as threatening.

Despite the generalized resentment of Latinos represented in the previous quotes, the newspapers also presented views that suggested who, among the perceived outsiders, is and is not considered members of "our country." Another report featuring H. R. Crawford helped establish certain people as legitimate members of the community. In an article commenting on Blacks irritated by the "sudden spotlight on the Hispanic community," the *Post* reported:

> He [Crawford] said that he did not want violence to be rewarded with city pro-grams, and added that the city needed to be concerned with "legitimate members of the community." ("The Painful Lessons of Mount Pleasant," *Washington Post*, May 12, 1991, p. A1)

The context of the story makes it clear that Crawford is referring to vio-lence by Latinos (not Blacks or Whites who participated in the distur-bances) and that those who engaged in violence do not belong within the community and have no right to city services. The idea that the city should look after only "legitimate" people is an oblique reference to undocu-mented workers in the city who, the Black community believed, were mainly Latinos securing employment and enjoying social services illegally. This article constructed the disturbances as solely criminal and carried out by people who did not have a right to be in the city or in the nation.

So who are legitimate members of the community when it comes to Latinos? Essentially, it is those who have either legal standing or cultural standing. Several articles refer to the need for "papers" that document legal status. One such article about Bell High School, attended by many of the community's Latino youths, quotes a teacher who makes the connection between legal status and various benefits:

> Diener told of a problem that needs a solution beyond Bell's doors: students who lack the proper immigration papers. "Scholarships programs are restricted only to those students who have papers." ("Bell High: Where Cultures Conjoin Instead of Clash," *Washington Post*, May 26, 1991, p. D8)

The connection made here is that with papers one is legitimate and eli-gible for benefits such as scholarships. Another benefit of having papers, in theory, is safety from deportation, which was an almost constant fear among many in the Latino community in the city. Although Congress had approved arrangements for temporary protective status for those without papers, there was enough uncertainty that "the level of fear [was] so high and so intense that it color[ed] their whole world" ("Mount Pleasant Anger Stirred by Distrust of INS," *Washington Post*, May 18, 1991, p. B5). But having the legitimacy accorded by papers should allay any fears, according to the INS officials: "'Nobody's afraid of the INS if you're here legally' INS spokesman Duke Austin said" ("Mount Pleasant Anger Stirred by Distrust of INS," *Washington Post,* May 18, 1991, p. B5).

However, according to an article in the Black press, papers not only protected Latinos from the INS, they also gave Latinos freedom to loot and burn with impunity. An editorial in the *Washington Afro American,* quoting an official from a conservative immigration-reform lobbying group, stated,

> As residents question why the Mayor took a hands off policy and refused to clamp down immediately, Dave Ray, public relations director of the Federation of American Immigration Reform pointed out that when police approached some of the rioters, they flashed their "protection" cards. ("Putting the Blame in the Right Places," *Washington Afro American,* May 11, 1991, p. A4)

The clear implication of this passage is that Latinos engaged in rioting while hiding behind their papers. Thus, even legitimate members of the community, if they are Latinos, may not be fit to be part of the nation.

Another basis for legitimacy in the community is cultural standing through assimilation, a process in which immigrants adapt to the culture of the new community and come to be accepted by the host community. Much of the coverage in the general circulation and Black press, however, suggests that Latinos are not willing to assimilate. For example, in an item in the *Washington Post,* Mayor Dixon refers to the "problem" of Latino assimilation:

> The Hispanic refusal to adjust to American culture is an additional problem, Dixon said: "They say when in Rome, do as the Romans do and that must be the order of the day. You cannot have people drinking liquor in public. . . . You cannot have people urinating in public. That is not allowed. And you have to respond to that symbol of authority in whatever form it takes in our culture." ("Black Power's New Dilemma," *Washington Post,* May 12, 1991, p. C1)

In another item, the *Washington Informer* reported that most of the Latinos in the community refuse to speak English ("The Riot in Adams Morgan," *Washington Informer,* May 9-15, 1991, p. 18). The *Washington Afro American* editorialized that the Latino community should expect the problems it has experienced because there are so many "who do not speak the English language" ("Putting the Blame in the Right Places," *Washington Afro American,* May 11, 1991, p. A4). In an article about the healing efforts in Mount Pleasant, the reporter ends with a quote from a longtime resident who clearly resents the Latino refusal to assimilate:

> The people of the neighborhood are tired of having to assimilate to the Hispanics. This is their adopted home. It's time for them to assimilate to the American way of life. ("Mt. Pleasant Begins Time of Healing," *Washington Post,* May 13, 1991, p. D1)

These articles suggest that some Latinos are unwilling to assimilate even though that is what it would take, from the perspective of the majority society, for them to be legitimate members of the community and nation. However, the articles also show that Whites and Blacks think most Latinos are capable of assimilating, and if they would adjust to the "American way of life," Whites and Blacks would accept them.

However, there are some articles that depict some Latinos as culturally unqualified to assimilate even if they wanted to. For example, a story in the *Washington Post* about the recent Central American immigrants describes "a thriving subculture" of immigrants for whom "the rule of law is an alien concept" because it is "seen as punitive [and] ignored when possible." These immigrants place "little value on order" ("Central America to Mount Pleasant," *Washington Post,* May 11, 1991, p. A21). A *Washington Post* guest column written by a White resident reported further "evidence" that some Latinos are culturally unfit to be part of the community:

> [Latinos] trash the neighborhood, use it as a public latrine, harass the women, ruin the area's trees, scare the elderly and kids out of the parks and pull knives and clubs on one another. ("How to Kill a Neighborhood," *Washington Post,* May 12, 1991, p. C4)

Aside from the images of Latinos who have the potential to assimilate but do not and Latinos who are culturally unqualified to assimilate no matter what, there are some Latinos, much smaller in number and mentioned in a handful of articles in the *Washington Post* only, who are portrayed positively by community residents. As suggested in the earlier discussion of heroes and villains, some Latinos are depicted as having fit in with and accepted by the community. Some non-Latino residents were quoted as saying that many Latinos were law-abiding ("Roots of the Riot," *Washington Post,* May 12, 1991, p. C8) and had expressed their sorrow and disgust about the disturbances ("The District's Storm From the Inside Out," *Washington Post,* May 12, 1991, p. B6). In another example, a writer commenting about the Latino immigrants in his community notes, "Many assimilate with surprising speed and are fine neighbors" ("How to Kill a Neighborhood," *Washington Post,* May 12, 1991, p. C4). But later, the writer reveals his vision of Latino culture and its place in the community and nation. In a nostalgic moment in the column, the writer said,

> I remembered the parties I used to throw each year when the feather-flanked dancers of the Hispanic Festival gathered around my steps to warm up for the parade. ("How to Kill a Neighborhood," *Washington Post,* May 12, 1991, p. C4)

Taken together, the items about acceptable Latinos reveal the social and cultural position Latinos must occupy in the imagination of the dominant White majority. Acceptable Latinos must conform to a vision of the ideal assimilated community member, be sympathetic to White misfortune, and be ready to denounce Latino protest, and/or play the role of the safely exotic object of the supposedly benign White gaze. Thus, there are "good" Latinos who assimilate toward the benchmark represented by dominant White society (or are capable of it), and there are "bad" Latinos who will not adapt. The latter are, in a nutshell, depicted as uncivilized and uncultured and therefore unfit to be part of the nation. This example of stratification within news depictions of Latinos shows that racial hierarchy is a matter of within-group as well as between-group differentiation.

El Tiempo Latino published a letter to the editor that dealt with a race and nation issue. The piece complained that "refugees from the former communist countries of Europe are treated well and receive all kinds of help, while Latinos only receive problems from the state" (Letter to the Editor, *El Tiempo Latino,* May 10, 1991, p. 5). So, in a twist on the Miami case, in which the Black press saw Latino immigrants escaping from communist Nicaragua as getting preferential treatment, in Washington, D.C., the Spanish-language paper depicts immigrants from Russia and other former Soviet bloc countries as getting preferential treatment. Thus, the article posits a perspective that suggests European immigrants who are anticommunist are getting more aid from the government, including the predominantly Black city government, than the Central American Latino immigrants who also are anticommunist.

Summary and Discussion

All the newspapers generally used "Black" and "Hispanic" or "Latino" as identifying labels for the two groups primarily involved in the disturbances as well as the issues surrounding them. The *Washington Post* occasionally used the term "Latino," but relatively infrequently. Both "Hispanic" and "Latino" as ethnic identifiers lump together a variety of nationalities and actual cultural differences that exist among these nationalities. Occasionally the *Washington Post* and *El Tiempo Latino* used a specific nationality as an identifier. For example, Gomez was identified as Salvadoran in several reports. A handful of *Post* stories used source attributions that identified nationality. The Black press consistently used the term "Hispanics" and never referred to a specific nationality that would fall under that umbrella term.

Blacks and Latinos are depicted as the main groups of people involved in the disturbances in all the newspapers. Latinos appear more frequently as actors than Blacks. Latinos are frequently depicted as villains. The most commonly appearing actor in all newspapers is the Black-dominated city government, including the police. The newspapers depicted the police, to some extent, as villains, but the more dominant image is of police as heroes. Several articles mentioned White predominance in key institutional sites such as local business and media. However, this near invisibility is precisely what reinforces White privilege: By not seeing White power and privilege embedded in the local political economy, the disturbances are seen as a function largely of Latino pathologies (depicted in the Black press and the *Washington Post*) and Black discrimination (depicted in *El Tiempo Latino* and the *Washington Post*). Whites and the institutions they control are largely exonerated from any historical or contemporary role they may have played in fomenting the disturbances.

All newspapers depicted Latinos as victims more often than any other group. Primarily, the Gomez shooting, discussions of police abuse, and government neglect of Latinos account for this image. In all newspapers, government (including police) is the second most frequently mentioned as victims. The newspapers depicted the police as victims in the context of injuries suffered during the disturbances. A Korean American store owner and a Black reporter were depicted once each as victims of the disturbances.

With conflict as the main theme in all the coverage, anger between Blacks and Latinos took center stage. The *Washington Post* portrayed the anger on both sides; that is, Black anger at Latinos and Latino anger at Blacks. The Black press almost exclusively focused on Black anger at Latinos. *El Tiempo Latino* gave more attention to Latino anger at Blacks but was more subdued in its language than the Black press was in describing Black anger at Latinos. All newspapers published stories that discussed the possible causes of the disturbances. Explanations falling into the individual, institutional, and structural levels appeared in the newspapers in discernible patterns. Individual- or institutional-level explanations appeared more than structural-level ones. All the newspapers discussed the implications of the disturbances, but these implications received less attention than the causes of the disturbances. One of the discussions of implications focused on the costs of the disturbances. The pattern of reporting emphasized economic and short-term costs to the city, police, and merchants (thereby giving primacy to a nexus of the social control-capital formation). The coverage mentioned almost nothing about noneconomic costs, long-term costs, and costs to rank-and-file Latino residents. Another set of stories about implications was coded as providing reassurance to readers. Mainly, these stories were about restoring law and order and assurances from the city leaders that the shooting of Gomez would be investigated.

Finally, stories about solutions to the problems revealed by the disturbances constituted another set of discussions about implications. Most of the proposed solutions reported in the press were conventional, emphasizing dialogue and lobbying government for resources and more effective policing. The only exception was one call for more agitation along the lines of the disturbances, which went against the dominant construction of the disturbances as criminal activity. The press infrequently discussed solutions involving close examination of structural issues such as distribution of various resources, perhaps because the sources journalists normally consult—that is, officials and prominent community leaders—rarely discussed these solutions.

The articulation of race and nation was accomplished through a particular understanding of "cultural fitness." Nation was racialized by suggesting that to legitimately "belong" in America, one must possess certain cultural values and traits, such as respect for law and order, property, neighbors, and the "American way of life." The implication of the press coverage in the *Washington Post* and the Black papers was that Blacks were more American that Latinos. Latinos may strive for those characteristics and may even internalize them, but as a group they also have primary and natural cultural characteristics—such as intolerance of authority, cultural insularity, disregard for others' privacy, and so on—that must be suppressed or eliminated if they want to become legitimate members of the nation.

PART II

PART II

4

Los Angeles, 1992

A mong the cases of unrest examined in this book, the civil disorder in
Los Angeles in April-May 1992 is arguably imbued with the most
complex set of economic, social, and political conditions. One facet of this
complexity emerged with the arrival of Asian and Latin American immigrants during the late 1980s. Simultaneously, federal policies contributed to
mounting alienation and economic vulnerability among the city's Black,
Latino, and poor people. These trends—increased immigration from Asia
and Latin America and the disempowerment of racial minorities and the
poor—created a simmering cauldron of racial tension in the City of Angels.
Analysts commonly viewed the Los Angeles riots as a violent expression of
Korean–Black or Black–White racial tension, typically downplaying the
long historical presence of Latinos in the region's politics, economy, and
race relations. But, in fact, the riots were a truly multiracial experience,
reflecting the full range of the main ethnic populations living in Los
Angeles.

The Political and Economic
Context of Los Angeles, 1992

In the decade or so before the Los Angeles rebellion, the city was undergoing
important changes on its economic, social, and political fronts. Global,
national, and local forces were contributing to the reshaping of the city.
Among these forces were a rapidly changing global and domestic economy,

global migration patterns related to U.S. foreign policy, new dynamics in Los Angeles city politics and housing patterns, growing interethnic tensions, and the always disturbing presence of a city police department with a reputation for arrogant and selective law enforcement.

Domestic Economics

As noted in the introduction, during the 1980s, there was an unmatched transfer of riches to wealthy Americans that hit poor Black communities particularly hard. While the salaries of chief executive officers grew from between 35 to 120 times faster than the pay of workers, the average American lost ground, especially the young, Blacks, and those without a college education.

In addition, during this time period, the U.S. economy underwent a drastic restructuring (Johnson & Oliver, 1992; Sojas, Morales, & Wolff, 1983) that caused a decline of traditional high-wage manufacturing jobs, which in turn devastated an already depressed area such as South Central Los Angeles County (Sojas et al., 1983). Capital flight and plant closings helped reduce access to well-paying unionized jobs for South Central residents (Johnson & Oliver, 1992). The few employment prospects opening up in South Central were in highly competitive simple service industries, which relied on undocumented labor and paid, at most, minimum wage. A high proportion of employees in these sectors were Latino immigrants willing to work menial jobs for low pay. Well-paying and stable jobs associated with high-technology manufacturing and advanced services, areas of rapid growth in the county, did not materialize in South Central. These developments, combined with the negative attitudes toward Black male workers held by many employers, helped push Black male joblessness in some South Central areas to 50%. Thus, given these racial and economic dynamics, many Blacks were among the jobless poor, whereas many Latinos were poor, but working (Johnson & Oliver, 1992; Luttwick, 1992; Sojas et al., 1983).

Policies implemented during the Reagan presidency were partially responsible for these developments. As such, these policies were possible factors contributing to the rebellion (Johnson & Oliver, 1992, p.125). The late 1980s and early 1990s were a time of a laissez-faire business climate marked by "trickle-down" supply-side economic policies, which were ostensibly an attempt to facilitate the competitiveness of U.S. firms. One of the consequences of these policies was capital flight to suburbs and overseas, leading to plant closings and unemployment in large urban areas such as Los Angeles. Federal policy dismantled the social safety net for racial minorities and the poor. For South Central especially, that meant less funding for community-based organizations. To fill the vacuum, poor people were encouraged to pursue mainstream avenues of social and economic mobility—avenues, at the very least, difficult to find and more often closed to the poor. The "savings" garnered by federal cuts in aid to the poor were often funneled into the criminal justice system, which in turn, not surprisingly, led to increasing numbers of jailed working-aged Black and Latino males unable to find the avenues to mobility in the first place—a vicious cycle of social control. Finally, many school initiatives, such as tracking and standardized tests, led to further disenfranchising of Blacks by placing them in special education classes and subjecting these students to extreme disciplinary sanctions for even minor transgressions. In this context, surveys of Los Angeles residents prior to and after the riots discovered rising alienation among Black men and women of all classes (Bobo, Zubrinsky, Johnson, & Oliver, 1994). The most important contribution to the increased alienation was growing economic hardship that trickled down into the region.

Immigration

Increased immigration, brought about by U.S. foreign policy in Central America that pushed refugees out of the region and by economic opportunities that pulled Asians to the city of Los Angeles, was another noteworthy factor in pre-riot racial tensions in Los Angeles. At least since the early 1980s, U.S. foreign policy backed oppressive governments in several Central American countries, which led to dire consequences for average citizens in the countries of the region. Between 1980 and 1992, the United States spent more than $4 billion in El Salvador to finance a proxy war that left thousands of Salvadorans dead (Hamamoto & Torres, 1997, p. 4). American involvement in Central American wars contributed to political and economic instability in the region. As a result, thousands of Salvadorans, Guatemalans, Hondurans, and others left the region—many heading for Los Angeles, where Central American immigrants joined both new and well-established communities of Mexican immigrants. By 1989, 40% of city residents were foreign-born and almost half spoke a non-English language. About 35% spoke Spanish (Miles, 1992, p. 41). Latino immigration to Los Angeles from Mexico and Central America, combined with high rates of natural increase, swelled the county's already large Latino population by 60%. By 1990, Latinos—primarily Mexican and Central Americans—had become the dominant ethnic group in Los Angeles, and "non-Hispanic Whites," previously the majority of the population, had become a numerical minority (Davis, 2000, p. 16).

On a slightly smaller scale, population growth among Asians in the city of Los Angeles was similar to the growth among Latinos. Part of the increase was, again, a result of U.S. foreign policy. Southeast Asians dislocated by U.S. military involvement in Vietnam, Cambodia, and Laos created large numbers of refugees, many of whom ended up in the United States working in low-wage jobs or as small-scale entrepreneurs. In 1970, 34% of the city's Asian Americans were foreign born and by 1990, 72% were. Koreans were among the newest arrivals, with 83% foreign born and 61% having entered the United States during the 1980s. Among other Asians of working age (24- to 64-year-olds), 90% were foreign born. These patterns began after the overhaul of immigration laws in 1965, after which the U.S. government gave preference to highly skilled and family-chain immigration. The effects were dramatic: In Los Angeles, the Asian American population increased fivefold between 1970 and 1990, from 190,000 to 926,000; 400,000 immigrated to Los Angeles in the 1980s alone (Ong & Azores, 1994, p. 102). Between 1980 and 1990, the Chinese population in Los Angeles grew from 94,000 to 245,000, whereas the number of Filipinos was up more than 118%, Koreans by 141%, and Indians by 134%. At the same time, the county's Anglo population decreased by 8.5% due largely to an exodus of Whites from the region.[10]

Housing

One of the most obvious and most visible consequences of changing demographics was in patterns of residential housing, which is related intimately to the development of ethnic tensions in the neighborhood. Many Asian and Latino immigrants settled in and around the area known as South Central Los Angeles, a large portion of land 6.5 miles wide and 18 miles long, where many of the city's middle-class and poor Blacks lived. In the 1980s, there was a rapid infusion of Asian and Latino groups into the area accompanied by almost nonexistent growth in the Black populace, which increased by less than 1%. By 1990, Blacks were moving out of South Central and into Inglewood and Hawthorne to the west and into Downey, Paramount, and Long Beach to the southeast. These housing shifts were signs of upward mobility as Blacks that prospered often took advantage of growing prospects for housing in areas away from South Central. Still, South Central remained home to some 278,000 non-Latino Black residents in 1990, accounting for 53% of the neighborhood's population.

As upwardly mobile Blacks moved out of South Central, newcomers from Asia and Latin America moved in. Some were destitute refugees but others—especially some of the Asians—came with graduate degrees or strong business credentials.[11] These new immigrants formed enclaves that nearly encircled, but did not infringe upon, the Black and older Latino core in the city of Los Angeles. These patterns of change, based mainly in immigration, infused the county with linguistic, cultural, and religious diversity.

One of the new ethnic enclaves created was Koreatown, about three miles north of South Central. It is of special interest to this discussion for it was a major target of arson and looting in 1992. Its identity derives less from its residents than from heavy Korean investment in the area's commercial enterprise. The vicinity between Koreatown and South Central, the West Adams–Exposition Park area, is mixed, Black and Latino. This pattern of ethnic division is the result of territorial rivalry and accounts for some of the underlying tensions between Koreans and many other groups (Oliver & Johnson, 1984). Black and Latino customers often resented Koreans who followed Jews as the primary local merchants. Blacks, Koreans, and Latinos also have clashed over jobs, housing, and scarce public resources. Moreover, the Black community, no longer the majority in the area, deemed the incursion of Latinos into "their" territory as a political and economic threat.

Residential patterns suggest that Asian Americans in Los Angeles have interracial contact with a variety of others (Ong & Azores, Table 4.8, p. 122). Overall, Asian Americans are most likely to have residential contact with Whites, followed by Latinos and Blacks. It is not surprising that Asian Americans had most contact with Whites and Latinos. In fact, Latinos and Asian Americans frequently live in the same neighborhoods—the areas that facilitate entry into social and economic activities. Thus, the pattern of where Asians live in the inner city does not occur randomly. Asians appear to avoid Black neighborhoods, partly due to prejudice, but also because of the structure of social and economic opportunities, patterns in housing and commercial properties that reinforce these structures, and spatial configurations that define the important arenas of intergroup interaction and conflict.

Perhaps as a result of their marginalized status, Central American Latinos often lived in depressed areas of South Central, where there were many Korean shops. As a result, these particular Latinos interacted with Korean Americans so extensively that, Davis (2000) suggests, Spanish rather than English is the second language of choice for many Asians. As Davis (2000) noted, this interaction was due to "Asian capital eagerly [seeking] out Latinos as workers and consumers" (p. 46). Asian firms employ thousands of Latino workers. Koreans control thousands of low-rent housing units and a majority of the "swap meets" in South Central Los Angeles. Thus, Central Americans were almost always in subordinate positions: They were customers and employees in Asian American–owned factories and stores and renters of Korean American–owned property. Thus, the level of economic powerlessness and frustration among the Central American population in South Central was very high. Not surprisingly, perhaps, post-riot arrest records indicate that for every type of crime except possession of firearms, Latino arrests exceeded Black arrests, and most of the Latinos arrested were Central Americans.

Politics

The two main components of Los Angeles city government are the mayor's office and the city council. Almost exclusively, White men had filled the mayor's office and city council for decades. Until about 1960, the structures of city governance gave considerable power to managers and experts for running the day-to-day affairs of the city; elected officials—the mayor and city council members—provided mainly political and philosophical guidance (Saltzstein & Sonenshein, 1991). During the 1960s, this relationship began to change as the civil rights movement gained momentum and the city's Black community, along with liberal Whites and some sections of the Latino and Asian American community, demanded more assertive leadership from elected leaders. A political coalition of minority groups and White liberals coalesced around maverick Democrat Sam Yorty and elected him to the mayor's office in 1961. Yorty had promised to hire more minorities in city government and put an end to police brutality. When Yorty came to power, however, his refusal to do either deeply disappointed minority leaders (Sonenshein, 1993, p. 41). During Yorty's term, both the mayor's office and the city council became more active in governance and gained power. Indeed, the two governing bodies often clashed. In a harbinger of the city council's independence from Yorty, in 1963, Tom Bradley and two other Blacks were elected to the city council with support from Blacks, Jews, Asian Americans, and some Latinos.

An important turning point in the racial politics of Los Angeles was the so-called Watts riots of 1965. On August 11, a White California Highway Patrol officer arrested a Black motorist for drunk driving near Watts, an area dominated by Black residents. Very quickly a confrontation broke out between Black bystanders and the White officer, who immediately called for backup. During the escalating argument, someone spat on one of the officers, who, enraged, grabbed a young woman from the crowd, threw her in the back of a police car, and hurried away from the scene. The gathered residents angrily threw rocks and bottles at the police cars and then at passing vehicles. Some of the residents pulled White motorists from their cars and beat them. Several days and nights of arson and violence followed. The rioting had led to 34 deaths—all but three were Black—more than 1,000 injured people, and more than 4,000 arrests. Estimated property damage was $40 million (Sonenshein, 1993, p. 77).

After the Watts riots of 1965 the city government became bitterly divided along racial lines, with Yorty refusing to do much to rebuild the downtown area, where many of the city's poor Black families lived, or to pursue liberal reforms. Bradley, on the other hand, was pushing vigorously for reform on several fronts including increasing minority representation in city government and employment, civilian control of the Los Angeles Police Department (LAPD), and the aggressive pursuit of federal aid to help rebuild downtown Los Angeles (Saltzstein & Sonenshein, 1991, p. 194). In 1969, Bradley challenged Yorty for the mayor's office, but Yorty prevailed after a racially divisive campaign. In 1973, Bradley again challenged Yorty and won with support from the growing liberal, multiracial coalition that had helped Bradley win a seat on the city council. Over the next ten years or so, Bradley and his supporters on the city council were able to implement liberal reforms that literally changed the face of city government. For example, affirmative action policies created a racially diverse public sector work force, federal funds expanded social services and revitalized downtown, and Bradley's allies succeeded in establishing some measure of civilian oversight over the police force (Saltzstein & Sonenshein, 1991, p. 195).

The multiracial alliances built during the civil rights movement began to deteriorate during the 1980s. With the passing of Proposition 13 in 1978, a statewide law that froze property taxes, and the election of Ronald Reagan, who immediately cut federal dollars to states, and the emergence of economic recession, the level of federal and state funds available to city officials shrank drastically. As levels of unemployment and homelessness increased, Bradley's administration could not adequately respond, and newly assertive groups of Asian Americans and Latinos criticized his administration. Bradley's multiracial coalition began to show cracks. Blacks and Latinos grew wary of Bradley's ties to downtown business interests, White liberals were disappointed after Bradley allowed oil drilling in the waters off western Los Angeles, and Jews were outraged when Bradley did not immediately condemn Nation of Islam leader Louis Farrakhan for his anti-Semitism (Sonenshein, 1993, pp. 191-192). Between 1985 and 1989, Bradley's control of the city council also began to erode as powerful Latino and Asian American leaders with independent agendas emerged, were elected to the council, and developed their own base of support. In several cases, new council members came to power by defeating Bradley allies (Saltzstein & Sonenshein, 1991, p. 198). By the time of the riots in 1992, Bradley's ability to hold together the multiracial coalition, which was the source of much of his influence, had diminished considerably.

Interethnic Tensions

As in Miami and in Washington, D.C., the growing size and power of the Latino population resulted in tensions with Black communities over social services, political representation, and access to local resources. The political friction was in addition to the job rivalry among working-class Blacks and Latinos. Add to the mix the declining economic conditions mentioned earlier, and we have the context for the hair-trigger tension in the heart of Los Angeles, where Blacks and Latinos were concentrated. Davis (2000) used the city of Compton to illustrate the racial dynamics between Blacks and Latinos. Compton's Black leadership, squeezed by cutbacks implemented by the Reagan and Bush administrations, heavily taxed residents of the city, who were mainly poor Blacks and new Latino immigrants. Latinos were angry about the heavy tax burden but also the favoritism showered on Black businesses and entrepreneurs—frequently absentee landowners—whereas city officials denied permits to their own groups to set up vending carts. Latino leaders pleaded with city officials to share power on the city council but were double-crossed in a 1993 election that brought Black mayor Omar Bradley (no relation to Tom Bradley) to power with an overwhelming show of support from Latinos. Bradley then reneged on a promise to appoint Latinos to the city council, angering Latinos further. The resulting racial tension between Blacks and Latinos in Compton is representative of many other parts in and around South Central.

The relationship between Blacks and Asian Americans was also tense—but for different reasons. Asian Americans are also one of the fastest growing ethnic groups in Los Angeles County. But unlike many Latinos, they entered South Central as shopkeepers, not as residents. Koreans and Filipinos are owners of many convenience stores in the area but make their homes outside of the neighborhood's traditional boundaries. Many Blacks saw Korean merchants as part of a long-term trend in Black communities, a link in the chain of outside exploiters, from White to Jewish to Korean. That each group in turn seemed to receive special privileges not bestowed on Blacks led some Blacks to believe in a conspiratorial relationship between Koreans and Whites. Added to this was personal experiences with behavior that showed many in the community that Korean merchants were at best insensitive to customer concerns and, at worst, racist. Many Koreans arrived in the United States having learned all the negative stereotypes of Blacks from American racial ideology perpetuated throughout Asia. They learned it from White U.S. troops that went to segregated bars and brothels, from globally distributed U.S. popular culture, and from friends and relatives returned from overseas (Abelman & Lie, 1995; Sturdevant & Stoltzfus, 1993). These perceptions were reinforced when Koreans encountered their low-income Black customers in high-crime areas such as South Central. In addition, an ethnonationalistic Korean self-image of discipline, sacrifice, family unity, and so on contrasted with and enhanced these negative images of Blacks.

Looters especially targeted stores owned by Korean Americans. Although Korean Americans had nothing to do with the verdict or police harassment of Blacks, tense relations between Korean Americans and Blacks had been heightened since March 16, 1991, when Soon Ja Du, a Korean American grocer in South Central, shot and killed Latasha Harlins, a Black teenager, during an argument about paying for a bottle of orange juice. The grocer was ordered to pay a $500 fine, perform 400 hours of community service, and serve a six-month suspended sentence. Many Blacks thought it was extremely light punishment and akin to being treated like a White culprit. In addition, the Black community was already sensitized to violence against Blacks, because only a few days earlier, on March 5, a local television station had broadcast the video of four police officers beating Black motorist Rodney King. Then, in June 1991, another Korean merchant shot and killed a Black customer. Black community leaders immediately organized boycotts of selected Korean-owned grocery stores, which raised Black–Korean American tensions to palpable levels. Thus, although it is too simple to suggest that the root cause of the riots was tense Korean American–Black relations, the conflicts between these groups were like smoldering embers that were ignited by the not-guilty verdict in the LAPD trial—and further stoked by long-simmering resentments among other racial groups.

Police

A discussion of the political economy of Los Angeles and race relations would not be complete without some mention of the LAPD. Noted for its technological sophistication and relatively small size, the LAPD has also been involved in numerous controversial altercations with the citizenry, chiefly with the city's residents of color (Davis, 1990). In late 1979, the LAPD came under fire for the police killing of Eulia Love, who had defaulted on her gas bill. The chief of police, Daryl Gates, defended the actions of his men before the Police Commission. In 1982, the LAPD was criticized for using a "choke hold" in which a police baton is used to restrict the blood flow to the brain. Several Black youths died as a result of this, but Chief Gates blamed the deaths on the victims' racial anatomy. In late 1990, police beat a defenseless Tracy Marberry so hard that they pierced his skin, even with the blunt police baton that they used. After the beating, they tied him up in a way that constricted his breathing so severely that he choked to death. Between January 1986 and December 1990, there were 2,044 allegations of police brutality made against the LAPD officers. Many of these complaints came from neighborhoods with large concentrations of racial minorities (Fukurai, Krooth, & Butler, 1994, p. 74).

On March 3, 1991, California Highway Patrol (CHP) officers tracked a car speeding down a local highway. CHP officers signaled the driver, Rodney King, to stop. King, on probation for a second-degree robbery conviction, panicked and sped up. King exited the highway as LAPD squad cars joined the chase. Eventually, King pulled to the curb. At this point, a resident in an apartment complex across the street from where King's car was parked began to videotape the encounter between King and police. The now-famous video begins with King on the ground. He has wires from a Taser gun (a mechanism that shoots a burst of 50,000 volts through the victim) coming from his body (Fukurai et al., 1994). He tries to stand up and as he does, the confrontation rapidly turns even more violent. Four LAPD officers, Sergeant Stacey Koon and Officers Lawrence Powell, Timothy Wind, and Theodore Briseno, beat King repeatedly with their batons and boots while 19 law enforcement officers—CHP, Los Angeles School District police, LAPD, Sheriff's Department, and others—stood by and observed. The beating was so severe that they knocked fillings out of King's teeth (Fiske, 1993, p. 154).

The district attorney indicted the four officers who beat King. Gates did not rise to defend the officers this time—perhaps because the amateur photographer had captured the incident on videotape. Indeed, for residents and activists who had for decades been pointing to a pattern of LAPD brutality and demanding reform, the videotape was the silver lining in an otherwise reprehensible situation. Many critics of the LAPD were convinced that the evidence of the videotape would lead to significant condemnation of the police force. The case against the officers went to trial March 4, 1992. The proceedings were held in Simi Valley, a predominantly White Los Angeles suburb, after the judge ruled that a fair trial was not possible in Los Angeles County. The jury comprised ten Whites, one Latino, and one Asian American. On April 30, 1992, the nearly all-White jury cleared the officers of criminal wrongdoing: The jury was hung on one count against Powell but dismissed all other charges. Within hours, angry demonstrators were on the street, igniting fires, destroying property, and looting stores.

The Los Angeles riots of 1992 were a truly multiethnic affair. Whites, Blacks, Latinos, and Asian Americans were all involved as victims, perpetrators, or both. Korean-owned stores were the primary targets of the looting and arson by both Blacks and Latinos (though some Blacks and Latinos came to the aid of Korean Americans too). Those arrested during the disturbances were slightly more likely to be Latinos. Although people of all racial backgrounds participated, the Asian American–owned properties were the hardest hit. Koreans felt deeply betrayed because they felt police and city officials had not come to their aid. The magnitude of the 1992 disturbances was larger than those in 1965. Nearly 2,500 people were injured, and 58 people died. More than 17,000 people were arrested. There was an estimated $785 million in property damage. The simmering racial cauldron had boiled over.

5

Los Angeles Times
Coverage of Los Angeles

The *Los Angeles Times* is one of the oldest and most powerful institutional forces in Los Angeles. Harrison Gray Otis joined the year-old *Los Angeles Times* in 1882 and four years later was in full control of the paper. Although Otis often published editorials against unethical businessmen and supported the Russian revolution, he was, in fact, reactionary in his outlook. He used the paper to promote his pet projects, such as bringing water to the region, annexing lands spreading west from Los Angeles proper to the Pacific Ocean, and breaking the printers' union in Los Angeles (Hart, 1981, p. 33). Editors slanted news stories in ways that would favor Otis's positions and interests. All the while, Otis was enriching himself by purchasing thousands of acres of land in Southern California and Northern Mexico. Otis was succeeded by his son-in-law Harry Chandler, who was in turn succeeded in 1944 by his son Norman Chandler and in 1960 by his grandson Otis Chandler, who is generally credited for making the *Times* a more balanced, more serious journalistic enterprise (Emery & Emery, 1996, p. 552). The *Times* has a circulation of about 1 million and is owned by the Times Mirror Company, which formed in 1970 when Otis Chandler bought major dailies in Texas and New York, and later in Connecticut, Colorado, Maryland, and Pennsylvania. Besides newspaper publishing, the parent company has interests in cable television, book and magazine publishing, and online interactive services. In 1990, the Times Mirror bought 50% of *La Opinión*, one of the nation's leading Spanish-language newspapers.

Table 5.1   Number and Percentage of Articles in the
Los Angeles Times Mentioning Various
Groups (*n* = 83 articles)

	Number	Percent
Blacks	41	49.4
Asian/Asian American	36	43.4
Korean/Korean American	27	32.5
Whites	19	22.9
Anglo	6	7.2
Latinos	8	9.6

The Coverage

The following sections report analyses of 83 articles about interethnic conflict published in the *Los Angeles Times*.

Ethnic Groups in Los Angeles

Table 5.1 shows that Blacks are the group mentioned most often in the coverage (in 49.4% of the coded articles). The coverage mentioned Asian Americans next most frequently (most were specifically referring to Korean Americans). The coverage mentioned Whites and Latinos least frequently. Thus, even though the coverage sometimes discussed the disturbances in terms of the "first multi-racial riots," the *Los Angeles Times* depicts the event as conflict mainly between Blacks and Korean Americans. The involvement of Latinos does not come through as strongly in the *Los Angeles Times* as it does in its Spanish-language partner paper *La Opinión* (analysis of which is in the following chapter). Most references to Whites were to Reginald Denny. Otherwise, Whites are infrequently mentioned, a fairly consistent pattern in all general circulation papers, which largely ignore the role of Whites and the economic power of Whites.

In terms of ethnic labeling, the *Los Angeles Times* consistently used the term "Latino" rather than "Hispanic," which was conventionally used by the general circulation newspapers in Miami and Washington, D.C., cases, or Chicano, a term used by many Mexican Americans in Los Angeles. "Latino" may be the preferred term for the *Los Angeles Times* because the label includes not only Mexican Americans but also the increasing number of immigrants from Latin America who have settled in the Los Angeles area. The *Los Angeles Times* was consistent in its use of "Black" and "African American" in that it used the terms interchangeably when referring to that group. However, the *Los Angeles Times* was inconsistent in its use of terms to describe Asians and Asian Americans. The paper sometimes used the term "Asian" and at other times the term "Asian Americans" with no discernible pattern as to when it used each ethnic label. The same held true when the coverage referred to specific Asian American groups such as Korean Americans—the paper would use both "Korean" and "Korean American." The interchangeable use of "Korean" and "Korean American" may reflect a misunderstanding on the part of reporters who did not distinguish or see significant political and cultural differences between recent Asian immigrants and Asian Americans who are long-time residents in the United States. The interchangeable use of "Black" and "African American," however, seems to be less problematic, as the terms have evolved as more-or-less synonymous even in Black and African American communities.

The paper referred to Whites as "Whites" and less frequently as Anglos. The paper used neither term often, as Table 5.1 shows, but it is interesting to note the use of the terms "Black" and "White" when *Los Angeles Times* coverage referred to the trial and verdict in the case of the four Los Angeles Police Department (LAPD) officers who beat Rodney King. Of course, not each of the 83 articles coded mentioned the trial or the verdict. The articles from the earlier part of the coverage cycle usually provided (in the "boiler-plate" language of journalism) a reference to the trial or verdict. Later in the cycle, the references became less frequent. In terms of labeling, the paper mentions the race of the police officers, White, twice, whereas it referenced much more frequently King's race, which is Black. The first reference to the police officers' race is in a story about Reginald Denny. The writer draws a parallel between the beating of Rodney King, "a White on Black beating," with the assault on Reginald Denny, "a Black on White beating" ("Beaten Driver a Searing Memory of Mob Cruelty," *Los Angeles Times*, May 1, 1992, p. A1). The second reference is in a story about preparations for a second day of violence. The writer reports that the city is on edge after "four White Los Angeles police officers" beat "King, a Black motorist" ("City Officials, Police Brace for Possible New Violence," *Los Angeles Times*, May 1, 1992, p. B3). Other than these references to the officers' race, the rest of the articles usually called them the "four LAPD officers," the "Los Angeles officers," or listed them by name.

The fact that the coverage attached the label "White" so infrequently to the four officers on trial for use of excessive force, whereas it attached the label "Black" frequently to the man upon whom the officers used excessive force creates a subtle but significant disassociation between Whiteness and

Table 5.2   Number and Percentage of Articles in the *Los Angeles Times*
Discussing Actors and Victims (*n* = 83 articles)

| | Actors | | | | Victims | | | |
| | Actual | | Potential | | Actual | | Potential | |
	#	%	#	%	#	%	#	%
Blacks	21	25.3	2	2.4	13	15.7	1	1.2
Government	20	24.1	1	1.2	6	7.2	0	0
Police	16	19.2	0	0	2	2.4	0	0
Asian/Asian Americans	12	14.5	0	0	21	25.3	4	4.8
Whites	11	13.3	0	0	10	12.3	1	1.2
Korean Americans	8	9.6	0	0	20	24.1	3	3.6
Latinos	8	9.6	0	0	4	4.8	0	0
Firefighters	0	0	0	0	2	2.4	0	0

use of violence. At the same time, the frequent mention of King and his race, even though it is as the victim of violence, makes an equally significant connection between Blackness and involvement in violence.

Actors and Victims

The coverage depicted Blacks as actors most frequently, and it portrayed the actions by these actors mainly in stories about the looting and arson in the aftermath of the announcement of the verdict in the trial of the four LAPD officers. (See Table 5.2.) Many of these depictions of Blacks were in the stories on the first and second day of the violence—that is, on April 30 and May 1. Several first-person accounts of being victimized by Blacks contribute to the imagery of Blacks as the primary actors in the disturbances (e.g., "'No One Else Made a Move to Help,'" *Los Angeles Times,* April 30, 1992, p. A23; "A Long Night of Anger, Anarchy," *Los Angeles Times,* May 1, 1992, p. A1).

Accompanying the image of Blacks as the primary actors in the disturbances is a less-dominant image of the "multiethnic riot" (though it seems the *Los Angeles Times* rarely used these words, it was a common catch phrase in some publications and broadcasts). In these portrayals, Whites, Latinos, and Asian Americans also were participants in the disturbances. Some of the descriptions used to capture this dimension of the disturbances included "Across South Los Angeles, Blacks, Whites, Latinos, and Asians met in scores of violent confrontations" ("View of Model Multiethnic City Vanishes in Smoke," *Los Angeles Times,* May 1, 1992, p. A1). Another story reports that "although young Black men constituted many of the rioters and looters, Latinos, Anglos, and Asians also took part" ("Opportunists, Criminals Get Blame for Riots," *Los Angeles Times,* May 1, 1992, p. A1).

The second most frequently mentioned actor was government. Federal government actors such as President George Bush, Vice President Dan Quayle, and former president Ronald Reagan, were the next most frequently mentioned government actors. Los Angeles Mayor Tom Bradley and California Governor Pete Wilson were among the least frequently mentioned government actors. The stories in which Bradley or Wilson are reported as actors are essentially those featuring these officials making announcements about policing strategy, sending National Guard reinforcements, asking for federal assistance, pleading for calm, and so on. Most of the references to police as actors were in the context of complaints about police brutality or police retreating in the face of escalating numbers of people involved in the disturbances. (Coverage heavily criticized Gates for not taking better control of his officers and for not having an adequate containment plan in place.)

Coverage mentioned Asian American, White, and Latino actors less frequently than Blacks and government. Asian American actors were mainly those who took action to protect their property and those involved in initiating attempts to reach out to the Black community following the riots. White actors, aside from the Whites engaged in looting, were coded in reports about Peter Ueberroth being named head of a commission to organize the rebuilding efforts ("Reaction Divided over Key Role for Ueberroth," *Los Angeles Times,* May 4, 1992, p. A1). Coverage also depicted Latinos infrequently as actors, suggesting again that the *Los Angeles Times* portrayed the disturbances largely as conflict between Blacks and Korean Americans and between Blacks and police.

In terms of victims, coverage mentioned Asian Americans most often as actual or potential victims, mainly in the context of Korean Americans having their stores burned and looted during the disturbances. Several stories depict angry or depressed Korean American store owners amid the wreckage of their stores. The following represents a typical portrayal of this kind:

> Dawn found Joe Tong, a Korean immigrant, shuffling though wet soot and broken bottles in his looted and fire-ravaged grocery store in Pacoima. ("Violence and Looting Spread Into Valley," *Los Angeles Times,* May 1, 1992, p. B1)

Imagery used by this writer, such as Tong "shuffling" in his ruined store, conveyed an image of the sympathetic victims.

Blacks are the group next most frequently mentioned as victims. Many of these depictions were in the context of stories recounting the beating of Rodney King by the four police officers. But another aspect of the depiction of Blacks as victims was in relation to suffering racial discrimination from Korean American store owners, police, and other government officials. These depictions are, on the whole, instances where articles portray the victims as deserving of reader sympathy. For example, a story based exclusively on quotes from various city residents includes several along these lines: "I feel like the system can do whatever it wants to Blacks" ("Voices," May 1, 1992, p. A8). Another sort of victimization was economic neglect by federal and local agencies created to provide grants and other funds to poor communities ("Life Has Been Hard in Neglected Areas for Years," *Los Angeles Times,* May 1, 1992, p. A1; "Group Formed to Oversee Rebuilding of Riot Areas," *Los Angeles Times,* May 31, 1992, p. J4).

Blacks also complained about discrimination by Korean store owners. The exemplar case illustrating their complaint, the shooting death of Latasha Harlins, echoed throughout the days of the disturbance. In a typical reference to the Harlins killing, one story summarized the situation in the following way:

> The acquittal of the White policemen who beat Rodney G. King was read in some neighborhoods as saying that a Black life is worth less than other lives. The lenient sentence of the Korean grocer who killed a Black girl in a dispute over a bottle of orange juice was read in some areas as a sign that foreigners have a better shot in the criminal justice system than blacks. ("Tale of Two Cities: Rich and Poor, Separate and Unequal," *Los Angeles Times,* May 6, 1992, p. B8)

Clearly, the writer conveys a sense of unequal justice and implies that it is based on racial hierarchy in which the bodies and lives of Blacks are devalued.

The mention of Whites as victims was almost exclusively in reference to the beating of Reginald Denny, which was accompanied by a few items in which White members of the LAPD claimed to be victims. For example, Laurence Powell, one of the officers on trial, is quoted without comment from the *Los Angeles Times* that he would not have been on trial if Gates had backed him up ("All 4 in King Beating Acquitted," *Los Angeles Times,* April 30, 1992, p. A1).

In another story, the *Los Angeles Times* reports that

> for the 14 months since the videotaped incident hit the airwaves, the officers of the LAPD have endured life under a microscope. A blue ribbon panel was appointed to examine their conduct. Their chief has come under fire, and there have been dozens of demonstrations by people railing against police brutality. ("Verdict Greeted With Relief and Elation Among LAPD Officers," *Los Angeles Times,* April 30, 1992, p. A18)

In this passage, depicting the police as having "endured" scrutiny, whereas their opponents are "railing" against LAPD practices, conveys the image of police as victims who deserve the sympathy of readers.

Coverage infrequently mentioned Latinos as victims. But one *Los Angeles Times* writer provided a particularly revealing account of feelings of persecution commonly felt among Latinos. The incident takes place as the reporter is interviewing a Latino youth:

> "The cops are always pulling us over, just because we're brown and poor," said Jesse Santoya, [a] 17-year-old associated with the Mexican 18 Street gang. While Santoya spoke to a reporter, an LAPD Black-and-White pulled up to the curb and ordered Santoya and his colleagues to line up and to be frisked. One of the youths was quickly arrested and charged with arson. ("Perspective on the Latino Community," *Los Angeles Times,* May 18, 1992, p. B5)

The juxtaposition of the Latino youth describing his humiliating experiences with police with an actual occurrence of what he is describing is effective in conveying Latinos as victims.

Government appears as victims in a fairly small number of articles. Most of these articles refer to the National Guard coming under attack from rioters. Police and firefighters as victims of physical assaults and sniper fire were mentioned a handful of times.

Conflict and Discontent

These were two major themes in the coverage, coded in about 70% and 60% of stories respectively. (See Table 5.3.) Also appearing frequently were the racism, fear, and cooperation themes. The pattern was that, in the coverage immediately following the outbreak of the disturbances, conflict and violence were coded often. Later, as many more analytical pieces appeared, reporters began mentioning more instances of cooperation. The theme of discontent was a constant in that reporters mentioned it in conjunction with stories about conflict and cooperation.

Another dimension of the fear that the *Los Angeles Times* conveyed was its long-term impact. A typical story of this kind is the following:

> The raging fires have long been extinguished, but fear still engulfs the daily lives of untold numbers of Los Angeles residents, one month after the worst civil unrest in a century ripped through city streets. ("Fear Distrust Linger After Riot," *Los Angeles Times,* May 30, 1992, p. A1)

Left unsaid is that, for most city residents, feelings of fear will eventually diminish. For many residents of South Central Los Angeles and other areas with high concentrations of racial minorities, on the other hand, fear of police brutality, gang violence, and general uncertainty has been a relatively constant experience.

It is important to note, however, that despite conveying the anger and fear in the Black community, many stories in this vein also fed the stereotype of the "out-of-control violent Black male" and the "justifiably scared White resident." These passages are indicative of the often-found ambivalence in general circulation news coverage of race and race relations.

For example, the instant characterization of the first-day events as "race-related violence" ("Rioters Set Fires, Loot Stores," *Los Angeles Times,* April 30, 1992, p. A1) immediately framed the disturbance as racial. Other issues such as economic inequality, legal injustice, and police brutality are secondary or are left out of the frame altogether. The choice of words to describe the trial and the verdict is another case in point. In the first and second day after the verdicts were announced (that is, April 30 and May 1), 21 stories referred to the case within the first five paragraphs. In four of these stories, the *Los Angeles Times* provides an unambiguous description of the case and verdict. Each of these is some version of the following: "Four officers acquitted of beating Rodney King" ("At Least 25 Killed in Riot Related Violence," *Los Angeles Times,* May 1, 1992, p. A6). In these four stories, it is clear who did the beating, who was beaten, who went on trial, and who was acquitted. Some of the other stories are less clear. For example, eight of the stories refer to the "Rodney King beating case" or the "Rodney King beating trial" (e.g., "The Challenge of Holding the City Together," *Los Angeles Times,* April 30, 1992, p. B2; "Five Firefighters Feel Raw Heat of Fear," *Los Angeles Times,* May 1, 1992, p. A3), which do not clearly indicate whether King was the aggressor or the victim in the beating. Even more confusing are descriptions such as "the Rodney King case" ("City Officials, Police Brace for Possible New Violence," *Los Angeles Times,* May 1, 1992, p. B3) and "the Rodney King verdicts" ("The King Verdict Aftermath," *Los Angeles Times,* May 1, 1992, p. A1), which suggest that it was King who was on trial, not the four police officers. In fact, in one story a reporter quotes without comment a Los Angeles resident sympathetic to King but who refers to the "Rodney King trial" ("Verdicts Greeted With Outrage and Disbelief," *Los Angeles Times,* April 30, 1992, p. A1).

Stereotypes of Blacks also appeared in a story about a police department news conference held immediately after the announcement of the verdict. The reporter pays significant attention to the boisterous, predominantly Black crowd yelling outside the building. The story quotes without comment from the reporter a city official who says, "The outbursts by these people are certainly in no way helping the healing process" ("All 4 in King Beating Acquitted," *Los Angeles Times,* April 30, 1992, p. A1). Another story highlights the observations of a probation officer who says, "This is just people who are greedy and immoral and opportunistic. They don't give a (expletive) about Rodney King." The writer later reported that Blacks "jammed the streets," "flash[ed] Black power signs," and "chanted slogans vilifying police" ("Opportunists, Criminals Get Blame for Riots," *Los Angeles Times,* May 1, 1992, p. A1). Coverage prominently quoted Bill Clinton, in the midst of his presidential campaign, referring to the "savage behavior" of rioters ("Political Leaders' Analysis of Crisis Varies," *Los Angeles Times's* May 1, 1992, p. A4). The use of the word savage by Clinton to describe a violent event in which Blacks are the primary participants and the *Los Angeles Times's* reproduction of his language without comment is a particularly damaging use of the term, given the long history of the pernicious stereotype of the "savage Black male." Other events selected for inclusion also reinforced this stereotype. In one story, a White resident of an affluent L.A. suburb reported his experience as he was going to his downtown office:

> As I approached my building several Black men, about eight, yelled out "Get back here honkey!" I ran for my building, and when I turned around, I saw them beating up another man. They were all over him. ("Edgy Residents Bracing for Spillover of LA," *Los Angeles Times,* May 1, 1992, p. B1)

Several aspects of this account need comment. First, the anachronistic term "honkey," associated with Black radical rhetoric in the 1960s seems oddly out of place in 1992. What does seem authentic is that a White man would put these words into the mouths of what he saw as a group of angry Black males. Second, the White man states that when the group of Black men could not reach him, they beat up another (presumably White) man, which suggests that the Black men were looking for anyone White to assault. Both elements reinforce long-held stereotypes of dangerous and violent Black men.

Another White male made the following observation: "There are unsupervised teenagers out roaming the streets, doing anything they want to. It's like a forest fire" ("City Officials, Police Brace for Possible New Violence," *Los Angeles Times,* May 1, 1992, p. B3). The comparison to forest fires suggests that the speaker sees Black men as out of control, wild, and indiscriminately destructive, like forest fires.

Korean Americans also were stereotyped. Popular culture and news has often depicted Asian Americans of all ethnic groups as "model minorities" (Hamamoto, 1994; Nakayama, 1988). Briefly, this image suggests that Asians and Asian Americans are naturally talented in academics, business, and technology. The stereotype further suggests that Asian American families work extra hard, make large sacrifices, and remain neutral on political matters to ensure family financial stability. Eventually, the stereotype suggests, the group enjoys high levels of achievement and prosperity.

The model minority image of Korean Americans in the context of the disturbances went through a significant metamorphosis over time. The first hint of change was an article referring to "frightened Koreans guarding their shuttered markets with guns" ("View of Multiethnic City Vanishes in Smoke," *Los Angeles Times,* May 1, 1992, p. A1). The image of the timid Asian American is somewhat consistent with the model minority image, but taking up arms in self-defense is inconsistent with the stereotype. The next major change in image is depicting a more aggressive Korean American reaction to the plundering of their stores: "Some Korean American merchants armed with shotguns posted themselves on the roofs of their properties" ("Looting and Fires Ravage LA," *Los Angeles Times,* May 1, 1992, p. A1). The change in description of Korean Americans from "guarding their markets" to "posting themselves on roofs" is a subtle but sure shift from a posture of self-defense to one of readiness to initiate action. To this point, there were no reports of Korean Americans actually using their firearms. That changed with a story reporting that "Korean American shop owners in South Los Angeles armed themselves with handguns, took cover behind their cars and fired on mostly Black looters" ("The King Verdict Aftermath," May 2, 1992, p. A1). At this point, the paper depicted Korean Americans as the aggressors, even though they were shooting people destroying and stealing their property. The next transformation is in a story printed two weeks after the disturbance recounting the scene in the following way: "Vigilantes nervously clutched pistols while patrolling the perimeters of their apartments while armed merchants in Koreatown and South Los Angeles barricaded themselves behind fortifications" ("Under Fire," *Los Angeles Times,* May 17, 1992, p. A27). This new imagery explicitly linked the actions of Korean Americans to more aggressive postures of patrolling and protection and transformed the model minority into the vigilante.

There also was somewhat of a bifurcation of the Korean American image in the press at about the same time the vigilante picture came into focus. Coverage gave attention to several Korean American political leaders, thereby creating the image of the politically active Korean American, something that was relatively rare in U.S. popular culture and the press. Although Los Angeles and California have had a number of Asian American leaders at the state and local levels, images of Korean American political leaders have been rare in the United States.

As for Latinos, not only were they relatively absent from *Los Angeles Times* coverage, but when they did appear, the articles often depicted them in stereotypical ways. In one story, a visiting Korean cleric suggests that Blacks and Latinos are not as culturally evolved as the White Christian missionaries that came to Korea when he was a child ("Christian Church Has Lost Its Force in the US," *Los Angeles Times*, May 16, 1992, p. B5). A second article made reference to "hundreds of Latinos taunting police" and to what is depicted as general disrespect for police and property ("Violence and Looting Spread Into the Valley," *Los Angeles Times*, May 1, 1992, p. B1).

Complicating the general trend toward negative stereotypes were a few stories about cooperation. A total of 31 stories contained the cooperation theme. Sixteen of these were about individuals helping individuals. The rest were about various types of cooperative efforts involving collective action. Of these 15 stories, 5 were about White businesses and political elites creating a committee to rebuild South Central (e.g., "Rebuilding LA, Picking up the Pieces," *Los Angeles Times*, May 26, 1992, p. D1; "Vast Expansion of Rebuild LA Adds Minorities," *Los Angeles Times*, June 27, 1992, p. A1). Another three stories were about White, Black, Korean American, and Latino clergy mobilizing assistance to families in need (e.g., "Groups Reach Across Ethnic Lines to Help Ease Pain of Riots," *Los Angeles Times*, May 23, 1992, p. B5). The image of the angry Black male had its counterpart in three stories of rival Black gang members cooperating to help the rebuilding effort (e.g., "Blacks, Koreans Seek Conciliation," *Los Angeles Times*, May 26, 1992, p. A1). Other stories about cooperation included coverage of students of various ethnic backgrounds rallying for peace (e.g., "Students Stage Peaceful Protest," *Los Angeles Times*, May 1, 1992, p. B1) and Koreans coming to the aid of other Koreans ("King Case Aftermath," *Los Angeles Times*, May 2, 1992, p. A31).

Heroes

Black Good Samaritans

The most prominent heroic figure in the coverage of the disturbances is the Good Samaritan—the average citizen who went out of her or his way to help someone in need. In some cases, the description was rather generic as in "countless scenes of South Los Angeles residents rushing to help strangers caught in the crossfire" ("View of Model Multiethnic City Vanishes in Smoke," *Los Angeles Times,* May 1, 1992, p. A1). But, over-all, the most prominent heroic figures were Blacks acting to prevent vio-lence or coming to the aid of people in need. In one case, for example, a Black man came to the aid of a White driver who was beaten for taking pic-tures ("Rioters Set Fire, Loot Stores," *Los Angeles Times,* April 30, 1992, p. A1). A Black reporter saved an injured Asian woman from an angry crowd and drove her to a hospital ("'No One Else Made a Move to Help,'" *Los Angeles Times,* April 30, 1992, p. A32). Another item reported the actions of a Black family that came to the aid of a White journalist. As he ran from an angry group of youths, the family took him into their home and cared for him until an ambulance arrived ("Free-lance Reporter Shot Four Times, But Family in South LA Saves Him," *Los Angeles Times,* May 1, 1992, p. A4). Finally, an additional example is of a group of Black men who spontaneously formed a fire line to help douse flames at a low-income housing facility ("LA Riots Escalate," May 1, 1992, p. A1).

Other Good Samaritans

Other racial minorities did not figure prominently as heroes. Only one story was coded as containing Latinos as heroes. It reports the actions of Latino families living near a Korean American–owned store and coming to the store owner's aid. The families are depicted viewing the store as a com-munity resource that needed protecting ("2 Cities—Under Siege and Under Threat," *Los Angeles Times,* May 1, 1992, p. B1). Korean Americans were never coded as heroes, perhaps because the dominant image was of Korean Americans as sympathetic victims (and a less dominant image as vigilantes). During the height of the disturbance, there were no Whites depicted as heroes. Toward the tail end of the events, the coverage gave Peter Ueberroth, the Los Angeles businessman appointed to head the effort to rebuild Los Angeles, a somewhat heroic image. In an article that presents several criticisms of the appointment based on fears that he would favor businesses outside the stricken area, the featured interview is with Ueberroth, who says,

> "Nothing can be further from the truth," he said. "I stated clearly that in this unpaid job, I will go forward only if I had the support of African-American, Latino, Asian and Anglo communities that were affected." ("Reaction Divided Over Key Role for Ueberroth," *Los Angeles Times,* May 4, 1992, p. A1)

Perhaps the writer wanted to convey Ueberroth's reference to the "unpaid job" with uncertain support from minorities in an ironic manner, but a casual reader may understand Ueberroth's comments as indicative of his selfless commitment to do the job without compensation and in the face of opposition.

Firefighters and the National Guard

Another set of heroes was military units and firefighters. Often these depictions were oblique. That is, by portraying the dangerous and difficult situations in which the National Guard and firefighters worked, the stories emphasized the heroic nature of their efforts. Coverage depicted firefighters as especially heroic.

> To the firefighters on the front lines, the sheer number of fires was overwhelming, but it was only a part of their problems. As new calls came—three or four every minute during the busiest time Wednesday—exhausted crews also found themselves facing assaults and threats from angry mobs in the streets. Some were pelted with rocks and bottles; others were shot at. Many firefighters said they were happy to make it through their long work shifts alive. ("Firefighters Feel the Raw Heat of Fear," May 1, 1992, p. A3)

Without diminishing the bravery of the firefighters, we should still note the use of language by the reporter to enhance the heroic imagery. Firefighters are not just working, but are on the "front lines" as if engaging in military action. They are also "exhausted," and many calls per minute overwhelmed them. Finally, they take their own lives in their hands as they do their jobs.

Coverage also depicted the National Guard as heroic but not as often as the firefighters and not in such clearly reverential language.

> By late afternoon, guardsmen armed with loaded M-16 rifles and riding in armored cars were dispatched to numerous hot spots. "It's scary, absolutely scary," said Staff Sgt. Jack Nix, a 19-year veteran who lives in the Bay Area. "When it gets dark," said Nix, "it gets much worse." As he spoke the ashes from a fire in the immediate area landed on his helmet.
>
> In some areas, the guard soldiers were welcomed, but in many areas they also were heckled and taunted with obscenities from motorists and small throngs of people. Many of the guardsmen, a number of whom served in Operation Desert Storm, appeared jittery. ("Looting and Fires Ravage LA," Los Angeles Times, May 1, 1992, p. A1)

This passage depicts the keepers of law and order as facing their fears, endangered by fires, and encountering hostile civilians. Even veterans of full-fledged wars are "jittery." The unstated conclusion: Yet they continue to do their jobs.

Police

In the *Los Angeles Times* coverage, there are almost no references to members of the LAPD as heroes, unlike in Miami and Washington, D.C., where the newspapers did portray the police as heroes. The only time coverage depicted them as heroes is when reporters quote members of the police force itself or their supporters. Chief Gates says in one story, "We will bring this under control, there's no question in my mind" ("Looting and Fires Ravage LA," *Los Angeles Times*, May 1, 1992, p. A1). The only references to heroes in the police force were about the four acquitted officers. Koon's attorney said, "He wasn't doing anything but making an arrest" ("All 4 in King Beating Acquitted," *Los Angeles Times*, April 30, 1992, p. A1). Only one story substantially reported the dangerous conditions in which the LAPD officers were working. This story reported on the random violence directed at police, making their work riskier than unusual:

> Three LAPD officers were fired on by a sniper about 7:30 a.m. near Vermont and Manchester, but escaped with superficial injuries. The three officers were driving south on Vermont when a sniper armed with an AK-47 assault rifle opened fire. . . . Later in the night, police reported that snipers fired at a plain-clothes officer driving on the Harbor Freeway. ("King Case Aftermath," *Los Angeles Times*, May 2, 1992, p. A1)

The language is less dramatic, perhaps, than in the constructions of the firefighters or National Guardsmen as heroes, but the image of police in danger doing a tough job clearly comes through.

Villains

Blacks

The most common depiction of villains was of people who engaged in violence and looting after the verdicts were announced. Blacks were consistently singled out as most numerous or most violent among the rioters. For example, in an article headlined "Criminals, Opportunists Get Blame for Riots" (*Los Angeles Times*, May 1, 1992, p. A1), the reporter wrote: "Although young Black men constituted many of the rioters and looters, Latinos, Anglos and Asians also took part." Another article reported

Black, Latino and White looters rampaging through ruined stores, White police officers and National Guard soldiers advancing to retake city streets by force, dazed White and Latino passersby beaten by angry Black assailants. ("View of Model Multiethnic City Vanishes in Smoke," *Los Angeles Times*, May 1, 1992, p. A1)

This passage depicts looting as a multiethnic activity, but it shows physical violence against people as an activity undertaken exclusively by Blacks. Many subsequent articles reinforced this image of violent Blacks.

Presenting victims of Black violence in a sympathetic and melodramatic way intensifies the image of the Black villain. A good example of this process is an article quoting a 10-year-old Korean American girl on how she feels about the disturbances. She says,

I'm angry at the African [*sic*] people because they went crazy and burned down the garage where my father worked. I'm afraid that now we're going to be poor. ("What Next for the Children," *Los Angeles Times*, May 6, 1992, p. A1)

Police

Another set of actors portrayed as villains were members of the police department. Police Chief Gates was the chief villain. In a story about the political fallout following the disturbances, the *Los Angeles Times* includes a quote that depicts Gates as a problem for the city: "The chief of police is unfortunately a liability. He symbolizes something that is very offensive" ("Outcome Rekindles Political Hostilities," *Los Angeles Times*, April 30, 1992, p. A20). Politicians and city residents also took Gates to task for attending a black-tie fund-raiser even though he already knew that the disturbances had broken out (e.g., "On a Block in South LA," *Los Angeles Times*, May 22, 1992, p. A1).

The coverage depicted the LAPD as one of the primary institutional villains of the story. It heavily criticized the department for lack of effort to control the outbreak of violence in South Central. L.A. District Attorney Ira Reiner was one of the prominent critics quoted on this point:

Officers responding to the violence retreated after the mob grew larger and angrier. The lack of response puzzled Reiner. "I would have thought they would have moved in immediately and quickly suppressed it," said Reiner. "The plan is a mystery to me." ("Rioters Set Fires, Loot Stores," *Los Angeles Times*, April 30, 1992, p. A1)

Some analyses linked the LAPD lack of action to the location of the disturbances. That is, the police force did not feel compelled to protect and serve South Central because the neighborhood contained a high proportion of racial minorities.

Coverage of a related issue villainized the police for not responding to emergency calls. Korean Americans were especially vocal about blaming police for their unwillingness to protect them and forcing them to take up arms to protect their property ("Korean Americans See Need for Political Power," *Los Angeles Times,* May 17, 1992, p. A1; "Korean Americans Criticize Police," *Los Angeles Times,* May 19, 1992, p. B3). A typical portrayal in the *Los Angeles Times* on this point is a quote from a business owner who ultimately had to take matters into his own hands. The story is about Ty Burgin, a tattoo shop owner who chased off youths trying to break into his store. "'Calling 911 is a joke, it just rang and rang,' said Burgin. 'So I stuck a .45 out the door and pointed at them. I said "Hey knock it off" and they all ran off'" ("Violence and Shooting Spread Into the Valley," *Los Angeles Times,* May 1, 1992, p. B1). This first-person account from a resident forced to deal with danger from potential thieves on his own magnified the police image as villains.

One other context that depicted LAPD officers as villains was in discussions of long-standing racism complaints against the department. One resident of South Central commented that he planned to move out of the neighborhood "because when he walks to the bus stop each night to meet his wife, police harass him. 'They ask me for I.D. I say we're not in South Africa'" ("Long Night of Anger, Anarchy," *Los Angeles Times,* May 1, 1992, p. A1). The reference to apartheid-era South Africa is particularly relevant given the hyper-segregation of the South Central area among Blacks, Latinos, Mexican Americans, and Korean Americans and the predominantly White demographics of the department that polices the area.

Causes of the Conflict

Most frequently, coverage attributed the cause of the disturbances to individual-level reasons (such as attitudes, values, and fear). The articles less frequently discussed institutional-level causes (such as discrimination and political problems) and structural-level causes (such as oppression, poverty, and inequality).

Individual-level Causes

The articles often presented individuals with a lack of appropriate values or bad morals as the cause behind the disturbances ("King Verdict Aftermath," *Los Angeles Times,* April 30, 1992, p. A1; "Quayle's Morality

Debate," *Los Angeles Times,* May 21, 1992, p. A1). Especially prominent were quotes from national politicians offering this view. George Bush, in the middle of a presidential campaign, argued that individuals with no "respect for people's rights or property" created the problems in South Central ("Political Leaders' Analysis of Crisis Varies," *Los Angeles Times,* May 1, 1992, p. A4). Bill Clinton, Bush's opponent, in a speech quoted in the *Los Angeles Times,* characterized the actions of those engaged in the violence and looting as "savage behavior" by "lawless vandals" ("Political Leaders' Analysis of Crisis Varies," *Los Angeles Times,* May 1, 1992, p. A4). Later, Clinton provided other individual-level explanations, summarized by the *Los Angeles Times* as a "need for minorities and the poor to exercise personal responsibility" and "the erosion of the family in many neighborhoods" ("Racial Unrest Presents a Touchy Dilemma for Clinton," *Los Angeles Times,* May 2, 1992, p. A32). Because Blacks were the group most often depicted as actors and because of deeply rooted cultural stereotypes, we can reasonably deduce from the larger context of news coverage that Bush and Clinton were referring mainly to Blacks as having no respect for property, behaving savagely, having no family values, and so forth.

Other explanations in this category blamed specific individuals for helping either instigate or perpetuate the disturbances. Police Chief Daryl Gates, and his history of "irresponsible and unrestrained remarks," was among the people frequently blamed as causing the disturbances. Other explanations accused Mayor Tom Bradley of causing the disturbances with comments deploring the verdict. The *Los Angeles Times* quotes a Latino activist, Peggy Estrada:

> How dare he make a press conference saying the system is wrong, that justice is not served. He gave permission for this (the disturbance) to occur. ("Outcome Rekindles Political Hostilities," *Los Angeles Times,* April 30, 1992, p. A20)

Another person singled out as a cause of the disturbance, especially by Blacks living in South Central Los Angeles, was Soon Ja Du, the Korean American grocer who shot Latasha Harlins in the back as she was leaving Du's store. Du was sentenced to probation and community service, a sentence that created outrage in the Black community and beyond. Black–Korean American relations were still tense at the time of the disturbances ("LA Losing Allure for South Korean Immigrants After Riots," *Los Angeles Times,* May 23, 1992, p. B1; "Fear, Distrust Linger Long After Fires Die Down," *Los Angeles Times,* May 30, 1992, p. B3). Some people involved in the disturbances told *Los Angeles Times* reporters that they were looting and burning "for Latasha" ("South LA Burns and Grieves," *Los Angeles Times,* May 1, 1992, p. A1).

Many police officers, White residents, and some of the jurors interviewed said Rodney King was the cause of the riots. One juror said, "Mr. King was in charge of the whole show," implying that if he had cooperated with the officers, there would have been no trial, no verdict, and no disturbances ("All 4 in King Beating Acquitted," *Los Angeles Times,* April 30, 1992, p. A1). Some other individual-level causes depicted in the *Los Angeles Times* were references to collective action by groups of individuals such as looters ("Looting and Fires Ravage LA," *Los Angeles Times,* May 1, 1992, p. A1), gangs ("View of Model Multiethnic City Vanishes in Smoke," *Los Angeles Times,* May 1, 1992, p. A1), and "White punk rockers" ("View of Model Multiethnic City Vanishes in Smoke," *Los Angeles Times,* May 1, 1992, p. A1). One group singled out perhaps more than any other as contributing to the "pre-conditions" that caused the disturbances was Korean Americans. The *Los Angeles Times* reported,

> [A Black man] admitted he could not help feeling hostile toward Koreans. "If they were more understanding and patient, it never would have happened," said Taylor, who refuses to patronize Korean merchants. "I felt they brought it on themselves." ("Tensions Add Awkwardness to Everyday Encounters," *Los Angeles Times,* May 4, 1992, p. A1)

Another article presented the "problem" underlying the disturbances as "the insularity of the Korean American community" ("Korean Americans See Need for Political Power," *Los Angeles Times,* May 17, 1992, p. A1).

Institutional-level Causes

At the institutional level, one of the most common causes depicted in the *Los Angeles Times* coverage was the legal system that handled the case of the officers accused of using excessive force on King. *Los Angeles Times* reported "experts" who claimed that moving the trial to predominantly White Simi Valley, which resulted in a predominantly White jury, was partly to blame for the verdict that triggered the disturbances ("All 4 in King Beating Acquitted," *Los Angeles Times,* April 30, 1992, p. A1; "Looting and Fires Ravage LA," *Los Angeles Times,* May 1, 1992, p. A1). Another cause related to racial politics of the region is raised in a *Los Angeles Times* column. The writer refers to the fact that Whites dominate political institutions in Los Angeles. This is so even though Whites are a numerical minority in the city. The column is important in that it is one of the only stories that brings up not only political dominance of Whites but also that it is a cause of the disturbances ("The Challenge of Holding the City Together," *Los Angeles Times,* April 30, 1992, p. B2).

The role of White discrimination as a cause of the disturbances is depicted in a slightly different way when the *Los Angeles Times* quotes an angry resident of South Central: "'It's all because of these (expletive) Whites!' a woman in a van screamed" ("A Long Night of Anger, Anarchy," *Los Angeles Times,* May 1, 1992, p. A1). The view represented in this quote is echoed by a quote from a Korean American who said tensions leading to the disturbances were caused by "'the White supremacy mentality' of the United States, the American media and the Los Angeles Police Department" ("LA Losing Allure for South Korean Immigrants After Riots," *Los Angeles Times,* May 23, 1992, p. B3). The LAPD and its reputation for a variety of bad policing practices was further singled out as an institutional cause in two articles ("Verdicts Greeted With Outrage and Disbelief," *Los Angeles Times,* April 30, 1992, p. A1; "Outcome Rekindles Political Hostilities," *Los Angeles Times,* May 1, 1992, p. 20). Finally, the *Los Angeles Times* covered presidential candidate Jerry Brown's view that the Democratic and Republican parties had failed "to create more job opportunities for Blacks" and should take part of the blame for the disturbances ("Brown Blames Parties' Failure to Help Blacks," *Los Angeles Times,* May 2, 1992, p. A32).

Structural-level Causes

Some articles also presented a set of structural issues that may have helped cause the disturbances. A general sense of "economic powerlessness and exploitation felt by the poorest" among racial minorities was a common explanation (e.g., "The Challenge of Holding the City Together," *Los Angeles Times,* April 30, 1992, p. B2). The tangible impact of this lack of power—and another cause of the disturbances—is a lack of jobs combined with high prices at local stores ("South LA Burns and Grieves," *Los Angeles Times,* May 1, 1992, p. A1). The final results are a perpetuation of poverty and a widening economic gap between the rich (many of them affluent Whites in the suburbs) and the poor (many of them racial minorities in the urban areas) ("Brown Blames Parties' Failure to Help Blacks," *Los Angeles Times,* May 2, 1992, p. A32). Globalization of the local economy represented by the export of manufacturing and increased immigration from Latin America exacerbated the situation significantly, according to two articles ("South LA Burns and Grieves," *Los Angeles Times,* May 1, 1992, p. A1; "King Case Aftermath," *Los Angeles Times,* May 2, 1992, p. A31). In an article in the *Los Angeles Times* Sunday magazine, a macrolevel historical explanation of causes more likely to appear in an academic journal than a daily newspaper, capitalism and colonialism, was offered as the fundamental reasons for racial tensions not only in Los Angeles but the world over ("Words to Live or Die By," *Los Angeles Times*, May 31, 1992, Sunday Magazine, p. 23).

Implications of the Conflict

Five broad categories of implications of the disturbances are represented in the *Los Angeles Times* coverage. The most common is the potential for community collapse. Several articles report the fear residents have that local businesses may not reopen (e.g., "South LA Burns and Grieves," *Los Angeles Times*, May 1, 1992, p. A1). Others report that investments in urban Los Angeles, where many racial minorities are concentrated, will dry up ("Years of Effort to Attract Investment Undermined," *Los Angeles Times*, May 1, 1992, p. A8). Perhaps magnifying these concerns is a *Los Angeles Times* report quoting Mayor Bradley: "This will have a negative impact on commerce in this city and the lives of those who live here" ("Looting and Fires Ravage LA," *Los Angeles Times*, May 1, 1992, p. A1). Another dimension of the community collapse was that longtime residents, the backbone of a strong community, started thinking about moving out. A typical report is the account of a Black couple who grew up in the South Central area about to move into the suburbs:

> Roy Walker, a state police officer, always felt his neighborhood was danger-ous but wanted to stay in the community where he had grown up, where his family members still live. Now, however, Walker feels as if he, his wife, and their 23-month-old daughter are living like prisoners. Laverne will not garden in the backyard when her husband is away. They avoid small neighborhood stores after dark and eat at restaurants outside the community. "I don't know whether we have changed or the community has changed, but after a riot starts at your doorstep, things will never be the same," he said. "I'm fed up. I've lived in the city all my life, but it just isn't worth it." Since the riot the Walkers, who are Black, have increased their efforts to find a new home in the suburbs— perhaps Lancaster, Canyon Country or even Simi Valley. ("Fear, Distrust Linger Long After Riot," *Los Angeles Times*, May 30, 1992, p. A1)

Whether or not the reporter intended it, this anecdote poignantly reveals several interesting twists and ironies about community collapse. For many people, the sense of family and community life ended when the disturbances began. Conditions became intolerable to the extent that Black residents changed their daily behavior and considered moving even to Simi Valley, the city where the verdict was determined and, in that sense, where the disturbances began.

A second category of implications depicted in the coverage is the fear of increased crime and disorder. One article carries the subhead "Proliferation of Guns May Be the Bloody Legacy of Riots," referring to numerous thefts from gun stores during the disturbances ("Under Fire," *Los Angeles Times,* May 17, 1992, p. A27). Another piece reports an interview the reporter conducted with gang members who say they will continue resorting to crime unless economic conditions improve in their neighborhoods ("Hope Takes Hold As Bloods, Crips Say Truce Is for Real," *Los Angeles Times,* May 21, 1992, p. A1).

A third category of implications was the impact on children, a category consistently mentioned in all three cases examined in this book (e.g., "What Next for the Children?" *Los Angeles Times,* May 6, 1992, p. A1; "Community Watch, Coming Together," *Los Angeles Times,* June 13, 1992, p. B7). One article reports a child psychologist who says that the disturbances may actually provide a long-term benefit by helping to shape children's moral development ("What Next for the Children?" *Los Angeles Times,* May 6, 1992, p. A1). Another article describes the potential for the disturbances to turn public opinion among sympathetic Whites against Blacks ("Opportunists, Criminals Get Blame for Riots," *Los Angeles Times,* May 1, 1992, p. A1). One of the potentially positive implications discussed in the *Los Angeles Times* is that the events could mobilize a large Black turnout for the presidential elections of 1992 ("Political Leaders' Analysis of Crisis Varies," *Los Angeles Times,* May 1, 1992, p. A1).

One of the inevitable implications of the civil disturbances is that individuals and groups began to propose solutions to what they believed are basic social problems. The most common solution to the problems that caused the disturbances and to the problems caused by the disturbances was racial solidarity. This was mainly in reference to the gangs "Crips" and "Bloods" declaring a truce and urging a united front. This category also included a few other articles calling for Korean Americans and Blacks to work together to decrease tension between their groups (e.g., "Blacks, Koreans Seek Conciliation," *Los Angeles Times,* May 26, 1992, p. A1), including a suggestion from the Korean American community for Black leaders to visit Korea ("LA Losing Allure for South Korean Immigrants After Riots," *Los Angeles Times,* May 23, 1992, p. B1). The next most frequently proposed solutions had to do with economics. Private and federal investment into the South Central area and other efforts to close the gap between rich and poor were mentioned as solutions (e.g., "Rioters Set Fires, Loot Stores," *Los Angeles Times,* April 30, 1992, p. A1; "Rebuilding LA, Picking up the Pieces," *Los Angeles Times,* May 26, 1992, p. D1).

Less frequently mentioned as a solution was direct assistance to Korean Americans ("Korean-Americans Criticize Police," *Los Angeles Times*, May 19, 1992, p. B3). Of the solutions proposed in the coverage, the paper mentioned legislative actions such as passing gun control laws and anti-police brutality laws (e.g., "Angry Legislators Demand Reform," *Los Angeles Times*, May 1, 1992, p. A8) as frequently as improving the educational system. Mentioned only once was a call from a pro-police group to allow police to use an outlawed maneuver in which officers constrict blood flow to a suspect's brain by compressing the carotid artery with a baton ("All 4 in King Beating Acquitted," *Los Angeles Times*, April 30, 1992, p. A1).

Race and Nation

The *Los Angeles Times* coverage of the disturbances included several articles and commentaries that dealt with a question about race and nation that talk-show host Charlie Rose raised. Reproduced in an article appearing in the *Los Angeles Times* Sunday Magazine, the question Rose asked his guest Cornel West was "Is this [the disturbances] an important moment in American history to define ourselves, to ask who we are?" ("Words to Live By or Die By," *Los Angeles Times*, May 31, 1992, Sunday Magazine, p. 23). This question brings us squarely back to the questions about national culture and identity raised in the introduction to the book.

The main element in the depiction of the intersection of race and nation in the *Los Angeles Times*, as it was in other general circulation newspapers examined in this book, is a normalization of Whiteness, that is, the idea of the nation as rooted in traditions of Western Europe. In the Sunday Magazine piece, one of the most coherent and easily accessible pieces on this complex topic published anywhere—not just by the *Los Angeles Times*—author Itabari Njeri clearly lays out the "America = White" logic:

> The lived American culture—as opposed to what usually gets funded by public television—has been shaped by many groups and at its base is European, African and Indian—not the Eurocentric artifact that [Pat] Buchanan, for example[,] has extolled during campaign speeches for the Republican presidential nomination. Jazz, the only uniquely American music, represents cultural synergy that is the best aspect of the melting-pot metaphor, but the aspect least celebrated. What we embrace as "high" culture is European. The all-American social identity that we celebrate is the ethnic smelter's homogenized end product: Jimmy Stewart in 1940, Kevin Costner today. ("Words to Live By or Die By," *Los Angeles Times*, May 31, 1992, Sunday Magazine, p. 23)

In this passage, the author shows that Whiteness of a particular kind is privileged and understood as the natural, obvious, racially hegemonic norm for America even though the country's history is actually profoundly multicultural. In classic hegemonic fashion, not only is Whiteness normalized, but the process of normalization is rendered largely invisible by a seemingly innocuous discourse of assimilation in which the normalization of Whiteness is displaced by a rhetoric of incremental movement by ethnic and racial minorities toward American-ness. This entire process is occasionally revealed in the *Los Angeles Times* news. In an article unusual for revealing the "America = White" equation hiding at the core of assimilation discourse, a reporter describes the life of minority police officers in the LAPD. The article features Lorenzo Glenn, a 24-year-old rookie police officer who is proud of his African American and Japanese American heritage. The article shows how Glenn tries to assimilate even as he is aware of the consequences for his racial identity.

But he puts that ethnic pride on hold when he steps inside the station house. When he is around his White colleagues, Glenn makes a point of trying to mix with the crowd. He doesn't ask "stupid" questions. He doesn't call attention to himself. He doesn't dress differently from anyone else.

> "I'm reluctant to wear my Malcolm X hat or my Black T-shirts." . . . For Glenn and other minority officers in Orange County, trying to assimilate into a police department—an environment dominated by Whites—often means discarding cultural ties. In some cases, it even means ignoring an occasional racial snub from some peer. ("Police Force Seeks Diversity," *Los Angeles Times,* May 4, 1992, p. B1)

The story reveals an Afro-Japanese American who feels compelled by the culture of his workplace—the "lived American culture" described in the Njeri article from the *Los Angeles Times* Sunday Magazine, a culture in the article described as White—to monitor his talk, his clothing, and his interaction with colleagues. Police officer Glenn polices his own actions so that he does not "call attention to himself." He wants to be as invisible—normalized, Americanized—as his White peers, and assimilation purportedly offers that chance.

The idea of America as a White nation is not an unchallenged construction in the *Los Angeles Times.* In an article recounting the first hours of the disturbances, Joseph Lowery, president of the Southern Christian Leadership Council, expressed anger and dismay over the verdict.

I am shocked, outraged and frightened for our nation," [he said]. "We all cried and prayed for our nation. Even in Johannesburg, South Africa, they have begun to punish White officers who assault Black people." ("All 4 in King Beating Acquitted," *Los Angeles Times,* May 3, 1992, p. A1)

Lowery is Black, and the Southern Christian Leadership Council is a predominantly Black organization that advocates for issues in the interest of the Black community. By referring to "our" nation, Lowery insinuates himself, his organization, and the community he serves into the construction of America. By including these quotes in the story, the *Los Angeles Times* joins Lowery in challenging the idea of a White nation.

However, Lowery tinges his challenge with a sense of irony in that he refers to the fact that "even in South Africa they are now jailing police for beating Blacks" ("All 4 in King Beating Acquitted," *Los Angeles Times,* May 3, 1992, p. A1). This allusion to South Africa reveals that Lowery is aware that even if Blacks claim a rightful place in America, there is no guarantee they can avoid inequality and injustice.

But by invoking the South Africa example, Lowery suggests that the main problem of race in the United States, as it is in South Africa, is the relations between Blacks and Whites. In other articles, however, the *Los Angeles Times* covers the story in ways that complicate the Black–White binary construction of the nation. In the Sunday Magazine piece, Njeri quoted Richard Rodriguez of the Pacific News Service:

We are not in the 1960s anymore. Certainly not in multiracial Los Angeles. To talk about America falling into two halves again ignores the enormous complexity of what America has become in the last 30 years. Los Angeles is a Mexican city . . . and is increasingly Asian. ("Words to Live By or Die By," *Los Angeles Times,* May 31, 1992, Sunday Magazine, p. 23)

Not only does the *Los Angeles Times* help circulate the image of a multiracial Los Angeles, it also helps to convey the tension, instability, and anxiety created by racial diversification. Some stories capture and convey these characteristics in discussions of racial hierarchy, though the articles do not name it as such. For example, one article reports that

in 1992, the Los Angeles riots again point toward a great and worsening divide in a city moving toward two societies, one rich and predominantly White, one poor and predominantly Latino and African-American—still separate and increasingly unequal. Asians, depending on their income and ethnicity, are caught somewhere in the middle. ("Tale of Two Cities," *Los Angeles Times,* May 6, 1992, p. B8)

There are several remarkable points about this passage. First, it uses the "two societies" metaphor in reference to class, not race. Second, it recognizes—despite using this metaphor—that Asian Americans are also a significant part of the social mix. Third, the story recognizes ethnic diversity within the Asian American community and links this diversity to class location. Fourth, the story clearly conveys a sense that a racial hierarchy, connected to class, exists in Los Angeles. Taken as a whole, the passage challenges the "America = White" idea but also illustrates racially based, hierarchical class segregation. Thus, America may no longer "equal" White, but Whites still dominate America.

Summary and Discussion

Blacks were the group most frequently mentioned in the articles, followed by Asian Americans (mostly Korean Americans). Whites and Latinos were among the least mentioned groups. That the articles did not frequently mention Whites is not surprising given the discussion in the earlier chapters about infrequent mention of White privilege, but the relative absence of Latinos was surprising given their large presence in the Los Angeles area. One of the consequences of this pattern of coverage is that the extent of Latino involvement in the disturbances does not come through.

The main actors are Blacks, mainly in connection to looting and arson, but a number of articles discuss Black Good Samaritans as heroes. The articles do not give much emphasis to the multiethnic dimension of the disturbances given that they make infrequent mention of Latino, Asian American, and White rioters as actors.

Not surprisingly, the main victims in the coverage are Korean American merchants and, to some extent, merchants belonging to other Asian American ethnic categories. The coverage also frequently depicts Blacks as victims, but most of these instances are articles that recount the beating suffered by Rodney King and articles that describe the long-term racial oppression and discrimination in Los Angeles against Blacks. The articles also occasionally mention Latinos as victims of racial oppression. The coverage mentions Whites as victims only in the context of Reginald Denny.

The main theme in the coverage is conflict and discontent. The conflict is mainly between Blacks and Koreans and Blacks and police. To a lesser extent, there is conflict between Blacks and Latinos. The usually unstated but clear conflict is between Whites and non-Whites. Later in the news coverage cycle, the theme of cooperation is significant as various groups attempt to formulate strategies for rebuilding and healing. Throughout the news coverage cycle, however, the theme of discontent seems to be a constant. The *Times*'s coverage shows the complexity of Black discontent with social and economic conditions, giving voice to several political sides, officials, as well as community residents. The Korean American discontent is also covered but appears to be less comprehensive than coverage of the Black perspective.

Another theme worth highlighting is fear. Coverage highlighted Black fears relating to police brutality and double standards of enforcement, a White backlash of violence against ethnic minorities, and long-term obstacles to rebuilding. White fear of Black reactions to the verdict also received much attention. But in explaining White fears, the articles often resorted to stereotypes of the dangerous, violent Black male.

Coverage of heroes was rather limited, highlighting the acts of various Good Samaritans, including Blacks. Coverage depicted firefighters and the National Guard as heroes in several articles. Coverage, however, rarely depicted police as heroes. The main villains in the coverage were Blacks engaged in rioting and violence and the LAPD. Coverage frequently criticized police for their abuses of power, for ignoring requests for emergency help, and for a long history of racist behavior.

The *Times* focused mainly on individual-level causes of the conflict. Primarily, these causes concerned bad values or bad behavior. Institutional and structural explanations were relatively rare. Implications of the conflict included negative outcomes such as community collapse and increased disorder and positive outcomes such as interethnic solidarity and cooperation.

The *Los Angeles Times* provided some sophisticated discussions of the intersections of race and nation highlighted by the disturbances. Even though the main effect of the coverage is likely to normalize Whiteness as a sign of American-ness, the *Times* also provided several perspectives on the issues and reported on the experiences of ethnic minorities; no other general circulation newspaper examined in this book has taken as penetrating a look at the question of Whiteness. Perhaps the polyglot character of Los Angeles and an increasing sensitivity to questions of race and ethnicity stirred the *Times* to consider the question more carefully than other general circulation papers.

6

La Opinión
Coverage of Los Angeles

Responding to a growing demand for a Spanish-language newspaper in Southern California, Ignacio Lozano founded the weekly *La Opinión* in Los Angeles in 1926 (Rodriguez, 1999). The paper emphasized news about Mexico and some domestic news, the latter especially in response to frequently derogatory coverage from the *Los Angeles Times*. The newspaper enjoyed high circulation figures among the Latino population of Southern California. The *Los Angeles Times*'s owners noticed the success of *La Opinión* among Latinos and for many years considered a strategy to compete for that market. In the mid-1980s, the *Times* launched a monthly bilingual supplement available in all predominantly Latino zip codes. The bilingual supplement experienced mixed results, and in 1988, it changed to an all-Spanish format. This effort also met with a lukewarm response from the Latino community, and the project was suspended. Two years later, in 1990, the Times Mirror Company, corporate parent of the *Los Angeles Times,* bought 50% of *La Opinión,* which then had a circulation of about 100,000. The editorial staffs were (and are today) completely separate, and members of the Lozano family retain key management positions at *La Opinión*. The arrangement allows the two newspapers to conduct joint marketing projects, but their management teams, reporting staffs, editorial page, and opinion pages are separate. In addition, the papers' printing plants and distribution systems are also separate (Rodriguez, 1999, p. 111).

Table 6.1   Number and Percentage of Articles in *La Opinión* Mentioning Various Groups (*n* = 127 articles)

	Number	*Percent*
Latinos	76	59.8
Blacks	70	55.1
Asian/Asian American	38	29.9
Korean/Korean American	24	18.9
Whites	31	24.4
People of Color	5	3.9

The Coverage

This chapter reports an analysis of 127 news stories published in *La Opinión* about interethnic conflict during the Los Angeles disturbances.

Ethnic Groups in Los Angeles

As Table 6.1 shows, coverage mentioned Latinos most frequently, which is not surprising given the target audience and topical focus of the newspaper (i.e., issues and topics of particular interest to Latinos). The term "Hispanic" was used frequently—more than specific nationality labels such as Mexican American (mentioned in only 11 items, even though Mexican Americans are the dominant Latino group in Los Angeles) or other nationalities (mentioned in 17 items). In reference to the Asian/Asian American category, the coverage mentioned Korean Americans most frequently in the context of their ownership of stores in the South Central area, but there were also some references to the Latasha Harlins case. Coverage specifically mentioned Korean Americans in 24 items. Other long-established Asian American groups in Los Angeles, such as Japanese Americans and Chinese Americans, were rarely mentioned (once and twice, respectively, in *La Opinión*). Again, this pattern is not surprising because of the prominent role of Korean Americans (primarily as victims) in the disturbances and because of the newspaper's emphasis on conflicts rather than cooperation efforts in which Korean Americans played a role.

Actors and Victims

Table 6.2 shows that *La Opinión* coverage focused more on actual rather than potential actors and victims. The articles cover only Asian

Table 6.2   Number and Percentage of Articles in *La Opinión* Discussing
Various Actors and Victims (*n* = 127)

	Actors				Victims			
	Actual		Potential		Actual		Potential	
	#	%	#	%	#	%	#	%
Government	55	(43.3)	0	0	15	(11.8)	0	0
Blacks	51	(40.1)	0	0	43	(33.9)	1	(0.7)
Latino	37	(29.1)	0	0	69	(54.3)	0	0
Whites	22	(17.3)	0	0	9	(7.1)	0	0
Asian/Asian American	17	(13.9)	5	(3.9)	21	(16.5)	0	0
Police	10	(7.8)	3	(2.4)	0	0	1	(0.7)
Judicial System	6	(4.7)	0	0	0	0	0	0
Korean/Korean American	4	(3.1)	0	0	13	(10.2)	0	0
People of Color	3	(0.7)	0	0	0	0	0	0
Firefighters	0	0	0	0	3	(2.4)	1	(0.7)
Society	0	0	0	0	3	(2.4)	1	(0.7)

Americans and police as potential actors. Government (e.g., mayors, officials, federal agencies, etc.) is the most frequently covered actor. Chief Daryl Gates and Los Angeles Police Department (LAPD) officers account for all the actors in the police category.

Among racial groups, Blacks were the most often mentioned actors, followed by Latinos, Whites, and Asian Americans. In terms of victims, coverage depicted Latinos as the primary victims, followed by Blacks, Asian Americans, and Whites. Coverage portrayed society as a victim least frequently. Thus, coverage depicted Blacks most frequently as actors but also second most frequently as victims. The pattern for Latinos was just the opposite: They were the most frequent victims and second most frequent actors among the racial groups. Korean Americans were the least mentioned actors, mainly in connection with initiatives taken to protect their stores. Whites were the least mentioned victims among the racial groups.

Coverage mentioned Blacks and Latinos as actors primarily in items reporting them as participants in the disturbances following the verdict in the Los Angeles police officers' trial for beating Rodney King. For example, one story reported, "Members of the Black and Hispanic communities were part of the looters" ("Causes and Origins of the Social Explosion," *La Opinión,* May 6, 1992, p. 11A). Another story reports, "[Blacks and

Latinos] attacked with violence a system that didn't give equal opportunity or legitimacy" ("Legal Isn't Always the Most Just," *La Opinión*, May 9, 1992, p. 15A). A final example: "[A] good part of the looting—as opposed to the fires and street violence, carried out by Blacks—was by the recently arrived Latin American population in LA" ("A Dream Turned Nightmare," *La Opinión*, May 17, 1992, p. 2B). The latter article is interesting because it distinguishes among nationalities—those from Mexico versus those from Central America—and implies that it was those from Central America that engaged in the looting.

Few articles depicted Korean Americans as actors. One article showed Korean Americans demanding assistance for reconstructing Koreatown ("LA Council Member Demands Urgent Measures," *La Opinión*, May 7, 1992, p. 1A). A second article is about a Korean American rally asking for calm in South Central Los Angeles ("Los Angeles Koreans Ask for Peace," *La Opinión*, May 1, 1992, p. 1A).

One incident undertaken by Black actors that received prominent mention was the beating of Reginald Denny, a White truck driver who was pulled out of his vehicle and beaten by several Black men ("A Sad Night in LA," *La Opinión*, May 1, 1992, p. 1A; "Trial of Four Accused in Denny Beating Postponed," *La Opinión*, May 15, 1992, p. 1C; "Bail Granted to Four Accused of Beating Denny," *La Opinión*, May 22, 1992, p. 1C). Aside from coverage of Denny as a sympathetic victim, Whites were infrequently depicted as victims ("A Sad Night in LA," *La Opinión*, May 1, 1992, p. 1A).

La Opinión also frequently portrayed Blacks as sympathetic victims. Blacks were the victims of "years of oppression and marginalization of the African American community" ("No to Violence," *La Opinión*, May 1, 1992, p. 11A). In one column in *La Opinión*, the author compared Black and Latino problems and concluded that Blacks have it worse than Latinos:

Signs of injustice in Hispanic America are clear but they are not signs of theological predestination. If Hispanics participated in the acts of looting, they did so for no greater or lesser reason than to get a better television. But for the Black community in LA, the idea of gross injustice is real and there is nothing they will not do to struggle against it. ("From Moscow to LA, an Unreal Dream," *La Opinión*, May 5, 1992, p. 1A)

Though *La Opinión* depicted Blacks as worse off and, it would seem, entitled to grievances, it also depicted Latinos as sympathetic victims. Although much of the reporting in other news outlets concentrated on damage and destruction in South Central, *La Opinión* discussed damage in Latino areas.

The fires, the vandalism, the devastation, the deaths and suffering these last days in the Latino barrios makes the already difficult situation more precarious. ("Violence Is Not the Solution," *La Opinión*, May 2, 1992, p. 15A)

La Opinión did not depict Koreans as victims in a particularly sympathetic manner, but they are clearly victims. In the context of an article on reconstructing the South Central area, *La Opinión* said that "many proprietors of big firms and powerful commercial Anglo institutions didn't hide their satisfaction in seeing the flames destroy medium- and small-sized businesses owned by ethnic minorities, especially the Koreans" ("The Difficult Path of Reconstruction," *La Opinión*, May 16, 1992, p. 15A). The only other Asian American group mentioned as victims were Indian Americans. A group of Indian American entrepreneurs said they were frustrated about the lack of assistance from police in the midst of the rioting and looting of their stores. The leader of the group complained,

The treatment received by recent immigrants like us is bad. We people don't get anything [from the authorities]. We don't know where to go or how to proceed. ("Indian Businessmen Complain of Abandonment by Police," *La Opinión*, May 18, 1992, p. 3B)

One other set of victims is children. In one article, a coalition of family activists denounces reconstruction plans because they ignore the needs of poor families and children ("Ignoring Women and Children Denounced," *La Opinión*, May 15, 1992, p. 3C). Another article highlights the efforts of school officials trying to deal with or stave off psychological aftereffects suffered by schoolchildren in post-riot Los Angeles ("Psychologists and Counselors in 200 Schools Deal With the Emotional State of Thousands of Children," *La Opinión*, May 17, 1992, p. 1C).

Conflict, Anger, Resignation

As Table 6.3 shows, conflict was a major theme in the coverage. However, in *La Opinión*, the underlying conflict was not between Blacks and Latinos, as it was in the other two cases examined in this book, but between a united Black and Latino community in conflict with governmental institutions—such as police, the Immigration and Naturalization Service (INS), and the judicial system—and their representatives such as Police Chief Daryl Gates, INS agents, and the mayor. Many of the items that depicted this image were coded as containing the ethnic minority

Table 6.3   Number and Percentage of Articles in
La Opinión Discussing Various Themes
($n = 127$)

	Number	*Percent*
Immigration	12	9.4
Fear	20	15.7
Racism	39	30.7
Culture/Values	10	7.9
Violence		
Verbal	4	3.1
Personal	65	51.2
Property	88	69.3
Causes		
Individual	19	15.0
Institutional	31	24.4
Structural	21	16.5
Reassurance	22	17.3
Discontent	24	18.9
Conflict	101	80.0
Cooperation	51	40.2
Pluralism	15	11.8
Assimilation	3	2.4
Attitudes	18	14.2
Minority Intersection	18	14.2
Role of Race		
Primary	55	43.3
Secondary	25	19.7
None	9	7.1
No Mention	38	29.2

intersection theme (as well as the conflict theme). One of these items joined-together Blacks and Latinos by referring to "enemies of minorities" who will use the violence as a reason to further oppress Blacks and Hispanics ("Violence Is Not the Solution," *La Opinión*, May 2, 1992, p. 15A). There was some mention of the racial tensions between Blacks and Korean Americans, but this conflict was not a central part of the coverage, and the breakdown of groups mentioned in the coverage reflected this. Another item made clear that by the term "minorities," *La Opinión* was not including other non-White groups. In this item, the writer pointed out the apparent double standard by which the Korean American woman who shot and killed a Black youth was given community service, and influential families "like the Kennedys" are freed of all guilt (a reference to the William Kennedy Smith rape trial). This article clearly did not place Whites or Korean Americans in the same group—Blacks and Latinos—who have to worry about enemies of minorities.

Issues of race and experiences of racism were apparently major factors in uniting Blacks and Latinos. About 63% of the items coded contained "role of race" as a primary or secondary theme. Nearly 40% of the items were coded as containing racism as a theme. Some of the items were quite explicit in the way these themes were presented. For example, one columnist wrote,

> There is little doubt that racism and discrimination is not only not diminishing in the US, but that it is growing dramatically and dangerously. ("A Sad Night in LA," *La Opinión*, May 6, 1992, p. 1A)

Another item questioned the ability of American society to "administer justice without distinguishing race" ("After the Storm," *La Opinión*, May 3, 1992, p. 2B). A *La Opinión* editorial clearly stated the frustration of Blacks and Latinos:

> We feel like obstacles to the Reagan-Bush philosophy that places corporate gains and the needs of the military industrial complex over human needs. ("The Problem of Explaining Injustice to Youth," *La Opinión*, May 3, 1992, p. 2B)

Other items were less direct but clearly invoked race or racism in their references to police brutality, media stereotyping, criticisms of President George Bush and Vice President Dan Quayle who engaged in a "blame the victim" strategy in their public pronouncements, and so on.

Another portrayal of the conflict was that it was inevitable given the socioeconomic conditions in South Central Los Angeles, and there is much sympathy for Blacks expressed. One item argued that

> this atrocious situation is an expression of the anger and frustration over society's inability to provide adequate justice in the case of Rodney King. This event sums up years of oppression, of marginalization of the African American community. It is a consequence of North American society's incapacity to overcome its racist attitudes, its prejudice, and its egoism. ("No to Violence," *La Opinión*, May 1, 1992, p. 11A)

Another writer said that years of injustice finally "exploded the frustration of the Black population in the US" ("Causes and Origins of a Social

Explosion," *La Opinión*, May 6, 1992, p. 11A). Yet another item argued, "It would be foolish to ignore the events preceding [the riots] and the injustice that characterizes our society" ("Don't Lose Perspective," *La Opinión*, May 2, 1992, p. 2B).

Despite the obvious sympathy *La Opinión* writers had for Blacks in Los Angeles, they also reminded readers that Latinos also faced specific problems during the disturbances. Specifically, several items noted that INS officers were using arrest records to target Latinos and identify possible undocumented workers in the community (for example, "Pretext to Persecute," *La Opinión*, May 6, 1992, p. 1A).

Villains

Police

La Opinión depicted the LAPD officers as insensitive, out of control, and out of touch with the Latino and Black communities. The LAPD is referred to as "treacherous and domineering" ("An Unusual Verdict," *La Opinión*, April 30, 1992, p. 1A), and several references are made to police brutality. For example, an article reports the LAPD use of force to break up a rally calling for peace. One of the marchers is quoted saying, "We were simply citizens marching peacefully against police presence in the streets and against police brutality" when police moved in and roughed up some of the protesters ("Protest Against Massive Police Presence," *La Opinión*, May 3, 1992, p. 3A).

The paper heavily criticized LAPD officers for their treatment of "illegal aliens." One column is especially critical of a police spokesperson who declared publicly without evidence that it was "mostly illegal aliens who participated in the looting" ("Latino Immigrants and the Disturbances," *La Opinión*, May 19, 1992, p. 11A). In an editorial, *La Opinión* criticized the police department for its "odd actions" in not taking more decisive action in response to the rioting in South Central.

> The LAPD, without clear reason, refrained from a rapid and effective response to the emergency [and] the police seemed a complacent witness to acts of looting and destruction. ("After the Storm," *La Opinión*, May 3, 1992, p. 2B)

This perspective is especially damning in light of the fact that the LAPD moved very quickly when they considered more posh neighborhoods in danger, as shown in the previous chapter on *Los Angeles Times* coverage of the disturbances.

In a story about undocumented people in Los Angeles, *La Opinión* criticized the INS for the essentially unfair strategy of "fishing in the river of revolt" to make "indiscriminate catches of undocumented people" and then "arresting several hundred people principally for lacking immigration papers and not necessarily participating in the riots" ("Pretext to Persecute," *La Opinión*, May 6, 1992, p. 1A).

City Officials

Many residents quoted in *La Opinión* coverage of the disturbances cite city authorities for their lack of concern and misperceptions of ethnic minorities. In an article about the effect of rioting in East Los Angeles, a resident said,

> I don't like the actions of those Latinos who participated in the riots but I think it's the fault of the city authorities mostly. They think the people, they are lazy and don't work. ("Residents of East Los Angeles Condemn Arson and Looting," *La Opinión*, May 2, 1992, p. 7A)

Among the specific city officials heavily criticized by *La Opinión*, LAPD Chief Daryl Gates is taken to task for attending a fund-raising event rather than taking control of the situation on the night rioting began ("The Response Is the Vote," *La Opinión*, May 8, 1992, p. 11A) and for not taking more forceful action in stopping the rioters in the South Central area, but mobilizing forces in the wealthier areas ("No to Violence," *La Opinión*, May 1, 1992, p. 11A). Another government figure mentioned as an actor is Mayor Tom Bradley. The paper criticized him for appointing a White businessman, Peter Ueberroth, to oversee the rebuilding of South Central ("Learn From History," *La Opinión*, May 4, 1992, p. 11A) and for a general lack of leadership ("Lack of Leadership," *La Opinión*, May 5, 1992, p. 11A).

Business Leaders

Big business and other predominantly Anglo institutions represent another villain. One article laments the looting and destruction but notes that the problems highlight that "there was a type of cooperation between police authorities and the Anglo sector that holds economic power in Los Angeles, with support of the federal government" ("The Difficult Path of Reconstruction," *La Opinión*, May 16, 1992, p. 15A). As in other ethnic minority newspapers, there is less reticence than in general circulation newspapers to discuss the impact of White dominance of key institutions on communities of color.

Looters and Rioters

There were several reports of Blacks as actors, where their actions were villainous, such as the report of "Black men" beating Reginald Denny ("A Sad Night in LA," *La Opinión*, May 1, 1992, p. 1A). Other than these articles, few articles depict Blacks in terms that could be described as villainous, such as insensitive, brutal, and treacherous, which were used as descriptions of police and some political leaders.

On the other hand, there were articles reporting the actions of villains that did not specifically mention race of the actors. However, the context of the story and the event made it clear that the perpetrators were racial minorities. For example:

> During a meeting for emergency workers, [Mayor] Bradley said while he could understand the discontent of the people over the verdict but asserted that most of the participants in the rioting were "criminals using the occasion as an excuse" to rob and commit vandalism. ("Curfew in Los Angeles," *La Opinión*, May 1, 1992, p. 1A)

> Nothing justifies the breaking of the law and the atrocious, delirious destruction that seems to carry the arsonists and looters these days. ("Don't Lose Perspective," *La Opinión*, May 2, 1992, p. 2B)

> Elements of the underworld infiltrated the area, robbing stores, setting cars and buildings on fire. ("A Sad Night in LA," *La Opinión*, May 6, 1992, p. 1A)

Although these reports, and others like them, do not specify race, a reader could easily understand that the "villains" in these cases were likely to be Blacks and/or Latinos, given the well-publicized location of the incidents reported in other media. However, the point here is that *La Opinión* did not feel obligated to report race in cases where the general circulation newspapers typically would report clear indicators of race.

General Circulation Mass Media

One other villain was the news media. The paper criticized local television for a breech of journalistic ethics. It took the stations to task for "broadcasting immediately the looting and arson without stopping any of the instigators" ("After the Storm," *La Opinión*, May 3, 1992, p. 2B). In another case, it criticized a radio DJ for "identifying 'pillagers' as illegal immigrants, based solely on their appearance [as Latinos]" ("After the

Storm," *La Opinión,* May 3, 1992, p. 2B). In another article, an African American leader criticizes local television news for selective use of images:

> The main strategy of the television news seemed to be tracking "savage" blacks. The rioting was illustrated by images of blacks. [But] we never saw the violence and brutality of the economic and judicial system. ("Black Leaders Complain About Television Role in Riots," *La Opinión,* May 10, 1992, p. 3A)

Heroes

Good Samaritans

La Opinión depicted a small number of individuals and groups as heroes for their actions. The general media coverage mentioned a number of celebrities, but Latino actor Edward James Olmos received prominent mention. In a reverential tone, the newspaper said that Olmos was a "comforting presence, who without being directly involved in political activities, was capable of delivering a message of trust and hope to the anguished people in a voice that resonated with strength and echoed throughout south-central LA" ("Lack of Leadership," *La Opinión,* May 5, 1992, p. 11A). Local residents volunteering for cleanup duties also received some coverage from the newspaper ("Residents Volunteer to Clean up Streets," *La Opinión,* May 3, 1992, p. 5A). Finally, the paper gave prominent coverage to four Blacks who "risked their lives to save two victims of the violence." Two Black men and one Black woman helped get Reginald Denny to safety after Black rioters left him for dead. The fourth Black hero helped an injured driver get to safety. An article contains detailed accounts of the actions of the four people ("Homage to Heroes," *La Opinión,* May 6, 1992, p. 3A).

East Los Angeles Residents and Gang Members

La Opinión praised another set of heroes for *not* taking action. For example, an article deemed Latino residents of East Los Angeles heroic because they did not leave their neighborhoods to participate in the rioting ("A Dream Turned Nightmare," *La Opinión,* May 17, 1992, p. 2B). The same article depicted members of the predominantly Black street gangs the "Bloods" and the "Crips" in this way as well.

> The Black gangs could have looted businesses and attacked police with their high-power weapons and disciplined troops, could have brought much more unfortunate consequences to the riots. But the groups robbed stores that were already burned but they did not loot or shoot at police. ("A Dream Turned Nightmare," *La Opinión,* May 17, 1992, p. 2B)

In this article it is important to note that whereas Latinos in East Los Angeles and Black gang members were, in one case, praised for not participating in the riots or, in the other case, for not taking total advantage of the anarchic situation, the article implied that participating more actively in the riots would have been the "normal" behavior for these groups. That the article had to highlight nonparticipation as a newsworthy occurrence belies a stereotypical understanding of certain sections of the Latino and Black communities.

Countertrends

One other set of heroes was notable because it goes against the predominant grain of coverage. *La Opinión* coverage was, in general, hostile to local and federal political leaders and to police and other law enforcement agents. One article, however, commended President Bush (although the praise is lukewarm) for taking the correct action in condemning the rioters and condemning the verdict in the Los Angeles police officers trial for beating Rodney King ("Bush Before LA," *La Opinión*, May 7, 1992, p. 11A). A second article commended the National Guard for quickly "regaining control of the most agitated areas, and promising a new investigation" ("Causes and Origins of a Social Explosion," *La Opinión*, May 6, 1992, p. 11A).

Causes of Conflict

As with the analyses of the other newspapers, the discussion of causes of conflict in *La Opinión* can be conveniently and usefully divided into explanations of cause at the individual, institutional, and structural levels.

Individual-level Causes

At the individual level, some representative examples stand out. *La Opinión* placed blame for the disturbances on ethnic-community leaders—and Black, Latino, and White leaders are implicated:

> Many are responsible for this sad and chaotic hour. Of course, responsibility falls to those political leaders who focus less on the community's needs than keeping their electoral support. This includes, of course, many African American leaders who take their powerful positions then forget about their communities to align themselves with the political and economic establishment. ("No to Violence," *La Opinión*, May 1, 1992, p. 11A)

In a second article, the paper also criticizes Latino leaders for driving a wedge between Chicanos, the Mexican Americans with typically deep and long-term roots in the region, and more recent Central American immigrants. The paper criticized certain unnamed Latino "spokesmen" for suggesting that Central Americans were the main Latino ethnic groups participating in the looting. The director of the Center for Central American Refugees criticized "certain leaders" of the Mexican American community for "lack of an adequate attitude in a moment when unity should be a high priority." She continued,

> The Chicano community enjoys power and we see injustice; it's not right for them to blame the poorer community. At this time what is important is cohesion among all the communities affected by the disturbances. ("Differences Among Latinos About Looting," La Opinión, May 6, 1992, p. 3A)

It is important to note also that this report again reveals the complexity of the Latino community, which the Los Angeles Times rarely noted. The other ethnic minority newspapers examined in the following chapters, at times note ethnic distinctions in the Latino community, but not always in contexts favorable to those communities.

La Opinión coverage also noted White leaders, especially those linked to the Bush administration, as contributing to the ongoing violence of the riots by enraging members of the ethnic minority community with their comments. For example, La Opinión quoted Vice President Quayle's claim that the "illegal social anarchy that we see is directly related to the breakdown of families, personal responsibility, and social order" ("The Uprisings and the Social Problems Debate," La Opinión, May 11, 1992, p. 11A). Commenting on Quayle's statement, La Opinión said that

> politics is a nauseating game, but there are things that are purely intolerable, such as the images of the vice president, who was born and raised with all the privilege and security money brings, discussing the importance of family values to residents of an impoverished California community. ("The Uprisings and the Social Problems Debate," La Opinión, May 11, 1992, p. 11A)

Quayle's position was again taken to task by a La Opinión writer who called Quayle's statement a "total distortion of reality" and an example of "the practice of making victims guilty of their own conditions" ("Welfare and Riots," La Opinión, May 9, 1992, p. 1A). Also responding to Quayle was LAPD police chief-designate Willie Williams. A La Opinión article reported that Williams said the disturbances "were in large measure a result of lack of leadership from government and called the problems 'much more than simply a lack of values' as claimed by Quayle" ("Failed Leadership Caused the Riots, Says Williams," *La Opinión,* May 21, 1992, p. 1A). Clearly, for *La Opinión* and Williams, Quayle and, by implication, President Bush and his staff, were among the individual-level causes of the disturbances.

Institutional-level Causes

At the institutional level, three categories of explanations were prominent. One related to the LAPD, perhaps the most reviled institution in the city among the city's ethnic minorities. One article criticized the LAPD for being unprepared or unwilling to deal with the rioting in the South Central part of the city ("No to Violence," *La Opinión,* May 1, 1992, p. 11A).

Other articles depicted additional aspects of the LAPD as central factors contributing to conditions that ultimately resulted in the disturbances. In one column, the writer indicates that the widely broadcast video of the police beating of King had compelled many people of color to come forward with similar treatment at the hands of the LAPD ("Legal Isn't Always the Most Just," *La Opinión,* May 9, 1992, p. 15A). An article reporting a meeting of Black leaders quotes participants as they criticized the LAPD. The article, containing several first-person accounts of police harassment of community members, reports,

A group of Black religious and community leaders from South Central Los Angeles said the behavior of the LAPD was the main cause of the disturbances last week. "The police don't treat us with respect and don't have good relations with the community." ("Black Leaders Blame Police for the Riots," *La Opinión,* May 9, 1992, p. 6A)

In a column, the writer suggests that the LAPD was interested mainly in protecting the interests of the White-dominated business community and their economic interests.

Gates openly declared that police troops were ready to intervene in predetermined priority areas. Since the affected areas were not Beverly Hills, Bel Air, Santa Monica, Pasadena and other rich neighborhoods, the police efforts were sluggish, or moved with reluctance. As Gates said, "South Central LA was not an important area for us." ("The Difficult Path of Reconstruction," *La Opinión,* May 16, 1992, p. 15A)

These items depict the LAPD as prepared to protect and serve only certain segments of the Los Angeles population and to engage in violence to control and contain other segments of the population. The articles imply a racial dimension to the pattern of policing.

Another set of institutional-level explanations for the conflicts dealt with what *La Opinión* depicted as failure of the judicial system in acquitting the four LAPD officers accused of assaulting Rodney King. Typical of the coverage was an article that criticized the jury by comparing their decision to what the writer depicted as "public opinion":

> The outrage the majority of the population experienced—independent of ethnic origin—at seeing a young Black man repeatedly beaten by a group of White cops didn't appear to be shared by the 10 Whites, one Hispanic, and one Asian member of the jury. ("Causes and Origins of a Social Explosion," *La Opinión*, May 6, 1992, p. 11A)

A second article criticized the verdict in even stronger terms:

> The verdict is an offense to justice, human dignity, and tacit approval of police brutality. ("An Unusual Verdict," *La Opinión*, April 30, 1992, p. 11A)

In a third article, the Latasha Harlins killing was raised in criticizing the "shameful way of running the judicial system." The article stated,

> It wasn't that long ago that another LA court sentenced to community service punishment a Korean woman who shot and killed a Black adolescent for the crime of faulty subtraction [referring to the allegedly insufficient money the young woman paid to the clerk]. ("The Necessity of Judicial and Economic Reform," *La Opinión*, May 8, 1992, p. 1A)

This piece suggests that the judicial system has double standards or a bias against Black victims of crime by connecting the light sentences received by the four police officers and the Korean American woman. Interestingly, *La Opinión* merges together Korean Americans, who also have been targets of racism and discrimination in Los Angeles, with White police officers as benefiting from the judicial bias against Blacks. It is unclear why *La Opinión* links White police and Korean Americans in this way. Is it because the public perceives Korean Americans as "law-abiding," and police are therefore sympathetic toward them? Remember, *La Opinión* depicted Korean Americans as victims but not sympathetic victims, even though their property was destroyed. Perhaps this coverage is indicative of the tensions emerging from Asian American and Korean American patterns of settlement throughout the South Central area of Los Angeles.

The third category of institutional-level explanations related to politics. Two articles made the argument that minorities do not have sufficient representation and clout in the political system. Beyond this lack of power, one article stated that "no one but the minorities seems to care" about their lack of political power, revealing a deep frustration ("Violence Is Not the Solution," *La Opinión*, May 2, 1992, p. 15A). Another column asking the question "Who Lost LA?" pointed to Republican policies that have neglected socioeconomic deterioration in the nation's urban areas. The writer argues,

> The middle class demanded that the government stop "taxing and spending," taxing us, the Whites, and spending on them, the Blacks. It's not that they were unaware of the problem of poor Blacks in the cities. But they were determined to ignore that they existed, in the same manner that the jury in the Rodney King case ignored the evidence displayed before their very eyes. ("The Latent Causes of the LA Riots," *La Opinión*, May 14, 1992, p. 13A)

This article portrays the political process as beholden to public demand, and it shows that public demand is racially intolerant. An important insight in the last sentence is that racialized justice and racialized economic neglect are cut from the single cloth of racism.

La Opinión also gives some coverage to the view that Democratic politicians are to blame. Representative of these types of articles is one in which President Bush claims that it was the "liberal social programs of the '60s and '70s that are the reason for the disturbances in Los Angeles" ("Wilson Gives Promise for Reconstruction," *La Opinión*, May 6, 1992, p. 1A). In another article, Bush names former President Lyndon B. Johnson and his plans for the Great Society as the reasons behind the "the urban crisis" ("Candidates Speak About Riots," *La Opinión*, May 11, 1992, p. 1A).

Structural-level Causes

A third set of explanations for the conflicts referred to structural reasons or, more specifically in the Los Angeles case, macrolevel socioeconomic conditions such as racism, unemployment, poverty, and global economic decline. One of the prominent themes in the coverage was persistent racism against ethnic minorities. In the context of a column in which the writer pondered how he would explain the verdict to his children, he suggested that most Whites in the United States accept the proposition that violence against Blacks by Whites is no crime because the law said that "Rodney King provoked his own beating" ("The Problem of Explaining Injustice to Youth," *La Opinión,* May 3, 1992, p. 2B). In another article, Black residents suggested that the racism in the community was deeply entrenched well before the trial verdict set off the disturbances. The leader of the Congress of Racial Equality is quoted as saying that because of racism "long ago, Whites abandoned South Central Los Angeles, and so did industries, insurance companies, clinics [and] the justice system treats us differently" ("Causes of Disturbances Discussed," *La Opinión,* May 7, 1992, p. 5C).

Another writer suggests that racism and poverty are "corrosive social forces" and must be included on the "list of sources of instability in our society" ("The Latent Causes of the LA Riots," *La Opinión,* May 14, 1992, p. 13A). Typically, the discussion of other structural conditions is brief and lacks any detailed discussion. For example, one article states simply that riots "may have had socioeconomic origins" ("Don't Lose Perspective," *La Opinión,* May 2, 1992, p. 2B). However, two items stand out as exceptions. In one of these, there is a fairly lengthy explanation for the "economic crisis" that contributed to the riots.

> The economic crisis is a result of the arms race initiated by Reagan, with the objective of breaking the Soviet economy. To achieve this, the country had to go into debt. The national debt totaled almost $300 million and the government had to take out close to $400 billion to pay the interest on money loaned from the bank accounts of the Japanese and the Arabs. This is why there are no loans for new businesses. The government operates with a deficit, spending more than it collects. But the President, like many Representatives and Senators, greatly pressured by the capitalists who contribute to their election campaigns, doesn't dare establish or raise taxes. ("Causes of the Disturbance," *La Opinión,* May 4, 1992, p. 11A)

This article is unusual (in the context of other coverage of the Los Angeles riots) for its detail and the causal arguments it makes linking the riots with foreign policy, international banking, and the U.S. electoral process. It is also unusual for explicitly stating that "capitalists," possibly a reference to wealthy bankers and corporate heads, must share the blame. Although, notably, the article does not say that capitalism itself, the principle and system of relatively unfettered opportunity for accumulation, is to blame. Thus, although explicitly suggesting that a particular type of economic system is at the root of unrest, the writer stops short of saying that the system must be rejected.

The second item is a column that makes a case for a class-based understanding of the disturbances. The writer argued, "In reality, the riots are based in class difference." He then provides his evidence:

First, though Blacks expressed their rage at Whites and destroyed Korean stores, they did not participate in a significant way in the looting. Second, Black gang members also did not loot or harass police. Third, Chicanos did not participate in a significant way in the looting. The largest proportion of the looters—who were different from those engaging in violence in the streets—was from Central America. These migrants—poor recent arrivals, unprepared to face an unimagined reality—looted the city of angels. ("A Dream Turned Nightmare," *La Opinión*, May 17, 1992, p. 2B)

Although this article does not castigate the Central American immigrants for looting, it does highlight the economic differences among the already deprived groups of Blacks, Chicanos, and other Latino groups that can compel the poorest of the poor to engage in illegal action (as defined by the state).

Implications of Conflict

One of the implications discussed in *La Opinión* is that the disturbances will worsen an already bad situation for Blacks and Latinos in Los Angeles. An editorial claimed that "a political style based on exacerbating anguish and social antagonisms will carry our society toward a social polarization that nothing can overcome" ("No to Violence," *La Opinión*, May 1, 1992, p. 11A). Other *La Opinión* items elaborated on this theme. For example, a column made the argument that the rebellion "loosened a conservative reaction against public welfare, the cities, and the poor, securing an electoral victory for George Bush in November" ("A Dream Turned Nightmare," *La Opinión*, May 17, 1992, p. 2B).

Another implication discussed in *La Opinión* related to the impact on children of the trial verdict and subsequent violence. A *La Opinión* columnist is concerned that

> [childrens'] young minds can't assimilate and accept the proposition that Rodney King provoked his own beating because he was a Black man and the accused are White police officers. For [the children], the fact is that safety for a Black person isn't the same as safety for a White person. ("The Problem of Explaining Injustice to Youth," *La Opinión*, May 3, 1992, p. 2B)

There was also some discussion about the negative impact of the disturbances on the local tourism industry. One article reported that tourism industry analysts feared that the disturbances and "images of chaos" televised around the world could lead to losses of up to $2 billion for

Los Angeles area businesses oriented toward tourism ("Chaos in LA May Affect Tourism," *La Opinión*, May 7, 1992, p. 6C). A second article, published in late May, reported that the negative impact on Los Angeles tourism jeopardized 31,000 jobs. The community hardest hit by the disappearance of these jobs would be Latinos ("Disturbances Put 31,000 Tourism Industry Jobs in Danger," *La Opinión*, May 22, 1992, p. 12A).

Another set of implications of the conflict is that people propose solutions to the problems they see as underlying causes of the conflicts. A number of items suggested specific solutions in varying amount of detail. One item in its entirety was devoted to calling on ethnic minorities to vote candidates into office that could enhance the community's political clout. The item goes on to name specific people who ought to be voted out of office and to explain an amendment on the ballot in the November 1992 elections ("The Response Is the Vote," *La Opinión*, May 8, 1992, p. 11A).

Another article implied a number of actions to create conditions to improve life chances for Blacks and Latinos:

> While the government doesn't face unemployment with decisive action; while education isn't considerably improved; while the public aid system is not modified; and no immediate plans are put into action to rebuild the city, the danger of new violence breaking out will remain like the sword of Damocles in the second largest city in the US. ("The Difficult Path of Reconstruction," *La Opinión*, May 16, 1992, p. 15A)

Other articles proposed more general solutions, such as encouraging community residents "to find a spirit of reconciliation and recovery" ("After the Storm," *La Opinión*, May 3, 1992, p. 2B), and another item advocated nonviolence ("Violence Is Not the Solution," *La Opinión*, May 2, 1992, p. 15A).

Race and Nation

There is little discussion of the articulation between race and nation (unless one takes the entire discussion of the disturbances to be about the issue). In a column, the writer says, "The 'American Dream' only works in the US, but the US cannot work without it." In essence, he means that the United States could not exist as a sociocultural national formation without the idea that unlimited opportunities in mobility, employment at fair wages, educational attainment, political freedoms, and so on are only available in America. This dream then attracts immigrants who contribute in myriad ways to the social and cultural fabric of the nation. But then, the article details the frustrations and hopelessness that Latino immigrants in Los Angeles feel as they eke out a living in menial jobs and live in poverty. This explanation of the context also makes a connection between race and nation. That is, that certain people in America, because of their race or ethnicity, are marginalized to the economic and then, by extension, the political, social, and cultural sidelines of the national mainstream ("A Dream Turned Nightmare," *La Opinión*, May 17, 1992, p. 2B).

A second article elaborates on this theme further by contrasting Martin Luther King's dream of a society based on racial equality with the racial "nightmare" of the country in a post-Los Angeles riot era. The article reports a series of statistics about the differences in education, employment, and life chances for Blacks, Latinos, and Whites and demonstrates that racial equality in all these areas continues to be a dream. Then the writer states that Blacks, Latinos, and Whites are "not equal before the law in the United States, which Americans saw was the root cause of the events in Los Angeles." For these reasons, the writer concluded (paraphrasing the Kerner Commission report of 1968), "The United States is effectively two societies, 'one Black and one White, separate and unequal' and with two kinds of justice: black and white" ("Martin Luther King Had a Dream, Los Angeles Has a Nightmare," *La Opinión*, May 4, 1992, p. 7A).

This article spells out the additional elements of the "American Dream"—equal opportunity for learning, accumulation, and justice—but the writer suggests that they seem to be reserved for Whites. The argument here does not seem to be that Blacks or Latinos do not belong in America or that Blacks and Latinos cannot, in fact, *be* American—as in some of the other newspapers examined. Rather, the argument seems to be that many Black and Latino communities are relegated to being "sub-American," living in the same geopolitical space as Whites, having many of the same legal rights as Whites (especially if they are U.S. citizens), but having only a fraction of White levels of political power and economic comfort.

One other article reports a rally demanding justice, fair treatment for all minority groups. The following passage reveals the articulation of race and nation:

> The program was delayed at the beginning as the crowd cheered when a White woman accidentally dropped an American flag that she held over her head. The incident [dropping the flag] symbolized what had been abandoned. Later, when the woman, with Bible in one hand and her flag in the other, shrugged off the polite concerns of an usher, a young African American took the flag and threw it to the ground while the crowd applauded. ("Violence and Civil Rights," *La Opinión*, May 25, 1992, p. 5A)

By publishing this passage, *La Opinión* communicated several things about the articulation of race and nation. The article is explicit about the race of the flag-waver, indicating that American-ness and Whiteness are closely linked. The article also reports the fact that the White flag-waver is also holding a bible, suggesting that the writer of the article is also linking a particular set of values with being White and American. Then the reporter describes the reactions to the women and her flag. When she drops the flag, people cheer. When the Black youth stomps on the flag, people cheer. These reactions indicate the crowd's displeasure with America and American values, symbolized by the flag and the White woman with a bible, which ignore the problems of unequal justice and continued marginalization of minorities in America. On the other hand, the actions of the Black youth could also signal to readers that Blacks are un-American.

Summary and Discussion

Latinos were the most frequently mentioned ethnic minority group, followed by Blacks and Asian Americans. Coverage specifically mentioned Korean Americans, but less than any other ethnic minority group despite the fact their properties were the primary targets of looters and arsonists.

Almost all the coverage centered on actual actors and victims rather than on potential actors and victims. Blacks were the most frequent human actors, followed by Latinos. Coverage mentioned both groups in this context as taking part in the looting. Overall, coverage mentioned most frequently government actors. This category included the mayor, the police chief, the state governor, and representatives of the federal government.

In terms of victims, Blacks and Latinos are the most often mentioned groups, surpassing even Korean Americans who were the primary targets of the violence. One possible reason for this pattern is the predominance of institutional-level and structural-level explanations for the cause of the disturbances. Many of the explanations highlighted the role of local institutions such as police and structural problems such as generalized racial oppression that daily victimize Blacks and Latinos. This emphasis may have precluded more attention to the victimization of Korean Americans during the disturbances themselves. But to some extent, it seems possible that in *La Opinión*, Korean victims, in the specific context of the riots, were less sympathetic victims than Blacks and Latinos, who had been victims of decades of racial oppression.

An interesting pattern emerged in the representation of Latinos as victims. *La Opinión* distinguished between new and old Latino communities to the extent that the newspaper acknowledged the INS would be more likely to scrutinize new immigrants. Yet, the coverage also suggested disapprovingly that it was some of the new immigrants who were participating in the disturbances.

Conflict is the main theme depicted in the coverage, but there is a clear underlying sentiment of anger against "enemies of minorities," minorities being Blacks and Latinos only. Coverage portrayed Blacks and Latinos not only as suffering together under racial oppression but also putting up a united front against villains such as the police. The paper repeatedly takes police to task for their brutality and for not protecting property in poor areas of South Central Los Angeles. Articles heavily criticized Police Chief Daryl Gates for his lack of action and leadership. Though Blacks were part of the violence and looting, generally the coverage did not villainize them to the same extent as police. Coverage seemed to criticize Latinos who looted—mainly the new immigrants, according to *La Opinión*—as villains more heavily than Blacks. One exception to this trend was the Black men who beat Reginald Denny, the White truck driver.

Discussion of heroes in *La Opinión* was not extensive. The paper occasionally featured local celebrities who helped with cleanup. Another set of heroes, though it was an ambivalent depiction, was the primarily Latino residents of East Los Angeles. The newspaper compliments the residents for not taking part in the arson and looting but in so doing suggests that it would not have been surprising if East Los Angeles residents had participated in the disturbances.

Coverage mentioned institutional-level causes and structural-level causes of conflict more frequently than individual-level causes. The stories providing these explanations sometimes did not provide much detail, but the breadth of explanations ranged from the local to the global. Individual-level explanations, when they were mentioned, focused on lack of values and morals on the part of the looters and arsonists. Interestingly, many of these types of articles report statements made by federal government representatives.

The implications of conflict highlighted by *La Opinión* centered on the potential for a conservative political backlash and worsening conditions in the short-term aftermath of the conflicts, worries about how severely children were traumatized by the riots, and proposing solutions for long-term social improvements for Latino communities.

In comparison to the other Spanish-language newspapers analyzed, *La Opinión* clearly is the only one that forcefully advocates coalition with another ethnic minority group. Of course, Los Angeles is the only one of the three cities where large numbers of Blacks and Latinos shared a common history and contemporary condition of racial oppression. In Miami and

Washington, D.C., Latinos (Cubans specifically) and Blacks, respectively, held power during the time period analyzed. Thus, in Miami, *El Nuevo Herald,* although to some extent sympathizing with the plight of the city's poor Black population, was more likely to take a condescending "we'll show you the way" stance toward the Black community. In Washington, D.C., where Blacks were virtually absent from the news coverage, *El Tiempo Latino* registered no gesture of solidarity with Blacks because the conflict was rooted in what Latinos saw as Black insensitivity to Latino needs.

7

African American Newspaper Coverage of Los Angeles

Although there are several treatments of the breadth and scope of the Black press, this chapter presents a focused analysis of articles from a range of Black newspapers covering the Los Angeles interethnic conflicts. In this chapter, we go beyond Los Angeles and include several Black newspapers published in other cities. In part, we made this decision to supplement the relatively scant coverage given to the disturbances by the leading local Black newspaper. Before presenting the detailed analysis, however, we provide an overview of the newspapers examined in this chapter, starting with the leading local Black newspaper in Los Angeles.

Los Angeles Sentinel. This weekly paper appears in four sections and has a circulation of 19,175. It is a politically moderate paper but takes strong pro-civil rights positions in its editorials. Founded in 1934, its goal is to report on events in the Black community, stressing political, social, and economic news at the local and national levels. It is highly regarded in the Black community, and in a study of its coverage of the Watts riots, a researcher concluded that the paper seems to be more a mirror of the thinking of various elements of that community rather than the thinking of community leaders.

Afro-Times (New York City). The *Afro-Times* covers current news and events taking place in the region to "enlighten the African American community about the issues confronting them." In addition to covering news found in most newspapers, the *Afro-Times* provides information specifically geared toward Black self-help such as stories of personal triumph and positive events that reflect the strength of the Black community. The weekly *Afro-Times* is part of the Challenge Group, owned by Thomas Watkins.

Bay State Banner (Boston). The paper was founded in 1965 and is currently edited and published by Melvin B. Miller. It is the weekly paper of record for the Black community in Greater Boston. It emphasizes news that keeps the community well informed about the issues that affect its welfare. The paper's policy is to actively confront and challenge leaders and citizens who may potentially harm the interests of the Black community. It is distributed weekly and has a circulation of 10,500.

Big Red News (New York City). The paper was founded in 1975 and by 1977 became one of the most widely circulated Black newspapers in New York City. It started as a four-page advisory sheet for gamblers. The publishers quickly recognized the opportunity to include breaking news along with the "numbers." It is distributed weekly in six counties in the New York City area and has a circulation of about 32,500. The publisher is Walter Smith Jr. In 1993, the weekly newspaper changed its name to the *New York Beacon*.

California Voice (San Francisco). *California Voice* is a weekly publication of the Reporter Group of newspapers, established by publisher Dr. Carlton Goodlett. The paper has a circulation of 37,000 and serves the African American community of San Francisco and surrounding areas. Its main editorial focus is education. It features in-depth reporting on local and national news affecting African Americans. According to cofounder and current executive editor, Thomas Fleming, the mission of the *California Voice,* as well as its partner paper the *Sun-Reporter,* is "to have an editorial voice in the community [and] to fight for first-class citizenship for all people regardless of race."

Call & Post (Cleveland). The *Call & Post* is a weekly that began publishing in 1917 when Garrett Morgan, an entrepreneur and inventor of "personal care products for Negroes," and a number of other investors, started *The Call,* to promote his products. Badly edited and poorly managed, the publication was on its last legs when bickering shareholders decided to merge *The Call* with the *Cleveland Post*. The new paper, christened *The Call & Post,* floundered until William C. Walker, a department store manager from Baltimore, took over the paper. Walker arrived in October 1932 to find the paper in financial trouble, which forced him to subsidize the paper from his own savings. Nevertheless the newspaper established a strong reputation for excellent coverage of local news and coverage of society, club, women's, and entertainment news. Circulation today is about 30,000.

Chicago Defender. Founded in 1905 by Robert S. Abbott, the *Defender* is an important source of national news about Black America. Through muckraking journalism and sometimes sensationalistic coverage of local news, the *Defender* had built its circulation to 230,000 by 1915 (Wolseley, 1990, p. 51). Though its circulation fell dramatically after World War I and during the Great Depression, the *Defender* remained influential among the Black community. Today, the newspaper carries much more Chicago area and regional news to its readers than the general circulation press. Its editorial page is moderate in political position, but liberal on certain problems affecting Black lives such as housing, employment equality, and educational opportunities. Its circulation is around 27,000.

Chicago Citizen. Gus Savage founded the Citizen Newspaper Group, to which this paper belongs, in 1965. William Garth, current president and publisher of the Chicago Citizen Newspaper Corporation, joined the organization in 1969 as an advertising salesman, moving through the ranks to become advertising sales manager in 1975 and vice president of advertising in 1978. In 1980 he became president and publisher. A dedicated activist and leader in the local business community, Garth maintains memberships and affiliations with several business organizations. The Citizen Newspaper Group recently expanded to include the *South End, Chicago Weekend, South Suburban,* and *Hyde Park Citizen.* The weekly newspaper's circulation is 26,400.

Michigan Citizen (Highland Park, Michigan). Charles Kelly founded the paper in 1978 to fill a niche for serious analysis of local and national civic issues in the state. The newspaper is the only Black publication to have a bureau in the state capital and correspondents across the state. Among its emphases are politics in cities led by Blacks. Circulation of this weekly is about 52,000.

New Pittsburgh Courier. Formerly the *Pittsburgh Courier,* this is one of the oldest Black newspapers of general distribution. Robert Vann and others founded it in 1910. In 1966, John Sengstacke purchased the newspaper. It was renamed the *New Pittsburgh Courier* and became part of Sengstacke

Newspapers, the largest and most influential Black newspaper chain in the country. The *New Pittsburgh Courier* serves as a vehicle for African American expression, publishing local editions twice a week. At one time, it had the largest circulation of any Black newspaper, estimated at about 300,000. Today, it has a circulation of about 30,000. Forty years ago, James Baldwin considered it the only Black paper worthy of unqualified praise (Wolseley, 1990, p. 104).

Amsterdam News. This paper is one of the most widely known and oldest of the Black newspapers in the United States (Wolseley, 1990, p. 102). The first of its kind in Black journalism, the *Amsterdam News* has had since 1963 a contract with the American Newspaper Guild, a labor union of editorial and nontypographical employees. From 1936 to 1971, Dr. C. B. Powell owned the paper. He was a physician involved in insurance, funeral services, and loan services businesses. In 1971, he sold the paper to an all-black group, including Percy Sutton, then Manhattan Borough president, and Clarence Jones, a lawyer and an officer in a major stockbrokerage firm. Although encountering financial difficulties during the 1970s and 1980s, the *Amsterdam News* continued to sell considerable advertising space, including space devoted to palm readers, spiritualists, and astrologers. This weekly once had many guest columns but now uses outside writers sparingly. However, it remains one of the few Black newspapers with a section devoted to relations between people of color. Circulation is about 60,000.

Philadelphia Tribune. Among one of the oldest continuously published Black newspapers in the country, it was organized in 1884 by Chris J. Perry Sr. One of the largest Black papers, it engages in various public enterprises, such as charities and scholarship programs. Published by Perry's widow after his death, E. Washington Rhodes, Perry's son-in-law, was publisher and editor until he died in 1970. Rhodes held the opinion that "affluent middle-class Blacks" were not doing enough to help the poor (Wolseley, 1990, pp. 43-44). This weekly newspaper's circulation is about 130,000.

Sacramento Observer. This newspaper was founded in 1962 by William Lee Sr., a local business owner and real estate developer. It is a family-run paper today with a circulation of about 49,000. The first issue was a 4-page newsletter-size publication. Today the weekly is tabloid size and often runs to as many as 300 pages. The newspaper has won several awards for reporting, including the John Russwurm Award for Journalism Excellence. Its mission is to inform, influence, and impact the existing and emerging African American community.

Table 7.1   Number and Percentage of Articles in Black Newspapers
Mentioning Various Groups (*n* = 43 articles)

	#	%
Black/African American	43	100
Asian/Asian American	38	88.6
Latino/Hispanic	31	58.1
Korean/Korean American	22	48.8
People of Color	16	36.4
White	16	37.2

Sun-Reporter (Oakland, California). This newspaper bills itself as the old-est, largest, and most influential newspaper in Northern California. The San Francisco-based weekly paper has a circulation of around 12,000. Businessman Frank Logan and editor Thomas Fleming founded the news-paper in 1944. Today, the Sun-Reporter Company owns several Black pub-lications, including the *California Voice* (established in Oakland, California, in 1917 and analyzed in this study), acquired in 1960.

The Coverage

All together, these newspapers published 44 articles about interactions among ethnic minority groups in Los Angeles (see Appendix B, Table 1 for a breakdown). Some papers provided little to no coverage of the riots, let alone anything to do with people of color interacting. Indeed, four papers provided most of the discussion of Los Angeles, and three were responsible for most of the articles dealing with interactions between people of color. Thus, a puzzling question from these analyses remains: Why did the Black press, which prides itself on speaking for and defending Black communities, give relatively short shrift to what happened in Los Angeles and interethnic relations?

Ethnic Groups in the Black Press

As Table 7.1 indicates, there are six ethnic labels used by the Black press to describe groups involved in the Los Angeles riots. The papers used "Black" or "African American" in each article. The articles used the term "Black" exclusively in 51% of the articles, whereas they used "African

American" alone in 25.6% of the articles. The coverage used both terms interchangeably in 23.2% of the articles. The articles never made specific reference to Black subgroups from regions of the Caribbean or Africa. This tendency implies that the newspapers saw Blacks as, at least racially, a homogeneous group.

The Asian/Asian American label appeared in 88.6% of the articles. Korean/Korean American was the most commonly used subgroup within the Asian/Asian American category (48.8%), followed by Asian (27.9%) and Asian American (11.9%). Infrequently used labels were Oriental, Korean American, and Vietnamese. Interestingly, the papers make a distinction between Asian/Asian Americans and Korean/Korean Americans, for the articles used the terms interchangeably in only 9.3% and 4.6% of the articles respectively. This tendency to not draw parallels between these groups suggests that Black papers did not see Korean American issues as generalizable to Asian American communities. This trend may also imply that Black papers were ambivalent about the status of Korean Americans in the United States: The Black press much more often labeled them Koreans or Asians than Korean Americans or Asian Americans.

About 58% of the articles included some mention of "Hispanic" (30.2%) or "Latino" (27.9%). Indicating an awareness of the diversity found among Latinos, 11% of these articles identified subgroups with labels such as "Mexican" (used in one article interchangeably with Latino), "Mexican American," "Hispanic American," "Cuban," and "Latin American."

Some kind of reference to a number of people of color simultaneously (attributing a common experience to being a racial minority) appear in 36.4% of the articles. "White" also appeared in 37.2% of the articles. The term usually was affiliated with the police officers involved in the Rodney King beating, Jewish merchants, or government and corporate executives and leaders. "Minorities" appeared in 10.9% of the articles, and other terms, such as "non-White" (4.6%), "multiracial" (2.3%), "rainbow" (2.3%), and "urban communities" (2.3%) appeared much less frequently.

Actors and Victims

Table 7.2 indicates the main actors and victims as perceived by the Black newspapers. Among the actors, Blacks and Whites appeared most often (both appear in 44.2% of the articles in this capacity; see Appendix B, Table 3 for a paper-by-paper breakdown of actors). When Blacks appeared as actors, it was usually as protestors. Whites appeared as police and

Table 7.2   Number and Percentage of Articles in Black Newspapers
Discussing Various Actors and Victims (*n* = 43 articles)

	Actors				Victims			
	Actual		Potential		Actual		Potential	
	#	%	#	%	#	%	#	%
Government	16	37.2	2	4.7	1	2.3	0	0
Society	2	4.6	0	0	1	2.3	0	0
Blacks	19	44.2	1	2.3	29	67.4	2	4.7
Whites	19	44.2	0	0	8	18.6	1	2.3
Asian Americans	6	13.9	0	0	9	20.9	0	0
Korean Americans	10	23.2	0	0	12	27.9	1	2.3
Latinos	9	20.9	0	0	11	25.6	0	0
Police	17	39.5	0	0	0	0	0	0
People of Color	13	30.2	1	2.3	14	32.5	0	0
Justice System	13	30.2	0	0	0	0	0	0
Capitalists	4	9.3	0	0	1	2.3	0	0
Working Class	8	18.6	1	2.3	5	11.6	1	2.3
Media	11	25.6	0	0	0	0	0	0

government officials or as (Jewish) merchants. Although it is not surprising that police were second most likely identified as actors, it is interesting that only about two in five articles mention them (39.5%) and usually when touching on the catalyst of the rioting—the acquittal of police in the beating of Rodney King. When police appeared in stories other than about the King beating, it was about police brutality as a normal course of Black life or about police racism. Almost as often mentioned were government officials such as the mayor and his associates, who appeared in 37.2% of the articles. Other actors of note in these narratives were politicians, normally depicted as not doing their job or as part of the overall mechanism of oppression encountered by Blacks.

As part of the reaction to oppression, people of color are also mentioned frequently (both 30.2%), followed by Koreans (23.2%), Latinos (20.9%), and Asian Americans (13.9%). When the papers mention people of color and Latinos, it is usually when they band together with Blacks to protest against racism, organize to change the system, or in some way unite in a common struggle. Korean Americans (23.2%) and Asian Americans (13.9%) usually appear when they link up to protect their rights or act to defend themselves during the riots.

Other actors were people involved in the U.S. justice system, or as often described in Black papers, the "injustice system" (30.2%). Here, the actors are lawyers, judges, and jurors who negatively impact Black life. The news media appear as actors in 25.6% of the articles, usually in reference to how they misrepresented issues, people, and events. Another actor was privileged segments of society—such as rich or middle-class people (i.e., capitalists and classes)—who either abuse Blacks or take advantage of the system for their own good.

Not surprisingly, about two of every three (67.4%) newspaper articles depicted Blacks as the most likely victim in the events covered. A distant second was "people of color" (32.5%). Given that they were often the target of attack in Los Angeles, it is perhaps surprising that Koreans appear as victims in only 27.9% of the articles. Asian Americans are victims in just above twenty percent (20.9%) of the articles. About one quarter (25.6%) of the articles mentioned Latinos in relation to the argument in Black papers that Latinos and Blacks have similar experiences with discrimination. Appearing in about 11% of the articles was the working class as victims.

Conflict and Racial Violence

As Table 7.3 suggests, several themes emerged from the news coverage. Personal violence and violence against property was a common theme. In the Black press, the context for this theme was either violence perpetrated by other individuals (such as Whites) or by White institutions. The latter pattern is in contrast to what we normally find in general circulation news depictions where violence is almost always instigated by individuals.

Given the heavy reliance on violence in their storylines, conflict is overwhelmingly the most common theme, appearing in each article analyzed. In contrast, cooperation appears in about one third of the articles. The articles containing the cooperation theme typically involved advocating Blacks' political mobilization or creating interethnic coalitions, usually with Latinos. Given the papers' heavy focus on structural factors (79% of the articles mention them) as causes of the conflict, it is not surprising that most newspapers depicted the riots as a manifestation of national issues (67.4%). The papers mentioned relatively few individuals as causes of conflict, and when they are mentioned they were usually the police involved in the King beating, which could be argued to be a manifestation of institutional factors at play. For most of the papers, the role of race was a significant factor in the conflicts, but nearly one quarter did not mention race at all.

Table 7.3   Number and Percentage of Articles in Black Newspapers
Discussing Various Themes (*n* = 43 articles)

	#	%
Violence		
Personal	28	65.1
Property	22	51.2
Verbal	1	2.3
Conflict	43	100
Cooperation	14	32.5
National Problem	29	67.4
Minority Intersections	36	83.7
Causes		
Individual	13	30.2
Institutional	2	4.6
Structural	34	79.0
Role of Race		
Primary	14	32.5
Secondary	17	39.5
None	2	4.6
No Mention	10	23.0

These themes were interwoven with a number of different narratives. The following discussion examines the narratives of villains and of causes and implications of the conflict.

Heroes

Unlike the news in the other cities we examined, for Los Angeles, there were no individuals or groups clearly identified as heroes by the Black press for the period of the riot. There were several *potential* heroes mentioned, such as those residents and entrepreneurs who prepared to rebuild their destroyed neighborhoods. We incorporate an examination of these individuals in the discussion on solutions at the end of the chapter.

Villains

Police

Police are the most commonly mentioned villains, especially in the context of the officers who beat Rodney King. The adjectives used to describe their behavior, both toward King and Blacks more generally, often telegraphed newspapers' perspectives. One paper reported that the police were guilty of a "vicious beating" ("Reflections From Los Angeles," *Afro-Times*, May 23, 1992, p. 4), whereas others asserted that the police action was a "savage beating," a "monster police beating" and involved "brutal, excessive FORCE" ("King Beating, Jury Makes $500,000,000 Verdict," *Call & Post*, May 7, 1992, p. 9A; "'We Can All Get Along,'" *LA Sentinel*, May 13, 1992, p. A1; "Trickle Down . . . and Hope?" *Michigan Citizen*, May 9, 1992, p. A8). Another paper characterized the actions as "police lawlessness and racial violence" ("King Verdict Sparks Rallies Around Hub," *Bay State Banner*, May 7, 1992, p. 1), whereas the *Amsterdam News* used the adjective "sadistic" ("Dinkins and the New York Riots That Never Happened," May 9, 1992, p. 12).

Some of the papers hinted at the pervasive and constant nature of police malevolence toward Blacks. The *Call & Post* quoted a journalism professor who noted, "African American males are beaten, harassed and sent to jail routinely" ("Black Media Professionals Debate Riot Coverage," May 7, 1992, p. 10A). And the *Chicago Citizen* wrote, "No matter if you are rich or poor, short or tall . . . ugly or cute, with a business suit or a starter jacket, with a '82 or a '92, a condo or shack, a GED or a MBA—you are not exempt from police brutality" ("The Verdict That Shook the Universe," May 11, 1992, p. 12). A teen in Boston said that the police are a problem in communities of color "because cops have no one to answer to, they believe they can do anything they want" ("King Beating, Riots Leave Marks on Youth," *Bay State Banner*, May 14, 1992, p. 11).

For the *Chicago Defender*, the message learned from the verdict was that "America's police don't have to be concerned about the amount of force used when stopping or arresting Blacks" ("King Verdict, Rioting Were Wrong," May 2, 1992, p. 13). In this regard, the *Michigan Citizen* suggested a link between U.S. foreign policy and police treatment of people at home. It asserted that the Reagan-Bush years was a time of a "macho, kick-butt attitude pitting superpower might against people of color in Grenada, Libya, Panama and Iraq" and "manifested itself on the streets of America in the epidemic of police brutality" ("Trickle Down . . . and Hope?" May 9, 1992, p. A8). The *Amsterdam News* went further:

In oppressed communities, police brutality is not random or arbitrary. It is not just the misdeeds of a few bad apples. It is one manifestation of a consciously conceived policy of forceful containment of those at the bottom of U.S. capitalism's social pyramid, those most likely to resort to "mindless" violence when their oppression becomes unbearable. It is this policy which has led to the militarization of the country's police forces. ("Sober Reflections on the Rebellion of Los Angeles," May 9, 1992, p. 50)

Jury Members of the LAPD Trial

Another set of villains in the drama was the jury that acquitted the four officers who beat King. The *Philadelphia Tribune* contended that the "verdict was racist, inhumane, insensitive and obviously rendered by short-sighted people who have no historical perspective about Blacks, the police and what often happens when the two encounter each other" ("Our City's Restraint Was a Model for the Nation," May 5, 1992, p. 6A). The *Afro-Times* reported that an "all-White jury cleared four White policemen of crimes" ("Riots Tarnish Martin Luther King Jr.'s Dream," May 9, 1992, p. 12), clearly implying that Whites were looking out for other Whites in the racially charged case. The *New Pittsburgh Courier* noted that the jury saw the "incident differently, causing them to rule that the four officers charged with beating King were not guilty of using excessive force to subdue him. In so ruling the jury had effectively turned the clock back a few decades on justice." It went on to "wonder" at "what kind of abuse would the jury consider excessive and what its members would have ruled, using the same evidence, if the bludgeoned man had been White and the police Black" ("King Verdict and Rioting Were Wrong," May 6, 1992, p. A6). For some, the excess was the final straw. John Mack of the Los Angeles Urban League declared, "The jury told the police it's still right to beat the hell out of a Black man. Enough is enough" ("Waiting for Justice," *New Pittsburgh Courier*, May 13, 1992, p. A18). The verdict, in the words of the *Los Angeles Sentinel*, "created a feeling of total powerlessness over our lives" and "a stunning blow to a dwindling belief in the American justice system" ("Opinions: A Diary of the Los Angeles Riots," May 23, 1992, p. A7).

Blacks

The papers occasionally depicted other Blacks as villains. Manning Marable, the prominent African American social analyst, wrote in the *New Pittsburgh Courier* that Whites were often the targets across a "race/class division" and that people of color were villains too. "This time, Black and Latino young rebels weren't content to destroy the symbols of ghetto exploitation": Indeed they attacked White-owned property across Los Angeles County ("Along the Race/Class Fault Line," June 6, 1992, p. A7). The papers depicted those Black leaders who had not condemned the violence of Black residents as villains.

The *Los Angeles Sentinel* explained why Black leaders were silent: "The word in some quarters is that any comment on the demise of Korean businesses might be interpreted as 'anti-Black,' 'pro-Korean,' 'sell-out,' etc."

Perhaps that is why they were also seen to ignore the conflict, for a "strange, perhaps telling, silence defines African-American leaders' public response" to the targeting of Korean and Asian American businesses. The "failure to acknowledge this [targeting] has serious implications for race relations. It is impossible to negotiate or embark on meaningful dialogue from positions of distrust" ("Re-Examining Traditionalism," *Los Angeles Sentinel,* June 11, 1992, p. A6).

Korean Americans

The Black press also depicted Korean American merchants as villains. The papers accused them of disrespecting Black communities and customers. The Black press suggested that Korean American merchants moved into the Black neighborhoods and exploited them by extracting profits from the area and funneling the gains into non-Black areas.

For many of the papers, the context of what happened during the riots related to the Soon Ja Du court ruling almost a year earlier. The *California Voice* noted, "Much of the hostility of African Americans toward the Koreans had been spurred by the acquittal of a Korean shopkeeper who had shot a 14-year-old Black girl over a $1.40 bottle of orange juice" ("Japanese Meet With African Americans," May 29, 1992, p. 1). The merchant received probation for the killing. The apparent disrespect for Blacks represented by this verdict fit into a broader historical context that reinforced a perception among Blacks that they were at the bottom of the racial hierarchy. Even Korean Americans seemed to be above them. According to some newspapers, Soon Ja Du was treated as "White" when she took the life of a Black girl ("Slanted Media Coverage of Uprising Is Disgraceful," *Los Angeles Sentinel,* June 25, 1992, p. A6; "Japanese Meet With African Americans," *California Voice,* May 29, 1992, p. 1; "L.A. Residents Watch Riots Set City Ablaze," *Chicago Defender,* May 2, 1992, p. 38, and "The Siege of L.A. and Black America," May 9, 1992, p. 47).

The Soon Ja Du verdict was only one variable in Black–Korean American relations. Another was the long history of outsiders entering Black neighborhoods and profiting without regard for the welfare of community residents. Ben Chavis, who later would become chair of the NAACP, summarized in the *Afro-Times* the general feeling toward Korean Americans entering into this process:

> We heard of countless accounts of fundamental disrespect for the dignity and personhood of community residents by the owners of some of the businesses in the community even though these owners made a profit from doing business in the community. ("Reflections From Los Angeles," May 23, 1992, p. 4)

The *Chicago Citizen* took a particularly strident stance on Black–Korean American relations, rejecting any kind of solidarity with the Korean American community. Responding to suggestions that Korean Americans' own struggles against persecution should shield the community from attacks by Blacks, the newspaper said,

> They say they sympathize with us. They can understand. [But] you can not understand because you did not come here, like us, bound in shackles around our hands and feet. . . . You cannot understand when you get pulled over by a cop . . . that it may be frustration for you, but it's a highly-probable-generally-anticipated-holy-hell-butt-kicking for us. ("The Verdict That Shook the Universe," May 5, 1992, p. 12)

The *Call & Post* went further in distancing itself from these "villains" by drawing a particularly chilling picture of Korean American participation during the riots, painting Korean American merchants as dangerous and sinister: "Many of the deaths in the disturbance have been attributed to Koreans who concealed themselves on the roofs of businesses and shot into the crowds of demonstrators with high-powered rifles. Many fear the problem is not over but is just beginning" ("King Beating, Jury Makes $500,000,000 Verdict," May 7, 1992, p. 9A).

General Circulation Mass Media

According to the Black press, the general circulation media—individual journalists as well as the organizations themselves—are another villain. The general circulation media, the Black press claimed, conducted an "assault" on Blacks and other people of color. In some cases, as in this passage from the *New Pittsburgh Courier,* the Black press depicted the general circulation papers as purposefully attacking or undermining Black concerns:

> For centuries, the White media have been the vermin upholding slavery, supporting segregation and under-girding bigotry in America. Their claim of objectivity in news reporting, to the ears of African-Americans, sounds more like the ravings of a false messiah than the argument of a credible authority. ("Further Evidence of White-Media Bigotry," June 17, 1992, p. A6)

The *Courier* went on to say that Black and White reporters in the *Los Angeles Times* "cite instances in which editors have criticized reporters for taking too seriously Black-Korean problems, have tone[d] down statements about Black distrust of Whites and . . . rejected stories suggesting the possibility of race riots" ("Further Evidence of White-Media Bigotry," June 17, 1992, p. A6).

Other Black papers implied that general circulation papers seek to divide communities of color. The *California Voice,* for example, claimed that general circulation media helped

create tensions between Asians and African Americans, and this was heightened during the Los Angeles rebellion where the media showed Korean merchants and friends armed with weapons, and feeling betrayed, alienated and abandoned by the Los Angeles community. ("Japanese Meet With African Americans," May 29, 1992, p. 1)

The *New Pittsburgh Courier* suggested that White media often "offend not only Blacks, but Hispanics, Asians and Native Americans" ("Along the Race/Class Fault Line," June 6, 1992, p. A6). Elsewhere, the Black press viewed the mass media coverage as part of a pattern in general news media to quickly "broadcast or write about Black anger and ethnic rage, but not as swift or diligent in reporting the peaceful nature of our people" ("Our City's Restraint Was a Model for the Nation," *Philadelphia Tribune,* May 5, 1992, p. 6A).

The Black press magnified the villainy of the general circulation press by pointing out what, to most Blacks, was an obvious social impact of negative portrayals of the Black community. One newspaper claimed, "Nearly everyone . . . agreed that negative stereotypes on television, radio and in newspapers have done much to fuel hatred, bigotry and racial tension" and "do not give a good understanding of the life of African American minorities" ("Japanese Meet With African Americans," *California Voice,* May 29, 1992, p. 1).

This pattern of representation also suggested to the Black press that the general circulation press is not interested in the real causes of the riot. In an article titled "Slanted Media Coverage of Uprising Is Disgraceful," the *Los Angeles Sentinel* left no doubt how it felt about general circulation coverage:

The media consistently displayed itself as a powerful medium with little social responsibility. We are outraged at the manner in which the media covered the events. They showed limited ability to analyze the events taking place and exhibited an overall lack of balance in its coverage of the uprisings. Additionally, the media sought to exploit and reinforce longstanding racial stereotypes while inflaming racial tensions. . . . It is unreasonable for one to nearly destroy a city over one racist verdict itself. ("Slanted Media Coverage of Uprising Is Disgraceful," June 25, 1992, p. A6)

Continuing, the *Los Angeles Sentinel* noted that when general circulation papers used "unprofessional and blatantly racist" terms such as "savages," "animals," and "thugs," or when showing footage of Black and Latino looters, they reinforced "deep seated racist images that dehumanize those to whom the terms are directed." The *Sentinel* raised the question of why general circulation news media "never seem to refer to members of the White community who are involved in similar activities . . . with these same terms." Persons who pilfered savings and loans under the guise of legitimate business arrangements, the *Sentinel* argued, were never referred to as "thugs" and "savages" even when their activities have a greater and widespread socioeconomic impact than is true for any activities of looters ("Slanted Media Coverage of Uprising Is Disgraceful," June 25, 1992, p. A6).

Causes of the Conflict

As seen in earlier chapters, general circulation papers couched causes of the conflict in terms of individual or group culpability, in the tradition of personal responsibility for one's actions and consequences, where power lies in individual hands. In contrast, for the Black papers, the causes of the rioting in Los Angeles came down to structural imbalance in power and resources, institutional neglect of and racism against Black communities, and a lack of community and individual responsibility for the "Black condition." Regardless of what kinds of causes were discussed, however, relationships between Blacks and Asian Americans received little notice. Thus, the focus is typically about Black–White relations or Black intersections with Latinos and the working class.

Individual-level Causes

One individual-level cause of the riots was political leaders who made little or no effort to understand the problems of Black Americans. A prominent White leader, Harris Wofford, argued,

> [Leaders] have not made the effort to deal with the serious problem, that of the connection between the current social environment and the polarization that has occurred in this country. . . . We've failed up and down the line—especially the president of the United States. . . . We have not sat down together and decided what steps we should take. ("King Verdict Clear Case for Federal Action, Says Wofford," *New Pittsburgh Courier*, May 9, 1992, p. A3)

In an editorial in the *Big Red News*, state representative Edolphus Towns argued that Bush did not understand that the riots were a symptom of deeply rooted social problems and policies:

The problems relate to issues such as poverty and unemployment, and feelings that include disgust and anger from citizens who believe the federal government has turned a deaf ear toward them [and] true to form and policy, the president's [solution] stresses traditional law enforcement responses instead of applying social program remedies. ("Talk of the Towns; Why America Must Develop an Urban Agenda," June 26, 1992, p. 2)

A lack of personal responsibility among residents was often an individual level factor cited as the cause of the disturbances—especially if the articles framed the disturbances as "riots" rather than "politics." In some reports, rioters' behaviors suggested this. The *Los Angeles Sentinel* called them "pilferers whose wrongful rampage" led to much damage ("City of the Stars Under Siege and Occupation," May 13, 1992, p. B3). The *Chicago Defender* suggested that the participants were out of control, a danger to themselves and others: "Thousands of residents from all racial backgrounds ran amok while destroying area businesses and injuring—and killing—innocent bystanders" ("L.A. Residents Watch Riots Set City Ablaze," May 2, 1992, p. 1).

Some accounts referred more specifically to the motives of the rioters:

For the vast majority of the rioting Black people, Latinos, and Whites, the Simi Valley verdict . . . was merely an excuse to do wrong. The plain fact was that few of the rioters were concerned about anyone's personal, civil or property rights. . . . It mattered not to them that . . . they were burning away jobs, that they were burning up goods and services . . . that they were bringing terrible misery to the young and the old, the impoverished and the immobile. ("'We Can All Get Along,'" *Los Angeles Sentinel,* May 13, 1992, p. A1)

One "community activist" argued that it was important for people to know that all the destruction was not "the product of an angry mob." He suggested, "We want to bring it to the attention of the public that it was just opportunists. People in business, who weren't doing well, came forward to see if they could get anything out of the riot" ("L.A. After the Holocaust, Resurrection: Up From the Ashes," *Los Angeles Sentinel,* May 28, 1992, p. A1).

Some of the papers portrayed the causes of the riots as Black self-hatred. The *Amsterdam News* suggested,

the enemy [is] from within. It is we ourselves. We hate each other with a passion unparalleled with anything our real enemy can muster. ("The Bloods and the Crips," May 23, 1992, p. 26)

In a similar vein, a column in the *Chicago Defender* suggested that a lack of unity and an unwillingness to take the fair share of the blame were the problems:

The African American community nationwide has failed to become supportive of themselves [and] has become a race of beggars and leeches. We can blame no one but ourselves. We want to place the blame on the White man. [T]he Black man is mad at the Korean because he has surpassed us in the area of economics. We have failed to do what they have done but we are mad at them. There is unity in their community and they are helping one another. We need to place the blame squarely on our own shoulders because that is where it belongs. ("The Siege of L.A. and Black America," May 9, 1992, p. 47)

The last two examples are rare not because of the criticism leveled at the Black community per se, but because much of the message is similar to that used by the general circulation press.

Institutional-level Causes

Perhaps the most frequently mentioned institutional cause of the disturbances was the judicial system, which the papers depicted as seriously flawed and deeply and historically racist, due in large part to White culpability. For example, the *New Pittsburgh Courier,* editorialized that images of

the [court] ruling smells of the putrid stench that rose from the trials of Whites in the murders of Emmett Till and Medgar Evers and the roles of Whites in beatings and murders of other Blacks prior to the Civil Rights Movement. ("King Verdict and Rioting Were Wrong," May 6, 1992, p. A6)

Another paper commented on the apparently unchanging racist character of the U.S. legal system:

The legal system has stereotyped [Blacks] and changed the rules over and over to accommodate their [Whites] needs. According to them, no one Black and Male is exempt from the billy club, the prosecution, the jail sentence and the death chamber. ("The Verdict That Shook the Universe," *Chicago Citizen,* May 11, 1992, p. 12)

The Black press also indicated that it was not only Blacks who are victims of unequal justice. A column in the *Amsterdam News* argued that Latinos demonstrated against the verdict because they understood its implications for themselves. Latinos expressed a resounding condemnation of an "entrenched racist system that allows for people of color to be beaten and even murdered by cops. Latinos along with Blacks have a long history of being traditionally marginalized in American society" ("Clarifying a Position on Black, Puerto Rican Relations," May 2, 1992, p. 9).

For others, the problems inherent in the justice system affect more than only Blacks. One paper wrote, "Some Asians experience the same problems Blacks do as non-Whites in a White-dominated society. 'We have to make sure they're not mistreated as minorities. We don't want to pass that legacy on. We have to find a way to meet and solve problems between the two groups'" ("Blacks and Asians Gather to Find Common Ground," *Philadelphia Tribune,* June 19, 1992, p. 3A). In a statement to the *Amsterdam News,* the group Young Koreans United in New York drew similar connections: "We stand with our African-American, Latino, Native American and Asian-American communities who suffer the daily indignities of racism and police brutality" ("Young Koreans in Solidarity With Malcolm X Day UN Rally," May 23, 1992, p. 8).

Several papers also commented on a more generalized racism. *Amsterdam News* editor Don Rojas noted,

> During the days of the rebellion, Black and Brown school children in ravaged cities across the land placed hands on heart and pledged allegiance to a land of liberty and justice for all. They were told to mouth loyalty to an ideal yet to be realized, to words that have been rendered hypocritical . . . by the objective realities of racial and social injustice. ("Sober Reflections on the Rebellion of Los Angeles," May 9, 1992, p. 4)

By pointing out the contradictions between the promise of liberty and the reality of racism, this article also hints at the existence of racism at institutional sites throughout the United States. Another paper wrote,

> It's been a "just-us" murder in and outside of the penal system, the employment sector, in education, business opportunities and anything else White America has taken for granted. ("The Verdict That Shook the Universe," *Chicago Citizen,* May 11, 1992, p. 12)

The police department drew special attention from the papers as the institution that has almost daily contact with minority communities outside the judicial system, contact that often led to Blacks ending up in the judicial system. The following article is typical of the Black press perspective:

> The legal system had not proven effective for people of color, and to make matters worse, those who had sworn to serve and protect, did just the opposite. To be young and Black meant an almost certain, ritualistic encounter with the police that was never pleasant. ("Where Do We Go From Here?" *Los Angeles Sentinel,* May 13, 1992, p. B6)

The *Amsterdam News* also noted that the Los Angeles police department had a history of running "roughshod in African-American, Mexican-American and Asian-American neighborhoods," clubbing, arresting, threatening, and abusing at will. The paper argued "that the explosive rage of African-Americans, Mexican-Americans and Asian-Americans was manifested after the not-guilty verdict freed those blood-thirsty racist cops [against all minorities]" ("There Will Be More Rodney King Cases," May 16, 1992, p. 13).

Here too the Black papers did not spare the Black community its own responsibility in helping to cause the riot. One Black newspaper gave some prominence to an institutional-level explanation that put blame squarely on what it presented as a cultural failing of the Black community. In an article reporting on a speech by a former member of the U.S. Civil Rights Commission, the *Afro-Times* reported, without comment, the official discounted racial discrimination as the main cause of the Los Angeles riots.

> "I don't think racism explains all of the problems afflicting our cities or why Los Angeles blew up." He said the problems of the Black underclass are complex but center on the disintegration of the family, given that more than "60 percent of Black children live in households without both parents and many grow up without any job skills." Most Black families are without two parents and grow up without job skills and this has produced young Black men who "are not working and not looking for work." Furthermore, because most of these people, and especially men, are lost, he "doubts that a costly government-funded war on poverty would help solve the problem." That the Black middle class is also struggling suggested to him that they are not likely to sacrifice their own souls to help the urban poor. ("Riots Tarnish Martin Luther King Jr.'s Dream," *Afro Times,* May 9, 1992, p. 12)

This extended quote represents a fairly standard conservative explanation for what some sources refer to as Black pathology. Not strictly an institutional explanation, this perspective also includes what it presents as Black cultural shortcomings.

Structural-level Causes

The following excerpt from the Black press represents the tenor about structural causes of the conflict. In an article quoting a local resident, the *Los Angeles Sentinel* reported,

> I feel that they—the power structure—are constantly doing things to remind us that they do not consider Black folks "equal" to them, and they'll do their best

to make sure we'll never become "equal." ("Where Do We Go From Here?"
Los Angeles Sentinel, May 13, 1992, p. B6)

There were three kinds of discussions in regard to structural-level explanations for the riots. The first referred to maldistribution of resources such
as jobs and to impacts such as poverty. The second focused on how race
and social class intertwined. Finally, some papers highlighted the role of
class alone, seemingly arguing that all working-class people are oppressed
no matter what their race or ethnicity.

For many of the papers, the cause of the verdict was old news. A *Los
Angeles Sentinel* article noted that "we have only to look at the past to
determine our future" and compared current conditions to the 1960s

> [when] Blacks lived in urban areas that were ignored by community improve-
> ment programs, jobs, government programs and politicians. Unemployment
> agitated the already-unbearable conditions of oppression, brought on by vir-
> tually unchecked racism. ("Where Do We Go From Here?" *Los Angeles
> Sentinel,* May 13, 1992, p. B6)

Another structural factor discussed by the Black press was the intersection of race and class. One direction this discussion took seemed to be that
the rich (implied as White) are to blame for the condition of poor minority
communities. A typical formulation of this perspective was in the
Amsterdam News, which complained in an editorial,

> The same old crap—rich folks stealin', wheelin', and dealin', then talking dirty
> about poor people who are essentially just trying to survive and who can never
> seem to get their land legs. When the rich get in a tight spot, they spew racism.
> ("A Righteous Rage," May 9, 1992, p. 26)

The race–class discussion also had an international dimension. In an editorial in the *Afro-Times* by Otis Graham and Ron Beck, the writers pointed
out the long history of Latino immigrant workers displacing U.S.-born
working-class people—mainly Blacks.

> The White-dominated news media has been loath to discuss the role of
> unprecedented levels of immigration in the deteriorating economic and social
> conditions for African Americans who live in the nation's inner cities. ("LA
> Riots Point to Need for Breaking Taboo," *Afro-Times,* May 30, 1992, p. 5)

Clearly, the writers hint at the fact that those at the upper reaches of the
economic structure—mainly Whites—benefit from cheap labor that depresses
living conditions for the working class who are disproportionately Black.

Another article condemns what it depicts as the source of race–class tensions and conflicts. The riot "is an indication of the sharpening of the social and economic contradictions of US capitalism, which if not addressed swiftly will lead to more spontaneous urban explosions in the future" ("L.A. Uprising Analyzed at Harlem Forum," *Amsterdam News,* May 9, 1992, p. 8). This article also reports on a Harlem forum at which the riots were described as "masses of Blacks and Latinos who took to the streets of LA and other cities across the US [because they] are the alienated, ignored and exploited underclass that is rapidly growing in numbers. These are people who have completely given up on the U.S. capitalist system because this system gave up on them a long time ago."

In the articles that raise the race–class interconnections, it is important to note an interesting pattern. In discussing the issue, the Black papers seem to fall into the same pattern as the general circulation press in that they conflate race *with* class by equating Blackness with being poor. Notwithstanding the fact that U.S. Blacks are more likely to be poor than other racial groups, the problem here is the implication that to be Black inevitably means being poor.

There are also articles in the Black press that point to class issues alone as causes for the disturbances. The perspective here is that all poor people— non-White and White—share experiences of powerlessness, exploitation, and discrimination. For example, the *Chicago Defender* ("L.A. Residents Watch Riots Set City Ablaze," May 2, 1992, p. 38) suggested that, quoting a former Chicago resident, the riot was not a "Black but a human issue," affecting working-class people of all colors. The *Call & Post* noted that many people were linked in their despair, for there were "a lot of different types of folks, not just Blacks attacking Korean Americans. It wasn't just African Americans, it was more a war between the haves and have-nots" ("L.A., A Clevelander's Perspective," May 14, 1992, p. 1A).

The problems of the working poor that cut across racial boundaries were the result of federal policies, according to the Black press. The *Amsterdam News* claimed the riots were due to "years of neglect and indifference to the urban agenda, and there is a price that must be paid now or later, up front or in the end." The paper called the transfer of wealth from poor to rich during the Reagan-Bush years a "prescription for civil unrest." The paper argued further that significant social and economic change would not come about until "middle class and poor Whites see they are niggers too" ("L.A. Uprising Analyzed at Harlem Forum," May 9, 1992, p. 8).

The papers raise capitalism as the root cause of the disturbance—this time to explain class-based conflicts. The editor of the *Amsterdam News* wrote in a column that complex forces are aligned against all working-class people. He suggested that as economic elites awakened to the riots, "they quickly used the coercive powers of their state to put out the fires of rage set by desperate and impoverished people of color." He argued further that, despite the attempt of the ruling class to have the world believe otherwise,

> [a] vast majority of Blacks, Latinos, Asians and Whites who participated in the Los Angeles insurrection were not thugs, hooligans, criminals and vandals. These were masses of alienated and dehumanized human beings for whom the American Dream is nothing but a living nightmare; people who are jobless and hopeless, powerless and voiceless—angry people marginalized and ignored by American capitalism. Yes they looted and pillaged, but their looting must be put into perspective. It is dwarfed by the $500 billion looting of the savings and loan industry by a coterie of White-collar criminals. ("Sober Reflections on the Rebellion of Los Angeles," *Amsterdam News,* May 9, 1992, p. 4)

This article not only provides an economic analysis of the riots that brings together the poor as suffering a common fate, but it also labels their actions during the disturbances as political behavior born of alienation.

Implications of the Conflict

In highlighting various sites that helped create the environment in which the riots were spawned, the analyses thus far suggest a complex set of issues, ranging from Black and White culpability, structural and institutional factors, general circulation media, and the justice system, just to name a few. Given the nature of the culprits explored by these papers, we were particularly interested in what they saw as the aftereffects of the riot and what solutions they suggested to alleviate the hardships encountered by their communities. The papers described a series of implications arising from the disturbances. One implication related to social links among ethnic minority groups. The second implication related to the various solutions suggested to alleviate the conditions that brought on the rebellion.

The Black press suggested that one lingering effect of the riot was increasing unity among minorities who realized they all shared outrage at the not-guilty verdicts and experiences with police. One paper wrote,

> Given the record in Black, Asian and Mexican America, it is easy to understand the cumulative rage that the not-guilty verdict uncapped. The not-guilty verdict unwittingly created an historical phenomenon: a unity in rage among African Americans, Mexican Americans, Asian Americans and some White Americans. ("There Will Be More Rodney King Cases," *Amsterdam News,* May 16, 1992, p. 13)

The notable feature of this construction is that all the racial groups involved in the riots were included in a united front against police.

Other Black papers presented similar messages. For example, one paper wrote, "This wasn't a Black riot so much as a minority riot" ("Arrests, Studies, and Videotapes: Blacks Not the Majority in the Uprisings, Experts Say," *Los Angeles Sentinel,* June 25, 1992, p. A1). Another article said that people of all colors were united in the verdict: "Asians, Hispanics and Whites joined the march, too, demonstrating the widespread outrage in the country" ("The March Begins," *Sacramento Observer,* May 7, 1992, p. A3). The *Afro-Times* suggested, "The victims of the Los Angeles riots were predominantly Black but also included Asian-Americans, especially Korean American shopowners, and Latin-American immigrants" ("Riots Tarnish Martin Luther King Jr.'s Dream," May 9, 1992, p. 12).

In the future, the *Los Angeles Sentinel* suggested that Blacks and Latinos and other groups of color should envision themselves as bound together:

> African-Americans must also deal with Latinos in new, non-traditional ways. More Latinos were arrested than any other group during the upheaval, providing a wrinkle to the worn stereotype of African-Americans as predators and rioters in the inner city. Socioeconomic and political factors that undergird the behavior of many poor and otherwise disenfranchised African-Americans also affect Latinos. Cultural backgrounds differ . . . but Latinos share with African-Americans and many Asians histories of struggle and oppression in their native countries and the U.S. as well. ("Re-Examining Traditionalism," June 11, 1992, p. A6)

Interestingly, however, although many Black papers made note of other ethnic minority groups as participants, victims, and concerned parties during and after the riots, only infrequently did they mention them specifically advocating solutions to the problems encountered. And when the Black press mentioned other groups in the context of solutions, the weight of initiating action was on the non-Black groups. In identifying long-term efforts to improve relations between Blacks and Asian Americans, the papers pointed to Asian American–sponsored initiatives, but they reported no such efforts emanating from Black communities or organizations. Examples of the Black press reporting the coalition building projects of other ethnic minority groups include an article about the Asian Pacific American Legal Center of Southern California developing the Leadership Development in Inter-Ethnic Relations program ("Volunteers to Work for Better Black/Korean Relations," *Los Angeles Sentinel,* May 6, 1992, p. A3) and the Asian American Congress, which hosted a conference for racial harmony ("Blacks and Asians Gather to Find Common Ground," *Philadelphia Tribune,* June 19, 1992, p. 3A).

Given the focus on structural causes for the conflict, the Black press also focused on structural solutions to prevent future disturbances. One solution focused on improving economic conditions in depressed communities of color. In one column, Ben Chavis suggested that there must be "a fundamental social transformation of this society" through a "long term sustained effort of dismantling American apartheid while at the same time reconstructing this society to ensure economic justice and racial justice for all" ("Reflections From Los Angeles," *Afro-Times,* May 23, 1992, p. 4). Still another set of solutions had to do with addressing poverty and unemployment. The *Call & Post* suggested "some fundamental changes in governance, halting the welfare cycle and in solving problem [*sic*] of joblessness" ("King Beating, Jury Makes $500,000,000 Verdict," May 7, 1992, p. 9A).

Another paper suggested

> fundamental change from the ground up: A public-private sector partnership to create jobs with a high skill level; a complete over-haul of the public education system and a government commitment to accomplish these goals that would equal the commitment undertaken in the Persian Gulf War. ("L.A. After the Holocaust; Resurrection: Up From the Ashes," *Los Angeles Sentinel,* May 28, 1992, p. A1)

That many Blacks, but particularly the young, would encounter what these papers commonly described as either a "just us" or "injustice" system would suggest that judiciary reform might be an important component to any solution. However, few of the papers made specific mention of changing the justice system as a central solution. One exception was an article devoted to the topic in the *Amsterdam News,* which wrote,

> America must take concrete steps to remove race discrimination from our legal system. People of color will continue to view the system as unfair and unjust until such steps are taken. ("Rodney King Verdict: Symptom of Pervasive Racial Inequalities in Our Judicial System," *Amsterdam News,* May 23, 1992, p. 13)

To deal with this systemic problem of "two systems of justice—one for Whites and one for people of color," the author urged several reforms: getting more people of color "into decision-making positions" in the justice system, giving Blacks an equal opportunity to serve as jurors, eliminating police brutality against people of color, and dealing with the racial disparity in sentencing ("Rodney King Verdict: Symptom of Pervasive Racial Inequalities in Our Judicial System," *Amsterdam News,* May 23, 1992, p. 13).

Given the primary focus on the structural causes of conflict and structural solutions, there is a surprisingly large emphasis on solutions predicated on Black individuals organizing for self-help. For example, one article suggested the gist of what Black communities needed to do:

> So please, people—get involved! Stop being crazy! Vote in every election! And parents, encourage your kids to be more socially responsible! Brothas and sistas, stay up, keep rising, and remember: We always have each other. ("What's It All About?" *Los Angeles Sentinel,* May 13, 1992, p. B6)

Others made a plea for unselfish behavior on the part of Black leaders. The *Amsterdam News* wrote under the subhead "Seize the Opportunity":

> While the violence in LA was excessive, it has created a parting of a dense cloud that has hung over the young people of color out there for a long time. If Black leadership is smart, and they too often are not, they would seize this opportunity—*not* to get jobs for themselves and their educated cronies as peacemakers, but demand that this government approach the day-to-day remedies. ("The Bloods and the Crips," May 23, 1992, p. 26)

Perhaps the most common set of solutions discussed in the Black newspapers emphasized the idea of community responsibility and involvement. One paper put it quite bluntly:

> If the African American community wants change, then it must come from our own efforts. We must take control of our own destiny. For too long we've been dependent on handouts from White society. It's time we reclaim our communities and, in the process, reclaim our futures. ("What's It All About?" *Los Angeles Sentinel,* May 13, 1992, p. B6)

Another paper emphasized the importance of role models for youth:

> Young fathers must understand the responsibility of parenting and young mothers need support and guidance. ("Wayne Budd Criticizes 'Myths' of LA Uprising," *Bay State Banner,* May 14, 1992, p. 1)

However, the most popular approach to the self-help solution was to strengthen the Black economy. In the *Chicago Defender,* Marion Moore, a state representative who, responding to complaints that Korean American store owners disrespected Blacks yet received more financial backing than Black stores, encouraged African Americans to invest some of their dollars in their own communities:

When Blacks give their money to the Koreans, when will they ever see that dollar again? We have to make sure that every dollar we spend just doesn't benefit our families. We want those dollars to benefit others in the community as well. I refuse to spend one Lincoln penny with any business that will not respect me. Not only will I refuse to shop there but I will organize a boycott." ("Power, Lack of Equality Sparked the L.A. Riots," *Chicago Defender*, May 16, 1992, p. 1)

However, although many criticized Korean American businesses for their exploitation of Black communities, some still argued that those businesses had something to teach Blacks. It is perhaps a real irony—given the relative inattention to Asian Americans—that when the papers advocated development of Black business, authors often turned to using the Korean American merchant as a role model. The *Bay State Banner* argued,

It is significant to note that Blacks seem to have considerable conflict with Koreans in Los Angeles and Cubans in Miami. Koreans in America have the highest percentage of men who are self-employed of any ethnic group. Blacks are near the bottom. In order to become entrepreneurs African Americans must exercise extraordinary discipline. First, they must learn to save to accumulate capital. Secondly, they must find the time to study to learn all about the business and about corporate culture. ("Let's Do It Ourselves," May 14, 1992, p. 4)

Muhammad Nassardeen, the president of Recycling Black Dollars, an attempt to develop Black communities economically, argued that rather than be critical of the Korean American community, Blacks should turn to them as a model:

We're upset with Koreans because they're able to outwork us. They're willing to work 20 hours a day to build a business. They're willing to pool their money together to put each other into business. Koreans are successful because they control their own money and that's what we need to do. They take the money from their communities and reinvest it, unlike Blacks. Koreans don't have $9 billion in White banks. ("L.A. After the Holocaust; Resurrection: Up From the Ashes," *Los Angeles Sentinel*, May 28, 1992, p. A1)

The *Los Angeles Sentinel*, which is located in the heart of the South Central area, provided detailed prescriptions for the Black business development solution. In one article, the *Los Angeles Sentinel* suggested that

our battle for respect will require discipline and diligence. We can begin by 1) requiring that any commercial construction in our community consist of crews that represent a significant percentage of the neighborhoods, 2) hold the media accountable for the images of us that they broadcast to the world, and if that doesn't work, actively support and create more of our own, and 3) to the "Black establishment," let's do away with the lip service about developing more Black-owned businesses. It's time to get busy and create a community which has viable business, owned and controlled by us. ("What's It All About?" May 13, 1992, p. B6)

Summary and Discussion

According to the Black press, the "riots" were about dashed hopes for racial justice. The case against the officers who beat Rodney King looked open-and-shut—after all, there was a video documenting the beating. Instead, the justice system held no one accountable for yet another act of police brutality against a young African American male. The verdict was additional proof, in the view of the Black press and many Black citizens, that the judicial system, law enforcement, and urban policy have not, do not, and will not work for Blacks. The beating and acquittal were really about how racism and economic disparities between rich, White capitalists and poor, exploited Blacks and Latinos are entrenched features of U.S. society.

In this formulation, the Black press gives relatively little coverage to Korean Americans, even though they were, statistically speaking, primary victims in the disturbance. The picture drawn of Korean Americans is ambiguous in these papers. They were not depicted as poor, but neither is it is clear that they are viewed as middle class and "White." There is little recognition that Korean Americans encountered prejudice and bias; only Blacks and Latinos did and still do. The coverage rarely depicted attacks on Korean Americans or other Asian Americans, nor did it depict these groups as imposing themselves on others—except in the cases when they are shown as being rude to Black customers. Solutions to the problems rarely included Korean Americans in the process. Ultimately, for the Black papers, the coverage would not be much different if Korean Americans had not been part of the demographic landscape in Los Angeles. Given that most of the articles addressing what happened in Los Angeles did not even *mention* another group of color suggests an ethnocentric and almost myopic view of the disturbances.

Many of the solutions to the ills faced by many Black communities appear in these papers as self-help efforts. Although the villains are Whites and the White-dominated institutions, there is little reference to them in helping to find solutions for Blacks. Indeed, this may reflect a long history of looking to the White establishment and finding little substantial response or responses that primarily benefit Whites in power. Thus, the Black press appeals to the Black middle class.

Although these papers had much to say about what caused the riots and, to some extent, about interminority bonding, the shortcomings of the coverage are summarized succinctly by one of the newspapers, although the reference was to White papers and their coverage of the rebellion. "Far more emphasis is placed on those who rioted as opposed to determining and rectifying the symptoms that precipitated the rebellion" ("Slanted Media Coverage of Uprising Is Disgraceful," *Los Angeles Sentinel,* June 25, 1992, p. A1). Black papers spent less time on the rioters and more on the context and the symptoms of the rebellion than did general circulation papers, but they too, with a few exceptions, would spend few words on solutions. Perhaps for the Black papers this discussion was "old news," or maybe the solution, like the problem, was so complex, based on a belief that the system was fundamentally flawed, that it was hard to know where to begin. In the final analysis, the solutions offered may reflect a real sense of bewilderment at what to do now after so many decades of effort to deal with persistent and, often times, seemingly intractable problems.

8

Asian American Newspaper Coverage of Los Angeles

Of all the news texts examined in this book, Asian American newspapers provide a most distinctive perspective. In part, the point of view is unique among the papers we cover—particularly in the case of the Korean American papers—because they report stories of the rioting even as their community is figuratively and literally under siege. Given this position, one could assume that the Asian American press coverage would reveal a simplistic bias against the people perpetrating the assault. Instead, overall, we found the Asian American press coverage of the Los Angeles disturbances to be more sophisticated than the coverage provided by other newspapers examined in this book.

We examine five Asian American newspapers in this chapter. Because there is relatively little known about the Asian American press and because the Los Angeles-based English-language Asian American papers to which we had access were only from the Korean American community, we decided to not limit our examination to only local newspapers. Following is a summary of these newspapers, after which we present an analysis of these newspapers' coverage of the Los Angeles disturbances.

Korea Times (Los Angeles). Launched in 1980, this bilingual monthly newspaper carried news articles, features, editorials, and opinion pieces on Korean American life. The editors viewed the paper as a forum of discussion for Korean-speaking parents and their English-speaking children. The editors tried to provide a window into the Korean American experience for non-Koreans. *Korea Times* ceased publication in October 2001.

KoreAm Journal (Los Angeles). This monthly newspaper was launched in 1990 as an English-language paper serving the Korean American community in Los Angeles. Its mission is to provide coverage on issues of concern to Korean Americans and report on the achievements of Koreans in America. Koreans and non-Koreans consider this monthly publication to represent the collective voice of the Korean American community. Its mission is to reach Korean Americans of all ages and backgrounds, including mixed race and adoptees, with stories relevant for the Korean experience in America. The circulation of this newspaper is 24,000.

AsianWeek (San Francisco). *AsianWeek,* a nationally circulated weekly publication with a "community" focus, is a weekly English language newspaper covering news of Asian Americans. The late John Fang founded the paper in 1979 in San Francisco. The mission of *AsianWeek* is threefold: to chronicle the Asian American experience, provide a national forum on issues important to Asian Americans, and involve Asian Americans in the American democratic experiment. As the only English-language, pan-ethnic news weekly, *AsianWeek* helps to set the agenda for Asian America. The newspaper's guiding principle is that an informed electorate is the key to a healthy democracy, and it aggressively advocates a more active role in the political process for Asian Americans. Further, by reporting on the struggles for personal and political empowerment and on other issues of special interest to readers, the paper helps to define the priorities of the national Asian American community and to create a stronger political voice among all Asian Americans. Circulation is 30,000.

India-West (San Leandro, California). Founded in 1975, the paper covers Indian communities in India and the United States. Its mission is to bring the latest and most engaging news about the Indian subcontinent to Indian American communities in the United States. The weekly has made an effort to cover news of interest to Indian American youth and women.

Pacific Citizen (Monterey Park, California). The newspaper is a weekly founded in 1932 and is the official publication of the Japanese American Citizens' League. The paper's predecessor was the Nikkei Shimin, founded in 1929 as a monthly. The purpose of the paper was to forge connections between first- and second-generation Japanese Americans. During the internment of citizens of Japanese heritage, the paper was published from a camp in

Table 8.1   Number and Percentage of Articles in Asian American Newspapers
Mentioning Various Groups (*n* = 135 articles)

Groups	#	%
African American	73	54.4
Black	97	72.1
Asian	44	32.3
Asian American	35	25.7
Korean	100	74.3
Korean American	87	64.7
White	39	28.7
Hispanic	18	13.2
Latino	26	19.1
People of Color, Minorities	27	19.9

Salt Lake City. Today, the paper has a national voice and appeals mainly to
affluent second-generation Japanese Americans. With a circulation of about
23,000, the reading audience may be close to 75,000 (see Miller, 1987).

The Coverage

In all, these papers published 135 articles about the Los Angeles disturbances that included some discussion about interactions between people of
color. The amount of coverage here exceeds that found in any of the other
ethnic minority newspapers in their coverage of Los Angeles.

Racial and Ethnic Labels

The group labels used in the reporting suggest something about who the
papers consider major actors in the Los Angeles disturbances. The labels
also give us clues about who did what to whom and for what reason. As
Table 8.1 suggests, there are about 12 ethnic/racial labels most commonly
used in Asian American papers. However, because the papers used several
of the terms interchangeably, there are about seven distinct groups actually
referenced. For these papers, the label "Korean" appears most often (in
74.3% of the articles), followed by "Black" (in 72% of the articles).
Although more of the papers used "Korean" rather than "Korean
American," 64.7% of the articles used the latter term at least once. In a similar way, the papers often used "African American" to describe what are
more commonly referred to as Blacks (54.4% of the time).

Much less common were the labels "White" (in 28.7% of the articles), "Asian American" (25.7%), "Asian" (25%), "Latino" (19.1%), "Japanese American" (17.6%), "Latino" (13.2%), and "Chinese/Chinese American" (12.5%). Although they used separate terms, many of the papers referenced some aspect that linked ethnic and racial minorities as one group. In 19.9% of the articles, the coverage referenced "multiethnic," "person of color," "fellow minority," or "red," "yellow," and "brown." Examples of terms appearing infrequently are "Jew/Jewish," "Asian-Pacific American," "Afro-American," and "Indian/Indian American" (see Appendix C, Table 1 for a full listing of the labels used).

Actors and Victims

The coverage depicted many of the groups mentioned earlier as actors and/or victims (see Table 8.2). The articles clearly most commonly viewed both Blacks/African Americans and Koreans/Korean Americans as the primary actors in the drama unfolding in April-May 1992. Coverage depicted Blacks in 48.9% and Korean and Korean Americans in 47.4% of the articles as actors. Following these groups, government (38.5%, including mayors and other officials), the mainstream media (27.4%), and the police (24.4%) appear as significant actors in the events. The coverage mentioned Latinos and Whites in 14.9% of the articles as actors. Also mentioned were social classes (most commonly the wealthy) and Asian Americans, minorities/people of color, capitalists, and the justice system.

In contrast there were basically two victims—only one of which could be considered a primary victim. The coverage viewed Koreans/Korean Americans as victims in 82% of the articles. A distant second were depictions of Blacks as victims in about 29% of the articles. Following these two groups are people of color (in 14.1% of the articles), Asian Americans generally (13.3%), specific Asian American groups (12.6%), Latinos (5.2%), society (5.2%), and Whites (4.4%). Few others appear to any significant degree as victims. (See Appendix C, Tables 2-6 for a detailed breakdown for each paper.)

Conflict and Isolation

The themes most commonly reported by the Asian American press are presented in Table 8.3. Most often conflict (appearing in 89% of the articles) is the center of discussion. This usually manifested in the papers as fear of people involved (55.1% of the articles) and violence of all kinds (72.8%). Cooperation was also a fairly common theme (appearing in 56.6% of articles), mostly about either Asian American groups working with Korean

Table 8.2   Number and Percentage of Articles in Asian American Newspapers Discussing Various Actors and Victims ($n = 135$ articles)

	Actors				Victims			
	Actual		Potential		Actual		Potential	
	#	%	#	%	#	%	#	%
Government	52	38.5%	5	3.7%	7	5.2%	4	3.0%
Society	9	6.7	—	—	7	5.2	—	—
Blacks	66	48.9	5	3.7	39	28.9	2	1.5
Media	37	27.4	—	—	—	—	—	—
Whites	20	14.9	—	—	6	4.4	4	3.0
Asian/Asian Americans	15	11.1	2	1.5	18	13.3	9	6.7
Other Asian/Asian American Groups	9	6.7	—	—	17	12.6	1	*
Korean/ Korean American	64	47.4	3	2.2	119	82.2	11	8.1
Police	33	24.4	5	3.7	—	—	—	—
Judicial System	5	3.7	3	2.2	—	—	—	—
Capitalists	5	3.7	1	*	—	—	—	—
Latinos	20	14.9	1	*	7	5.2	—	—
Jews	11	8.1	—	—	5	3.7	—	—
People of Color/ Minority	16	11.5	2	1.5	19	14.1	2	1.5

Note: * = less than 1%

Americans or interethnic cooperative efforts between Blacks and Korean Americans (the latter topic alone appeared in more than 42% of the articles). A majority of the articles (55.9%) made no mention of race or said race played no role in the disturbances (55.9%), whereas the remaining 44.1% of the articles said race played a primary or secondary role. (See Appendix C, Table 7 for a breakdown of themes for each paper.)

Conflict, the primary thematic emphasis in the Asian American newspapers, ironically sprung from a sense of Asian American groups' alienation from Whites, Blacks, Latinos, and other Asian American groups. This sense of isolation was true particularly for Korean Americans, who also felt ignored by the city's centers of power, especially the government and police.

Table 8.3   Number and Percentage of Articles in Asian American Newspapers Discussing Various Themes (*n* = 135 articles)

	#	%
Pathology	9	6.6
Invasion	9	6.6
Fear	74	55.1
Racism	16	11.8
Culture/Values	20	14.7
Violence		
Verbal	9	6.6
Person	40	29.4
Property	50	36.8
Causes		
Individual	15	11.0
Institutional	25	18.4
Structural	18	13.2
Discontent	35	25.7
Conflict	120	89.0
Cooperation	76	56.6
Pluralism	18	13.2
Assimilation	11	8.1
Attitudes	31	22.7
Minority Intersection	58	42.6
Role of Race		
Primary	35	25.7
Secondary	25	18.4
None	50	36.8
No Mention	26	19.1

Eui-Young Yu, a Korean American sociologist, described the feeling of isolation in an article for the *Los Angeles Times:*

> By Wednesday morning, we knew the mobs would soon reach Koreatown. Desperate calls for help to city authorities were not answered. Koreatown leaders thought they had many friends in City Hall as they gave generously to their campaign coffers. At the time of crisis, no one provided us with police protection. We had to stand alone in times of danger. We felt under siege by police, news media and mobs, and have never felt so betrayed, helpless and lonely. ("We Saw Our Dreams Burned for No Reason," *Los Angeles Times,* May 5, 1992, p. B7)

This sense of isolation helps explain the post-riot emphasis on two questions: "How did we get here?" and "How can we prevent this from occurring again?" Answers to these questions, similar to those posed by President Lyndon B. Johnson when he established the Kerner Commission, focused on political power and involvement. The newspapers emphasized the need to reach and influence the offices of the governor and the mayor, demand and receive timely police protection when needed, and encourage better relations with members of the community, especially other Asian American groups and Blacks. Relations with Latinos did not seem to be a concern.

The sense of abandonment is obvious in an editorial written by the K. W. Lee, editor of the *Korea Times,* and published in the *KoreAm Journal:*

> Across the other ocean we came. We saw. It was our Warsaw. Of all places on earth, we have met our own latter-day pogrom in the City of Los Angeles. After 35 years with mainstream dailies, I have gone through an eerie three-year roller coaster ride in L.A.'s bloody Balkanization. I have come to bear witness to America's first media-instigated urban assault on a hapless tribe of newcomers who have no voice or clout. ("How the Media Endangered Korean Americans," August 1996, p. 13)

Even though the sense of isolation was a dominant underlying context, there was no corresponding sense of hopelessness expressed in the coverage. Much of the conversation in the Asian American papers centered on revealing the impact of the riots in ways that went beyond the general circulation press coverage, which generally ignored the proposition that the riots were not merely about conflict between Blacks and Asian Americans. In fact, the Asian American papers saw a wide variety of actors as both heroes and villains.

Heroes

There were three categories of heroes in the Asian American press coverage of the riots: business owners, advocates of racial solidarity, and non-Asian American Good Samaritans.

Family Business Owners

The first category was the Asian American family business owner. Within this category are two types. One was the merchant who struggled through the classic formula of hard work and personal sacrifice to achieve the "American Dream." Though the riots led some to question whether the dream was still attainable, for most the future was not a question of whether to rebuild, but where to rebuild and continue pursuing their dream. For these merchants, the riots represented only the latest impediment to surmount. The *Korea Times* reprinted one article from the *Wall Street Journal* that epitomized this view. The article titled "How the Kims of LA and other Koreans Made It in the US," with the subtitle "How do Korean Americans do it?" began: "While many businesses have fled the inner city and others have never entered, a new ethnic mercantile class has emerged in little more than a decade." The article featured Byung Kim, a merchant determined to reopen his store. The article links his heroism to his belief in the "American Dream" and his determination to succeed:

> [Kim] achieved success the same way other Koreans have: hard work, financial support from fellow immigrants, free labor from family members and a cultural tradition of pride and self-reliance. The riots merely were an obstacle to overcome. Like other Korean immigrants facing limited opportunities in mainstream U.S. business, Mr. Kim dreamed of being his own boss. . . . And despite being hard hit in the riots, his wife was shot and one store burned, Byung Kim still believes America is the land of opportunity he first saw in 1950 as a Korean army officer. ("How the Kims of LA and other Koreans Made It in the US," *Korea Times*, June 22, 1992, p. 3)

For other merchants, although they planned to reopen their stores, the decision was not so straightforward. For them, dramatic descriptions of the hardships they face enhanced their heroism. An example is a story about the Pack family, who had moved to a predominantly Black area to save money. The story begins,

> Hang Suk Pack had promised Wendy, her 8-year-old daughter, that she could take swimming and piano lessons. But that was before Pack's and her husband's beauty supplies store and market in South Los Angeles were set ablaze. More pressing needs and concerns are occupying Pack and her husband, Nak Jun, these days: How to qualify for an SBA loan; putting food on the table; not getting evicted from their apartment; conquering depression; and finding work so they won't have to receive welfare. ("Dead-end Recovery for Merchant Couple," *Korea Times*, June 15, 1992, p. 1)

Pack felt relatively safe in her predominantly Black neighborhood but after the riots was afraid to go out. Her children's feelings about Blacks were also affected:

They think Black people are bad to us. Especially my four-year-old boy, when he sees Black people, he says "They are the Black people who set your store on fire."("Dead-end Recovery for Merchant Couple," *Korea Times,* June 15, 1992, p. 7)

The second type of family business owner depicted as a hero treated customers well despite the circumstances—operating in depressed areas of the city, susceptible to robbery and assault, and having his store destroyed. For the men (only men were noted) in this group, there is a sad irony: They had their stores set ablaze despite being good to their customers; they are tragic heroes trying to succeed but running up against America's racial dynamics.

This issue is most prominent in depictions of the ways Korean American merchants interacted with their customers. Clearly, it would be reasonable if the merchants were angry with the customers who may have joined in looting their stores. The papers, however, highlighted merchants who were not angry with their patrons. Indeed, many merchants believed the looters were not local residents. One said, "I have no trouble rebuilding. I get along with my customers. I found out the majority of those who burned down my store were from the outside. My customers call me everyday, asking me when I'm going to come back" ("Victim to Social Activism," *Korea Times,* July 6, 1992, p. 8). Other merchants said that the looters might have been local but not likely to be regular customers. An article titled "Not Angry at Blacks" quoted one owner as saying, "My neighbors [are] good people. We had lots of good customers" (*Korea Times,* May 18, 1992, p. 1).

Many of the Asian American merchants said that they have a special rapport with their patrons and held no grudge against their customers. One merchant said that sometimes she "felt her customers were as much family as her children," and as she stood in the vacant lot that had been their store "dozens of former customers stopped by on foot, car and bicycle, chatting and offering consolations." The article ends on this note: "Blacks complain of Koreans who care only about money, never take time to know their neighbors. The Lees broke the stereotype" ("Merchant Leans Toward Leaving Riot Ruins," *Korea Times,* July 27, 1992, p. 3).

Although these were Korean American merchants, the papers recount similar refrains from South Asian American merchants. One suggested that his mostly Black customers "are very good people. I don't blame them for whatever has happened. . . . I never had any problems with my neighbors [who were Black]. They may roam round the restaurant but had never bothered us nor our customers" ("Healing Touch for Riot Victims," *India-West,* May 15, 1992, p. 38). Unlike what may have haunted some of the Korean American merchants, according to *India-West,* race was not a problem for South Asian Americans.

The Indian business owners were unanimous in declaring that the losses of their operations had nothing to do with the racial overtone of the riots. "Absolutely not racial[.]" Mr. Anubhai Patel exclaimed. Mr. Patel asserted this even after his store was "reduced to ashes after mobs set it afire and looted it completely" ("Healing Touch for Riot Victims, 'No Racism,'" *India-West,* May 15, 1992, p. 1).

Another dimension of this type of heroism was that the papers highlighted merchants who regularly invested in the community and their customers. For example, some South Asian American merchants said that they were relatively unhurt because their community led drives for the poor ("Indo-American Pledge to Riot Victims," *India-West,* May 15, 1992, p. 38). Another Asian American merchant said that his efforts to treat his customers well led to 30 Black neighbors trying to help him save his store. This merchant said that he felt a bond—he called it love—with his Black customers, with whom he felt more comfortable than with Whites ("Watts Market Burns," *Korea Times,* May 11, 1992, p. 1).

Perhaps Michael Yoon epitomizes the hero in this category. The *Korea Times* described him as "a classic example of a Korean American businessman who has taken an active role in community affairs in South Los Angeles." The article explains that Yoon

> struggles to explain in English why helping the community is important to him personally. He feels it is important to help those who are less fortunate. Merchants simply have to do it, he said. "People are the same[—]White, Black, Koreans. Blood is the same color. That's why we have to do community work." ("L.A. Slauson Reaches Out Through Ad," June 8, 1992, p. 3)

The *Korea Times* also highlighted a merchant who dedicated himself to his community in a different way. With the outbreak of rioting, Jim Moo Chung stayed behind to protect his swap meet and factory because "many people depended on it for their livelihood." But when his store was attacked, he refused to defend himself because "he didn't want to kill people and worsen tensions between Korean merchants and Black customers" ("Jim Moo Chung's Darkest Night," May 26, 1992, p. 7). Instead, he was wounded in the attack. As he lay bleeding from two gunshot wounds, Mr. Chung

> sounded a conciliatory note as he spoke from his bed at the California Medical Center. . . . "We need to understand the different cultures. It's really difficult, but we must try," he said in Korean. ("Jim Moo Chung's Darkest Night," *Korea Times,* May 26, 1992, p. 1)

Despite "callous treatment by the police and the burning of his business by rioters," Chung insisted that all members of the community should be respected: "Gang members have families too. If I build good relations with families, then I won't have any problems" ("Jim Moo Chung's Darkest Night," *Korea Times,* May 26, 1992, p. 1).

Advocates of Racial/Ethnic Solidarity

The second category of heroes in these newspapers are those who argue for better relations within Korean American communities, between Korean Americans and other Asian Americans, between Korean American merchants and their Black customers (rarely are Latinos mentioned), and between Asian Americans and the political establishment (i.e., government, city council, police). Those advocating collective action faced formidable challenges because they were going down paths of cooperation and community building much more inclusive than ever before attempted in the city. The coverage viewed treading this ground after the riots as a heroic act because of the risk of backlash and cynicism from within and outside Asian American society.

The ultimate sense of isolation for much of the Asian American community, at least as reported in their newspapers, was that they perceived few outsiders as caring about what happened to them. Police and fire trucks went first to other neighborhoods as stores were burned and looted. The general circulation media snubbed their concerns, framing the issues as either a Black–White conflict or emphasizing Blacks' hatred of Asian Americans. Not surprisingly, this feeling of isolation was unsettling and ultimately developed into a clarion call for organizing coalitions to protect their rights. The Asian American press depicted those taking up the call as heroes.

Edward Chang, professor of ethnic studies and women's studies at California Polytechnic at Pomona, suggested the need to organize. He argued in the *Korea Times* that "after two decades of pursuing the American dream in relative isolation, the recent riots and three-day siege of Koreatown have shattered the insularity of the Korean American community and awakened it to the need for building political power." Later he suggests,

Although Korean Americans have begun the rebuilding process, leaders, activists and merchants say they have learned that the community can no longer afford to work solely on building economic strength while ignoring political context. We have no allies in City Hall or Sacramento. Politically, we are on the bottom of society. ("Korean Americans See Need for Political Power," *Korea Times,* May 26, 1992, p. 1)

Some in the Asian American community were already heeding this call to act. In many cases, mobilization for collective action involved a rainbow of Asian American groups. The titles of articles disclose the nature of this support, most often targeting Korean Americans for help: "KAGRO [a national Korean grocers association] Launches Relief for Embattled Merchants" (*KoreAm Journal,* May 1992, p. 1), "Indo-Americans Pledge Assistance to Riot Victims" (*India-West,* May 15, 1992, p. 39), "Asian American Group Organizes Help for Riot Victims" (*Pacific Citizen,* May 15, 1992, p. 1), "KAs [Korean Americans] See Need for Political Power"(*Korea Times,* May 26, 1992, p. 1), and "Riot Flames Ignite Korean American Political Activism" (*Korea Times,* June 15, 1992, p. 1).

Although many argued for assistance and organizing for change, the scope of social change is limited. Typically, the vision of solidarity is multicultural, but the society in which the papers want Asian Americans included is assumed to be Black and White. The vision is one in which Asian Americans will "squeeze" into the creases. There is little or no acknowledgement of Latinos (and none of Native Americans), and these writers apparently concede that a Black–White society is the obvious starting point from which to build multiculturalism.

Non-Asian American Good Samaritans

The coverage rarely mentioned the third category of heroes, which involved non-Asian American community members. These were people who showed selfless sacrifice in that they put themselves in harm's way to help Asian Americans. In the overall context of isolation and abandonment conveyed as the underlying theme of the coverage, the fact that non-Asian Americans came to the rescue of Asian Americans makes the individuals especially heroic. One article described how a Japanese American was saved from death by concerned citizens, among whom were four Good Samaritans honored for their heroism ("2 Asian Americans Killed," *Pacific Citizen,* May 15, 1992, p. 2). Following are the details of the rescue efforts:

Only hours after a jury in Simi Valley acquitted four Los Angeles police officers . . . a jeering mob stopped a Japanese American motorist at a street intersection, smashed the windows of his Bronco truck, and attempted to beat him to death. The victim had been mistaken for Korean. Black actor Gregory Allen Williams risked his own life and carried the man to safety. ("The Los Angeles Riots: An Asian American Perspective," *Asian Week,* May 8, 1992, p. 14)

Other examples of this type include the following:

Sim [a Korean shop owner] said he stood guard round the clock for five days with a friend and a Black neighborhood resident. ("Merchant Struggles to Rebuild," *Korea Times,* July 13, 1992, p. 3)

Charles Lloyd [who is Black] was honored because he "displayed his commitment in the field of law and justice by defending Korean American grocer Soon Ja Du while receiving over 100 threats from the African American community" ("Du Lawyer Honored by Christians," *Korea Times,* June 29, 1992, p. 2).

Scenes of Blacks helping Korean shop owners clean up fire-gutted stores and reports of a Latino guard killed trying to protect a Korean business from looters gives evidence that hope and humanity is not lost in South Central. ("Healing Wounds Includes Emerging From Isolation," *AsianWeek,* June 5, 1992, p. 2).

The passage including the Latino security guard is one of the few mentions of Latinos in the Asian American press coverage. Other articles in the Asian American press mentioned Good Samaritan awards given to Blacks who saved Reginald Denny from possible death.

Villains

There were several villains in the news coverage. The rioters are the most obvious. The coverage often used this term synonymously with Blacks, but just as often without a specific racial referent. Coverage also commonly depicted police and government (including politicians and government officials) as villains in reference to their failure to assist Asian Americans during and after the rebellion. Finally, the papers often pointed to general circulation media as exacerbating the pre-riot tensions between Blacks and Korean Americans and as directly liable for the riots. Although not often directly depicted as villains, the papers implicated Whites in the discussion about the general circulation media.

Rioters

The most commonly mentioned villains were the rioters. The coverage usually referred to them generically as looters rather than by a specific ethnic or racial label. But often, stereotypes and language use clearly implicated Blacks as the perpetrators. All the Asian American papers, but especially the Korean American papers, made clear that members of all ethnic groups were engaged in the rioting and looting. *KoreAm Journal* argued that "most importantly, people of all races, not just African Americans linked only by poverty and disregard for the law, were engaged in the looting and burning" ("Media Bias Aggravated Riot Damage," June 7, 1992, p. 7). Earlier, the same paper suggested that the "White" verdict lead to senseless violence and self-destruction among groups of color ("After the L.A. Riot: Time to Deliver," *KoreAm Journal,* May 1992, p. 3).

One way the papers magnified the villainy of the looters was through depictions of what appeared to be organized violence. *India-West* suggested that Indian businesses were affected not because of their ethnicity, "but because the rampaging looters were on a destructive spree, unwilling to spare anything." In fact, the newspaper asserted, "It was a premeditated hit," an organized effort to vent vengeance ("Healing Touch for Riot Victims, 'No Racism,'" May 15, 1992, p. 1). Others suggested that it was more specifically hostility toward anyone who was not Black:

> A local resident, demanded that Vic Lee [a television newsperson] interview him. The reporter recalled, "This big Black guy said, 'I don't care if they're Koreans, if they're Japs, Arabs or Jews. I'm going to kill them if they come into my neighborhood! They're taking businesses that we ought to be running.'" Lee paused, "This guy was pretty scary. He was looking me down! I thought he was going to pull a gun and kill me." ("The Los Angeles Riots: An Asian American Perspective," *AsianWeek,* May 8, 1992, p. 14)

This passage not only suggests that Blacks are out to harm all non-Blacks, it also perpetuates stereotypes by including references to a "big Black guy" who is "scary" and might "pull a gun." Violence, and this level of hostility, might appear to be the natural tendency of Black males, according to this construction of the event.

In an editorial, the publisher of *KoreAm Journal* also emphasized the rioters' callousness. He wrote that the disorder was "violent destruction and senseless looting," even though it was "sad to see minority ethnic groups destroy themselves" ("From the Publisher's Desk: After the L.A. Riot: Time to Deliver," May 1, 1992, p. 3). Even as he engages in a bit of hyperbole (is there nonviolent destruction of property or sensible looting?), the writer helps construct the image of the out-of-control looter. Not only that, he racialized the idea of "looter" as members of "minority ethnic groups," even though Whites also participated in the looting, something his own paper mentioned on several occasions.

The Asian American press rarely mentioned Latinos as villains in the riot and, in fact, rarely mentioned them in the coverage. But there were at least two accounts of Latino participation in the riots, again reinforcing the villainy of the rioters. One paper reported, "Some people drove by and shot several times through the door. Then a mob of mostly Hispanic people bashed through the door and started taking things" ("Burning Koreatown," *KoreAm Journal*, May 1, 1992, p. 4). Later, in the same article, the story reported that "many Hispanic looters said 'everyone is doing it, so it must be O.K.,' in a perverted form of Korean Americans' categorical imperative philosophy, which argues that if an action could be universalized to generate a common good, then it is acceptable."

Korea Times also published a letter from a reader that was critical of "leftist rhetoric." The letter allowed the newspaper to inject a critique of Black rioters into the public debate without itself having to do the criticizing. The writer asserted that most observers on the left played down the

> most vicious racist rioting in California in over 100 years since the Chinatown riots of San Francisco. The Black community has never been attacked by mobs of White people in California the way Koreatown was deliberately ransacked. ("Polemic Against 'Leftist' Rhetoric: The Second Looting of Koreatown," May 26, 1992, p. 6)

Perhaps to fend off accusations of bias against Blacks, one article quoted J. Paul Brownridge, an African American city treasurer of Los Angeles, who wrote about Black rioters:

> In a nutshell, the failure to recognize the self as a source of problems imprisons people in their own illusions. No theology, whether Black or Calvinist, can allow someone to assume "I am God's elect, therefore, I can do no wrong." ("My Black Fellow Clergy: Isn't It Time for Introspection?" *KoreAm Journal*, June 1992, p. 6)

By including a perspective critical of Blacks from a prominent Black leader, the newspaper can inoculate itself from criticism that it published only the views of non-Blacks who were critical of the Black community.

The Asian American press also reported some moderate opinions. Michael Yamaki, L.A. Police Commissioner, cautioned that the rioters and looters were a "criminal" element:

> It's up to the leadership here to make it clear to the African American community that this is not a race issue. Unfortunately, I've heard a lot of rumors and been able to see unfortunate things that are happening to Korean merchants, and it's clear to me that the people who are doing this are basically criminals. It's not the leadership of the African American community. I've seen them respond very well to the Asian American community. . . . They

understand this is not a race issue. However criminals in the community are using this as an opportunity. ("APA Leaders Support Retrial of Officers Who Beat Rodney King," *AsianWeek,* May 8, 1992, p. 11)

Local Politicians

The second group portrayed as villains in these papers is local politicians. The argument in some Asian American papers was that, given conditions in South Central, the riots were inevitable. As such, the authorities should have been better prepared to protect the Korean American community and its property. Because the police and city failed to shield them, the newspapers argued that Asian Americans, and Korean Americans particularly, are owed damages for the destruction of their homes and stores.

A common theme in the papers was that politicians were derelict in their duties. *India-West* quoted a UCLA student, Nirlip Syan, who observed, "For too long the politicians, the White community, have been ignoring the plight of the inner city. So it was very understandable to us how it could happen and why it did happen" ("LA Riots Destroy Indian Shops," May 8, 1992, p. 23). Another theme was the lack of response from political institutions, including the mayor and the police. The *Pacific Citizen,* among several papers, noted that government officials failed to consult Asian Americans after the riots. "The President met May 1 with leaders from the African American and Hispanic American communities to seek their advice in the aftermath of the verdict. No Asian American individual or group was invited" ("Where Do We Go From Here? Asian Americans Take Steps, Say What Needs to Be Done After L.A. Riots," May 8, 1992, p. 1).

Several lawsuits were filed after the riots claiming the city was ultimately responsible for what happened by its neglect. Jun Ho Lee, general secretary of the Coalition of Asian Americans, filed suit "for financial and emotional damages that Korean American and other merchants suffered because of the riots. 'The city is responsible for this riot. They let it happen on purpose. We are going to have to prove it'" ("Victim to Social Activism," *Korea Times,* July 6, 1992, p. 1).

Human-rights lawyer and activist Angela Oh wrote,

We all were bewildered by the abandonment by our city officials and law enforcement agencies in the midst of a community crisis. Had we not been faithful supporters of our local politicians and police force? Had we not contributed significant amounts of money (and time) to show our faith and appreciation? Had we done something wrong to cause our city protectors to ignore us in our hour of need? ("Shaping the Political Agenda," *KoreAm Journal,* June 5, 1992, p. 1)

But others also pointed out that the neglect by politicians was nothing new, and it only indirectly related to Korean Americans. Jin Ho Lee, spokesman for the Korean American Victims Alliance, stated, "I don't hate the looters, arsonists or people involved in the riot. I'm more angry with the government and the media. These problems existed during the last three decades" ("Victim to Social Activism," *Korea Times,* July 6, 1992, p. 7).

General Circulation Mass Media

Depicted in some cases as the main catalyst of the riots, the general circulation media contributed to the general public understanding of Black–Korean American relations: by suggesting Korean Americans were anti-Black and in support of the verdict exonerating the four LAPD officers in the beating of Rodney King. The general circulation press, claimed the Asian American press, focused narrowly on racial conflict and failed to provide a broad range of perspectives, which helped to instigate the open conflict that ensued.

These papers saw the general circulation media as focusing on racial prejudice and personal issues and not economic factors and structures of oppression, issues going beyond the immediate context. For example, the Asian American newspapers attacked the general circulation press's coverage as misrepresenting the connection between Blacks and Asian Americans, and these portrayals exacerbated the troubles between the groups and distorted how those outside the community viewed the conflict. Indeed, much of the Asian American press suggested that the problem lay elsewhere. The *KoreAm Journal* described this media as speaking "to the public of this incredible tension between Korean Americans and Black Americans, as if it were the cause of the rioting, avoiding the real problem of racial injustice that has existed between Blacks and Whites for hundreds of years" ("The Riot of Greed," May 1992, p. 8).

Several Asian American organizations complained of media coverage that "resulted in inadequate attention to the verdict and community responses to that verdict." Other Asian American groups complained that

images of Korean Americans as gun-toting vigilantes and African Americans as vandals and looters dominated the media. In addition to exacerbating Asian-Black tensions, this characterization trivializes complex social and economic problems in favor of stereotypes of opportunistic vigilantes and looters. ("Bay Leaders Speak Out Against Verdict, Press," *AsianWeek,* June 5, 1992, p. 25)

AsianWeek also reported on a forum of journalists and community leaders that assessed the role of the media during the riots. "There was a general consensus that the mainstream media had failed to cover the rebellion accurately." Brenda Sunoo, former editor at the *Korea Times,* suggested that "the [mainstream] TV and press took a string, which was the inter-ethnic tension between Koreans and Blacks . . . and made it a real peg for exploitation for the riots. [I]t was secondary to all the economic conditions and political and social problems that were causing the initial revolt" ("Media Blamed Once Again for Bad Reporting During the L.A. Riots," June 26, 1992, p. 11).

Police

Although rarely mentioned, the Asian American press did not consider the police their friends. In an interview with Ton Soo Chung, founder of the Korean-American Coalition, a "group that included among its initial goals the fostering of understanding between the generations in the Korean American community," asserted that the LAPD treated Korean Americans "pretty shabbily . . . even before the riot." He went on to suggest that they were unsympathetic to Korean Americans and that many who live in Koreatown have felt that they have not gotten adequate police protection. He continued,

> But during the riots it reached gigantic proportions. I think it will be a number of years before we can create a feeling of trust toward the police. Many have come to a conclusion . . . that they have to protect themselves. And that's a sad situation, because that is one function that government is supposed to undertake." ("Seeking to Coalesce the Korean American Community," *Korea Times,* June 8, 1992, p. 6)

In the same vein, *AsianWeek* cited an excerpt of a statement from representatives of 23 community, health, and political organizations: "The police non-response to the initial outbreak may represent a conscious sacrifice of South Central Los Angeles and Koreatown, inhabited largely by African American, Latino and Korean Americans to ensure the safety of more affluent White communities" ("Bay Leaders Speak Out Against Verdict, Press," June 5, 1992, p. 25).

Causes of the Conflict

The source of the strife was once again a frequently mentioned topic. As with the treatment in other newspapers and in other cities, we can classify into three categories the Asian American coverage explaining why the riots happened: individual, institutional, and structural.

Individual-level Causes

The publisher of the *KoreAm Journal* cited one of the individual-level causes of the riots in an editorial. He blamed members of the nearly all-White jury who found four LAPD officers not guilty of excessive force in the beating of Rodney King. He wrote, "The Rodney King verdict . . . made Afro-Americans, Latino-Americans and Korean Americans in the LA area complete losers" ("From the Publisher's Desk: After the L.A. Riots: Time to Deliver," May 1, 1992, p. 3).

Another article singles out individuals, who could have been anyone, who seem possessed: "People, like animals in a feeding frenzy, mindlessly trashing about. They were your neighbors, maybe even your friends" ("Burning Koreatown," *KoreAm Journal*, May 1, 1992, p. 4). Other articles suggested that the looters simply were interested in destruction and revenge and had little concern for how their actions affected others. Reporting on an angry rally, one story reported the actions of some of the participants:

> It became painfully clear that some segment of the widening crowd were there for more than a rally. Small factions led by rambunctious and lawless individuals bent on destruction marched toward the commercial center. Storefront windows and parked automobiles were shattered along the "parade route," as violence became the order of the day. Looting and pillaging ensued. Public transportation came to a screeching halt as a war zone enveloped Market [Street]. Whether or not looters had visions of Steven Biko, Nelson Mandela, Martin Luther King Jr., Malcolm X or Rodney King dancing in their heads didn't seem to matter, all some wanted were a pair of Air Jordans or a new Radio Shack CD player. Rodney King seemed like a distant memory once the looting began. Some felt like venting their frustrations against the recession and stagnating economy by taking what they believed was theirs. Others simply wanted to "Off the pigs!" ("The City Riots Over King Case, Providing Fuel to Racial Tensions," *AsianWeek*, May 8, 1992, p. 1)

The passage is remarkable in the ways that it creates an image of the protestors as Black without ever referring to race. First, the point is made that these were "lawless individuals bent on destruction," linking the individuals to deep cultural stereotypes of Blacks. Their aim was to destroy a specific kind of property, the "commercial center," not residential or public property, so they could get Air Jordans and CD players, stereotypical markers of Black urban life revolving around athletics and music. The writer gives no political meaning to the actions. In fact, the suggestion that the symbols of Black activist politics Biko, Mandela, King, and Malcolm X were insecurely anchored in the motives of the protestors completely obliterated the potential political significance of their actions.

Similarly, *AsianWeek* depicted the young as particularly destructive, led not by ideology but by greed. Blacks were depicted as purposefully conflating the political act of "taking back the city" with "taking merchandise." Blacks have "nothing to be happy about today," but they were "glad that LA is in flames." Frustrated by years of oppression and lack of opportunities for upward mobility, for many young Blacks, taking back the city actually meant taking merchandise ("City Riots Over King," May 8, 1992, p. 1).

Some Asian American papers took Black leaders to task for a lack of leadership, which helped create a culture of defensiveness that blamed the "establishment":

> One conspicuous development of Black churches has been the increasing inability to be self-critical. Much like the Fundamentalists who blame all America's problems on secular humanists, Black churches have become the mouthpiece of the Black underclass, which tends to construe any criticism directed at them as being racially motivated. It is time to stop blaming the establishment as the primary course of attack against "systematic oppression." ("My Black Fellow Clergy: Isn't It Time for Introspection?" *KoreAm Journal*, June 1992, p. 6)

AsianWeek criticized two Black politicians running for office as endorsing racial stereotypes directed at Asian Americans. The paper quoted Marcia Choo, program director of Asian Pacific American Dispute Resolution:

> I am disappointed with the African American leadership. In the midst of the L.A. riots, [these politicians] inferred that Korean Americans receive free money and greater government support. These so-called African American leaders pandered to the emotionalism of the Korean-Black racial tension. ("L.A. Supervisorial Runoff Sparks Controversy," June 19, 1992, p. 1)

Here the article levels its criticism not only at these two politicians, as it perhaps should, but instead it lays blame on "African American leadership."

One writer in the *KoreAm Journal*, with a reference to the Japanese American internment experience, makes a similar point about inadequate leadership:

Not since the end of WWII, has a minority's minority—voiceless and powerless—been singled out for destruction by a politically powerful, but economically frustrated minority. Another LA pattern is emerging: Racism has come to wear a different garb called nativism, with an anti-foreigner, anti-immigrant undercurrent. Ironically, it is a growing number of African American leaders—politicians, preachers and activists—who voice this new form of racism in symbiotic alliance with the guilt-ridden White media. Why blame the American culture and not those who did the damage? ("Polemic Against 'Leftist' Rhetoric: The Second Looting of Koreatown," May 1992, p. 6)

In contrast, others blamed Asian American communities for causing the riot. A writer in *AsianWeek* said that Asian Americans have a tendency to place themselves above others. The writer quoted Lloyd LaCuesta [KTVU newsperson], who noted,

Some Asian groups think of themselves as "the Better Race" or "above other groups of Americans." That kind of attitude will continue to create divisions in this country, until they start realizing we're all people; we are all trying to make a living; and we're all trying to improve this country." ("The Los Angeles Riots: An Asian American Perspective," *AsianWeek*, May 8, 1992, p. 14)

Finally, the papers also at times singled out Korean American merchants themselves, the primary victims of the burning and looting, for their role in causing the riots. In *AsianWeek*, a business owner in South Central commented on Korean American racism toward blacks:

Koreans come with the perception of Black and White. White is good[.] Black is no good. We have someone who perceives that all Blacks are thieves, which is untrue. A very small minority of any group, African Americans and any other groups, are really thieves. But the same person, who is calling the African Americans thieves, will pay under the table for a case of merchandise so he can get more money. What's the difference in thievery? Both people are trying to make it. [But in the Korean merchant's mind,] "my" taking is ok because I'm servicing a debt. "His" taking is not ok because he's taking from me. ("Korean and Black Symposium Raises Tough Issues & Questions," June 5, 1992, p. 12)

Some observers claimed Korean American merchants should be faulted for the products they sold in their markets. For example, a South Central tenant was especially angry at Korean American merchants for selling alcohol in his area ("My Black Fellow Clergy: Isn't It Time for Introspection?" *KoreAm Journal*, June 1992, p. 6).

Institutional-level Causes

A second set of causes for the riots was institutional. Primary among these causes was the general circulation news media. The *KoreAm Journal* noted that

> if the media had played its role of reporting the news responsibly, most of the damage done would have been structural, something that some government generosity and community solidarity could have repaired. [I]nstead, the media inflamed racial tensions between the African- and Korean American communities, and aggravated what could have been minor wounds that the riots inflicted on both. [There is] no excuse for having every outrageous statement made by an African- or Korean American make its way to the TV screen or the front pages, for having every incident involving people of different races portrayed as a skirmish in a race war. ("Media Bias Aggravated Riot Damage," *KoreAm Journal,* June 1992, p. 7)

By focusing on tensions between Blacks and Asian Americans, the general circulation media missed other kinds of ethnic relations. But more important, they ignored other contexts altogether, frames that could suggest alternative versions of the Los Angeles disturbances. Indeed, as many of the Asian American papers asserted, there was much more amity and potential goodwill than was appreciated by general circulation news media. The Asian American papers suggested that two main factors were typically absent from the general circulation press coverage.

One was discussion of factors providing the context that could explain why Blacks were frustrated and why the community exploded in rage after the King verdict. The "root causes are many. Racism, economic classism, greed, militarism, sexism [and] a 'we versus they' mentality" ("A Message to the People of the United Methodist Church," *KoreAm Journal,* June 1992, p. 5). One writer claimed,

> [Black] anger and rage was primarily directed at the institutionalized, White racism of the legal system and [was] a "wake-up" call to America that poverty and injustice were no longer tolerated. Interethnic tensions played a role, but it was not the cause of the riots. ("From Third-Generation Eyes: Crenshaw, Still My Home," *Korea Times,* May 26, 1992, p. 4)

Another paper noted, "African Americans have been direly exploited in this country: two centuries of slavery, another one with Jim Crow standing by and three decades of deterioration have landed patches of the third world scattered throughout the nation's urban centers" ("Work Forum:

Advocates Communication, Cooperation," *KoreAm Journal,* June 1992, p. 11). "The heart of the matter is," asserted another *KoreAm Journal* article, "the failure of the media along with the government to address the real issue of social-economic inequalities and racial injustice prevalent in our society" ("Can People of Color Obtain Justice?" June 1992, p. 20).

The second issue typically missing from general circulation news media coverage, the Asian American papers asserted, was a discussion of factors that would encourage Blacks and Asian Americans to see their common experience. For example, Stewart Kwoh, executive director of the Asian Pacific American Legal Center of Southern California, said,

> [There was] collective outrage at the unjust, not-guilty verdict. Justice for Rodney King is an Asian American issue. It is not just an issue affecting African Americans. We believe that some people in the press are trying to pit Koreans against Blacks. We don't want any of our communities to fall into scapegoating any particular ethnic group. We know that African Americans, Korean Americans, and other Asians are victims of this tragedy. ("APA Leaders Support Retrial of Officers Who Beat Rodney King," *AsianWeek,* May 8, 1992, p. 11)

Bong Hwan Kim, executive director of the Korean Youth Center, described the tension [between Blacks and Koreans] as "nothing more than a predominant symptom of a larger Black-White problem. The interests of the power structure in America are best served by minority groups being divided, fighting each other for the crumbs" ("KAGRO Launches Relief for Embattled Merchants," *Korea Times,* May 26, 1992, p. 8). The same theme appears in the *Korea Times.* The writer suggests that both their past and futures intertwine:

> The Korean merchants cannot rise by themselves. They cannot rebuild their shops without rebuilding the Black community. When the merchants rebuild by themselves, there is more danger. You have to rise together. ("KAGRO Leaders Meet Bloods, Crips," *Korea Times,* June 1, 1992, p. 8)

Still others mentioned a history of oppression shared by Blacks and Koreans. For example, at a meeting of the Asian Law Caucus honoring Supreme Court Justice Thurgood Marshall, the keynote speaker Ben Chavis said,

> Asian Americans and African Americans have the same interests. We've been historically victimized by the system that instituted racial discrimination and injustice. ("Asian Law Caucus Celebrates Its Birthday," *AsianWeek,* June 12, 1992, p. 10)

The lack of discussion around the two factors described earlier was ultimately, many of the Asian American papers stressed, the reason why Blacks were misdirected in targeting Asian Americans. In that sense, too, the general circulation newspapers contributed to causing the riots.

Another institutional-level cause for the rebellion cited in the Asian American press is the government. As the *KoreAm Journal* noted, despite the millions in damages and "the loss of two Korean American lives, the greatest tragedy may have been the neglect of and lack of response from those charged with responsibility, the police, government and media" ("A Plan to 'Rebuild' the Korean American Community," June 1992, p. 4). The same paper also observed that, at a meeting of community leaders, they protested the "lack of police response, [and] the desertion of the community by some politicians" ("Community Leaders Coordinate Rebuilding Effort," June 1992, p. 9).

The *Korea Times* also quoted another merchant to that effect: "I just blame the government. They should have protected the community. They were slow and irresponsible. Poverty is up in this country. Because many Hispanics and Blacks are poor they blamed their poor economic state on Koreans." In July, the *Korea Times* quoted a Korean American grocer, whose store was a casualty of the riots: "The city is responsible for this riot. They let it happen on purpose" ("Victim to Social Activist," July 6, 1992, p. 1).

Structural-level Causes

At the structural level, the Asian American press discussed poverty, class conflict, and institutional and societal racism as root causes of the riots. One article begins, "They [Blacks] have been economically depressed for so long" and offers the following analysis:

> The root causes of the violent outrage are poverty, racism, alienation and neglect by the political and economic system controlled by the White power elite. The sometimes violent squabbling between African Americans, Korean and other ethnic minorities are an ugly by-product of insensitive and racist policies created largely by White politicians. African American leaders should stop scapegoating Korean Americans and concentrate their rage at the correct target. ("Don't Blame Koreans for Chaos," *Korea Times,* July 6, 1992, p. 6)

Aside from this structural-level analysis, another notable feature of this quote is the explicit reference to White power, politics, and privilege, themes less prevalent in the general circulation newspapers.

A related structural-level explanation for the riots offered by the Asian American press were references to deep divisions between the haves and have-nots, creating a growing underclass with few job and educational options. For example, the *Korea Times* noted in a statement from a Korean grocers' association that "the real issue is pervasive racism and poverty," not a Black–Korean American rift ("National KAGRO's Statement on the Recent Riots in Los Angeles," June 1, 1992, p. 3). A *KoreAm Journal* article mentions the role of White privilege as a cause of race-based class inequities. The article quoted Jung Min Choi, a member of the Korean American Alumni Association of the University of California, Berkeley, who noted that

> the processes that maintain dominant control of Whites over non-Whites are built into the major institutions. These institutions . . . either exclude or restrict the full participation of minorities by rules, laws and/or popular convention.

This problem, the author argued, is not "a figment of a demented imagination, but is central to the economics, politics and culture of this country" ("The L.A. Story: The Product of Institutional Racism," *KoreAm Journal,* July 1992, p. 27).

In getting reactions to the verdict from a cross-section of Asian American leaders, this community's press illustrated similar opinions from a variety of sources. For example, one paper noted that the actions of rioters represented "not the evils of looting but racism, poverty and despair, which were the catalysts for the rebellion" ("Amnesty Urged for All," *Korea Times,* May 15, 1992, p. 1). In another article, Jim Tokeshi, regional director of the Japanese American Citizens League, said that neglect of inner-city communities and "institutional racism, economic and inequitable neglect of a lot of disenfranchised people" were issues that prompted the riots. "It was not so much a race issue. It is fundamentally how economically deprived some communities in L.A. are. The problems are about education, crime, jobs. . . . There are so [many] inadequacies and inequities. The constant neglect of the inner-city community is the problem" ("City Riots Over King," *AsianWeek,* May 8, 1992, p. 1).

Other Causes

One commentary indicated that the cause of the riots was broader than individual, institutional, or structural. A writer in the *KoreAm Journal* suggested that the cause of the disturbances lay in American cultural trends, and all of America was thus responsible:

Should they [the looters] be punished? No. We are all responsible. What happened was not about Rodney King or Soon Ja Du. Some who partook in the looting may not even be aware of who King or Du are or what incidents sparked the whole thing. . . . Our failure to educate our children, our gravitation toward materialism, our inability to correct problems before they arise, and our general short-sightedness all contributed to this uncontrollable eruption of rage, frustration and revenge. ("Burning Koreatown," *KoreAm Journal,* May 1992, p. 5)

Here, in pointing to American culture as a source of the problems, the writer also reveals a desire to be a part of America. By using pronouns such as "we" and "our" in the context of national cultural trends, the writer injects himself and by extrapolation, Asian Americans, into the American society.

Implications of the Conflict

The coverage mainly framed the consequences of the rioting and disturbances in the context of solutions proposed to avoid similar situations in the future. To avoid riots in the future, the Asian American press contemplated three solutions. First, Korean Americans must commit themselves to rebuild their properties and the communities in which they did business. The second proposal was that merchants work more closely with the Black community to help foster better relationships with customers and other people of color to create a united effort to protect their rights. Third, the papers suggested placing greater emphasis on organizing Korean American communities (with cooperation from other Asian Americans as well) to enhance political power.

As part of continuing to strive for the "American Dream," the papers made note of Korean Americans who did not merely rebuild, but who transformed themselves. One article highlighted a story about the Slauson Swapmeet, a local discount goods store. After surviving the "fury of the recent riots," the writer said its managers "knew they could not go back to business as usual." Even with its already well-known "support of youth programs and neighborhood projects," the store owners felt an obligation to place a full-page ad in the Black-owned *Los Angeles Sentinel* proclaiming their desire to remain in the community. In part, the ad read: "Now, the fiery torch of rebellion has touched us all. And only the building of a true brotherhood will cool the flames. Our intentions are not to pacify, but to ratify our community commitment" ("L.A. Slauson Reaches out Through Ad," *Korea Times,* June 8, 1992, p. 3).

Rebuilding would require a renewed effort to build bridges. In making a case for renewed collaboration between Blacks and Asian Americans, many of the papers pointed out that the communities had shared a long history of mutual support well before the riots ("Black-Korean Alliance May Chart New Mission," *Korea Times,* June 15, 1992, p. 1; "Asian American Leaders Blame Economy, Lack of Leadership for Violence After King Verdict," *AsianWeek,* May 8, 1992, p. 1; "APA Leaders Support Retrial of Officers Who Beat Rodney King," *AsianWeek,* May 8, 1992, p. 11). Asian American observers hoped that the riots would lead to other sites of increased solidarity (e.g., "The City Riots Over King Case, Providing Fuel to Racial Tensions," *AsianWeek,* May 8, 1992, p.1; "Korean-Black Conflict in L.A.: An Inner City Problem, Not a Racial Thing," *Korea Times,* May 26, 1992, p. 6; "Work Forum: Advocates Communication, Cooperation," *KoreAm Journal,* June 1992, p. 11). Right after the riots, the *Korea Times* reported efforts of Korean Americans to join with Blacks, Latinos, and other Asian Americans to brainstorm about ways that their communities could work together ("Korean and Black Symposium Raises Tough Issues & Questions," *AsianWeek,* June 5, 1992, p. 12). However, some Asian American organizations (e.g., the Asian Law Caucus) planned to be more cautious: "To find true justice, the ALC was still awaiting word from both Korean and African American sectors before going forward with a concrete plan" ("The City Riots Over King Case, Providing Fuel to Racial Tensions," *AsianWeek,* May 8, 1992, p. 1). Stories of this kind helped counteract the White newspapers' tendencies to stress a seemingly universal hostility between Blacks and Asian Americans.

Perhaps the most common solution to the problems leading to what transpired for Asian Americans during and after the riots was to enhance efforts at intra- and inter-Asian American political and community organization. For example, the writer of a *Korea Times* article argued that

> after two decades of pursuing the American dream in relative isolation, the recent riots and three day siege of Koreatown have shattered the insularity of the Korean American community and awakened it to the need for building political power. Although Korean Americans have begun the rebuilding process, leaders, activists and merchants say they have learned that the community can no longer afford to work solely on building economic strength while ignoring political context. ("Korean Americans See Need for Political Power," May 26, 1992, p. 1)

Among Asian Americans, it was not only Korean Americans who advocated political organization. Leaders of the South Asian American community expressed similar views. For example, *AsianWeek* published the views of Rajen Anand, chairman of the Asian and Pacific American Caucus of the California Democratic Party, who predicted that "the need for national representation and political empowerment should bring Asian Americans together" ("Can APAs Find Common Ground?" May 15, 1992, p. 1).

Some articles provided quite specific prescriptions about how to gain political power. A representative article on this point is from the *Korea Times*:

> "The key to gaining power . . . lies in the immigrant community's ability to integrate with the larger society, overcome generational rifts and forge coalitions. I'd like to see an umbrella organization emerge from this crisis, something like the Jewish Federation Council," said T. S. Chung, a Korean American lawyer who lost a recent bid for a state Assembly seat. . . . Chung, 36, represents an emerging professional class of young, increasingly assertive Korean Americans whose Western ideals and values are in contrast to the dominant first-generation Koreans. ("KAs See Need for Political Power," May 26, 1992, p. 1)

This passage reveals a number of issues related to Asian American political aspirations. One is that the vanguard of Asian immigrants, those who came as adults and remained culturally rooted in their home countries, may be unable to lead the political efforts. The article suggests not only that the "young, increasingly assertive" Asian Americans must lead, but that they must have "Western ideals and values." Clearly, the article suggests that a necessary (but not sufficient) ingredient of political power is a certain type of assimilation based on acceptance of "Western" (or "American") values.

The articles proposing political organizing as a solution focused on two additional and interrelated aspects of the issue. The first was a discussion of how other ethnic minorities had organized, and the second was whether those strategies would work for Asian Americans. *AsianWeek* ("Can APAs Find Common Ground?" May 15, 1992, p. 1) reported a debate about whether it was reasonable to expect Asian American political unity. The article first observed that Jews, Blacks, and Mexicans have organizations that "have enough clout to give their communities a strong voice in government policy" and that no national organization representing Asian Americans existed with the "same weight held by such organizations as the Urban League and the NAACP." Participants disagreed about the feasibility of organizing a broad-based Asian American political organization. Henry Der, from Chinese Affirmative Action, argued that "too many differences exist for all Asian Americans to come up with a common agenda. It's not reasonable to expect a first generation Chinese immigrant to have full dialogue with a Korean immigrant. As Asian immigrants these people have to feel they are part of the solution[, but] to formulate one common agenda that would fit all is not realistic."

In contrast, Joy Morimoto, of the Japanese American Citizens League (JACL), commented that the violent aftermath showed that "anti-Asian violence is not just a Korean issue or a Japanese issue. History has shown time and time again that Asians have been mistaken for other Asians. . . . The whole area of civil rights in general is something all Asians have in common." Others noted that increased anti-Asian American hate crimes, "national origin discrimination," and the extension of voting rights and bilingual ballots affect all Asian Americans and give them a common agenda ("Can APAs Find Common Ground?" *AsianWeek*, May 15, 1992, p. 1).

Summary and Discussion

According to the Asian American press, the riots were ultimately about how one group, mainly Korean Americans, got caught up in a conflict between two others, Blacks and Whites. The verdict frustrated Blacks because they have encountered generations of discrimination and have been locked out of economic opportunities. This frustration was the result of discrimination and neglect by government and other institutions, which Blacks and other minorities equated with White privilege. Thus, Blacks were angry at Whites, but because they could not get to them, they attacked the group most accessible to them—Asian Americans and especially Korean Americans. To some degree, the Asian American press saw the Blacks' feelings as justified but misdirected.

Much of the Asian American community seemed to be surprised to be the focus of Black rage. As the press coverage made clear, much of the context of the discussion among the Asian American papers related to the sense of isolation experienced by Korean Americans from other Asian Americans and people of color, the larger community in which they worked, and the sites of community power, including city hall, police, and banks. They were indeed surprised to find that they were not considered part of the larger (White) community. This sense of isolation helps explain the journalistic emphasis on the underlying disappointment and shock regarding the depth of rage Blacks felt toward Korean American merchants as well as the sobering realization that they needed to become politically active to prevent similar incidents in the future.

The solutions proposed, it could be argued, suggest that the Asian American press promoted the idea that Asian American communities ought to move toward becoming part of middle class White America, following a classic assimilation scenario. Although there is criticism of neglect and discrimination by government policy and governmental representatives, there is relatively little critique of American institutions or values. Instead, proposed solutions for change focus on fine-tuning these institutions through political pressure so that Asian Americans can accrue benefit from "the system" just as others (i.e., Whites and the wealthy) already do. That there is no explicit critical discussion of connections between race and nation perhaps relates to this underlying desire for assimilation.

Although the coverage of the Asian American press was extensive and incorporated many more viewpoints than did the other presses, it also was limited in one important aspect of the riot coverage: It paid scant attention to the role of Latinos, mirroring the general circulation press coverage. This pattern suggests, as with the other ethnic newspapers, that the papers understand the dominant racial configuration as Black–White; other racial minorities struggle to insert themselves into the dichotomous mix, ignoring the plight of other non-Black minorities.

9

Conclusions

I n Chapter 1, we described Omi and Winant's theory of racial formation and how it helps us understand the role of news in constructing inter-ethnic conflict. We argued that the press should be seen as racial projects that mediate between cultural representations of race and the social structures that influence how races will be organized, monitored, and controlled. Because they operate as racial projects, we expected the general circulation press to produce news that reinforces the prevailing hegemonic ideology of White privilege. Conversely, we expected ethnic minority newspapers, even as the prevailing racial hegemony circumscribes their practices, to reveal ideologies that challenge notions of White privilege and promote alternative worldviews. Despite these expected differences in orientation between the two types of newspapers, we also expected to find some common themes and emphases in the news coverage, primarily because all media institutions operate in an environment of common commercial, organizational, and cultural pressures.

In this concluding chapter, we first outline the specific ways we believe the general circulation and ethnic minority media participated in the process of racial formation. By telling the story of interethnic conflict in specific ways, these newspapers help define how issues of race and race relations are understood in the United States. By examining this news coverage, we hope to show how the articles construct narratives about interethnic conflict and how these texts relate to racial formation. We also offer some insight into the important role that ethnic minority newspapers assume in offering an alternative perspective on racial life in the United States. These papers provide a vital public service by fleshing out a range of views not covered by the general circulation papers. Indeed, without the perspectives provided by ethnic minority papers, there would be few or no truly competing views in the public sphere about interethnic relations among ethnic minority groups.

Main News Narratives

The coverage of race relations in all the papers focused on race as conflict. With few exceptions, any time the news mentioned interaction of two or more ethnic minority groups, the main theme was conflict. This unrelenting focus in all the newspapers speaks to a prevailing journalistic bias toward conflict in coverage of race relations. It is why the analysis for this book began with an attempt to look at news about all aspects of race relations among ethnic minority groups and ended as an exploration of ethnic minority groups in conflict in Miami, Washington, D.C., and Los Angeles.

Within this context, the newspapers produced three patterns of coverage through certain framing choices for representing racial conflict. These choices resulted in themes that then channeled the narratives in specific rhetorical directions and, importantly, away from other possible directions and understandings. Three such patterns were readily apparent in the coverage. They were (1) definition of problems and solutions, (2) characterization of heroes and villains, and (3) debate over "American-ness."

A Focus on Problems and Solutions

To some extent, almost every newspaper discussed individual, institutional, and structural causes and solutions for a variety of problems. In the general circulation newspapers, a predominant narrative is that individual actions cause and can then solve various problems. In the ethnic minority newspapers, however, the problems have primarily institutional-level and structural-level causes and solutions.

Problems

In Miami and Washington, D.C., the general circulation press attributed the disturbances to confrontations between individual Blacks and Latinos, whether they were ordinary citizens, community leaders, police officers, or other government officials. In Los Angeles, the *Los Angeles Times* depicted the disturbances primarily as a conflict between Black rioters and Korean

American store owners, and to a lesser extent between Blacks and police. In general circulation news coverage in each of the three cases, shortcomings of individuals or ethnic groups—such as inappropriate values, bad behavior or intentions, or failure to assimilate—were given much attention as causes of conflict. In the *Miami Herald,* Latinos discriminating against Blacks, White police officers' brutality against Blacks, and inadequate values of Blacks appeared as causes of conflict. In the *Washington Post,* it was the skirmish between Officer Jewell and Gomez, along with a number of inappropriate behaviors and values of Latinos, that caused the conflict. In Los Angeles, the *Los Angeles Times* said bad values, Korean American insularity, and incompetent people in government and in the police force were to blame for the conflicts.

In the ethnic minority press, the focus was more on institutional and structural causes as explanations for the disturbances. Although the Black press often cited parts of the Black community and individuals within other minority communities as contributing factors to the riots, in each of the three cases, this ethnic press focused on the oppressive nature of structural conditions such as economic inequity, lack of resources, unemployment, and so on. In addition, the Black press cited White racism and White-dominated institutions such as the police, media, and judicial system, and Blacks (particularly Black leaders and the Black middle class) unwilling to help other Blacks as underlying causes. The *New York Amsterdam News* named capitalism and elites as causes of the problems. The *Miami Times* presented similar reasons but added discrimination by the city government. The coverage also explicitly mentioned Whites in their affiliations with various institutions as causes of the problems. In the coverage of Los Angeles, the Black press infrequently mentioned Korean Americans as primary culprits. When another ethnic minority group appears in the Black press, it is typically Latinos—especially in Miami and Washington, D.C.

La Opinión depicted Latinos and Blacks fighting in an alliance against various institutional actors and agencies that the paper viewed as major causes of the disturbances. *La Opinión* cited a sense of hopelessness and desperation and Black and White politicians as causes. In *El Nuevo Herald,* however, the focus was solely on the inadequate values and work habits of Blacks as the cause of the disturbances.

In the Asian American press, Black rioters are part of the disturbances, but the main causes are major institutions such as government agencies that failed to deal with Blacks' problems. The Asian American press also pointed to Black rioters, Blacks' misunderstanding of Korean culture, and insensitive politicians and police as causes. In addition, these newspapers frequently observed that White (general circulation) newspapers' depiction of the supposedly "inherent" conflict between Blacks and Asian Americans contributed to the riots. Many writers suggested that without the incendiary messages coming from White newspapers, the riots may not have happened, or at least would have been much less severe. For the Asian American press, Asian American store owners are the main victims, but the papers also regularly point out White institutions oppressing Blacks.

Solutions

In all three cases, ethnic minorities were the primary actors and the primary victims. The coverage infrequently mentioned Whites as actors or victims—except in Los Angeles where Reginald Denny was the subject of several articles. In the general circulation newspapers, the narrative theme of individuals causing problems is specifically played out as ethnic minority groups either hurting their own neighborhoods or, as in Los Angeles, hurting other ethnic minorities. Because the general circulation news coverage understood the problems as created by individuals, it also emphasized solutions that could be enacted by individuals. In Miami, Black self-help measures received much coverage, along with the need for police officers to improve community relations. In Washington, D.C., improvement of Spanish-language skills by police officers was one of the main solutions discussed. The *Los Angeles Times* was somewhat exceptional in that it suggested a more varied range of solutions, such as enhanced solidarity across ethnic groups, private investment, political mobilization, and ethnic business development.

The ethnic minority newspapers presented a wider range of solutions. Almost every newspaper mentioned enhanced interethnic cooperation and unity as a possible solution to racial tensions. Similarly, most ethnic minority newspapers suggested economic investment in depressed urban areas to improve access to resources for poor minority groups. In addition, there was near unanimity among the ethnic minority press in the call for political mobilization, grassroots organization, and development of ethnic businesses.

Conflict Involves Heroes and Villains

Usually, the coverage explained the interethnic conflicts in relatively simplistic terms of heroes and villains. Although members of the same group or a specific institutional actor are sometimes both hero and villain, the overall explanations are seldom more complicated than a story about "good guys" and "bad guys."

The depiction of heroes and villains typically focused on the actions of individuals. The *Miami Herald* and *El Nuevo Herald* portrayed mainly Blacks as villains for their role in the disturbances. Although reports that mention a history of brutality in policing the Black community in Miami occasionally villainized police, for both the *Miami Herald* and *El Nuevo Herald,* police are primarily heroes. *El Nuevo Herald* depicted local Latino leaders as heroes. In the *Miami Times,* police officers and city government officials are villains, and Blacks are the main heroes. All of the Washington, D.C., newspapers showed mainly Latinos as villains for their participation in the disturbances and, particularly in the *Washington Post* and the Black press, for their "cultural pathologies." In Los Angeles, in the *Los Angeles Times, La Opinión,* and Asian American press (though not as strongly), the villains were "lawless" Black rioters engaged in looting and arson, as well as members of local government (including the mayor and the police department). The Black press de-emphasized Blacks as villains and villainized a system of White racial oppression against Blacks.

The heroes in the *Los Angeles Times* were Good Samaritans coming to the rescue of citizens who were accidentally caught in the disturbances, the National Guard, and firefighters. Interestingly, for the Black press there were no readily identifiable heroes. In the Asian American press, Asian American store owners committed to their neighborhoods and rebuilding their businesses were heroes, as were those from Asian American communities who helped Asian Americans cope with the aftermath of the riots. In addition, the Asian American press portrayed as heroes non-Asian American outsiders who went out of their way to help people in trouble. Most often these were Blacks, and on some occasions, Latinos. In *La Opinión,* the main heroes were Latino Good Samaritans.

Minority Groups Portrayed As Un-American or "Less" American

Whites are never un-American; in fact, they usually represent the benchmark by which other groups, at least implicitly, are compared.

The patterns of representation had a bearing on the subsequent reports on the issue of "American-ness," which was used to signal a set of positive personal characteristics and qualities typically associated with Whites. In two of the cities studied—Miami and Washington, D.C.—the minority groups better suited to be Americans were those whose members held political power in the city. In Miami, Cuban residents and Nicaraguan refugees were valued as potential citizens. The *Miami Herald* depicted both groups, thought to have impeccable anticommunist credentials, as more preferable potential citizens than Haitian asylum seekers (who were, at any rate, lumped together with African Americans). *El Nuevo Herald* claimed that Blacks do not know what being a "real American" means—that is, to work hard, not complain, and be anticommunist. On the other hand, the *Miami Times* aggressively asserted the Black community's fitness to be American.

In Washington, D.C., there was no explicit statement about Blacks being preferred, but the coverage depicted Latinos—especially recent immigrants from Central America—as clearly unfit to be Americans. The *Washington Post* and the Black papers both reported claims that certain Latinos were unfit to be American, whereas *El Tiempo Latino* complained that Latino refugees were treated worse than White East European refugees even though both groups were anticommunist.

In the *Los Angeles Times*, however, there was no simple depiction of one minority group being more fit to be American than another group, even though the paper villainized Blacks more than any other group. In the coverage of Los Angeles by the Black press, the message was that Blacks have not been allowed to fully become American (i.e., having all the rights that citizens should have).

The ethnic minority newspapers examined for the Los Angeles case rarely discussed the issue of "American-ness" in the ways that the ethnic minority newspapers in Miami and Washington, D.C., did. For the Black papers that covered Los Angeles, the primary concern was with White machinations affecting Black communities. The only other group receiving any significant attention in the Black press was Latinos. Perhaps the focus on Latinos allowed the Black press to discuss the deeply embedded nature of the problems faced by urban America. Including Latinos in the discussion may have created rhetorical space for the Black press to suggest that discrimination was widespread and affected other minority communities and to indicate to its readers the possible allies in any effort at redressing the problems.

In the Asian American papers, underlying much of the discussion about merchants was the theme of immigration. However, explicit discussion of immigration status almost never came up. The assumption in the Asian American newspapers seemed to be that Asian Americans were already solidly middle class before the riots—living out the "model minority" lifestyle. They had worked and sacrificed to enter the American mainstream. But the community learned during the riots that Whites did not view them as either "American" or "White." After the riots, the major concern for the Asian American press became how to actually live out Asian Americans' pre-riot self-perception as "real" Americans.

Some Anomalies

These three patterns of presentation were not seamless, however. In other words, despite the significant weight of framing choices and the significant momentum of the subsequent narratives, there were occasional exceptions and apparent anomalies in the dominant pattern for each press. For example, the general circulation newspapers occasionally described structural-level explanations for the disturbances. Also, the general circulation press occasionally depicted Blacks as heroes in Miami, Latinos as heroes in D.C., and Blacks and police as heroes in Los Angeles. Again in the general circulation press, a small number of news stories pointed out the dominance of key institutions by Whites in each city. Finally, the *Los Angeles Times* printed stories that challenged the notion that the cultural history of the United States is exclusively rooted in Europe.

Among the other unexpected findings was the comparatively scant attention the *Washington Post* and *El Tiempo Latino* gave to Blacks during the Washington, D.C., riots compared to the city's large Black population and the active participation of Black youths in the disturbances there. All other newspaper coverage in the three cities mentioned Blacks in one half or more of the stories analyzed.

Equally anomalous, perhaps, was the pattern in coverage of Latinos in Los Angeles. Only the Black newspapers and *La Opinión* mentioned Latinos in a large proportion of articles. The *Los Angeles Times* and the Asian American newspapers covered Latinos relatively infrequently. When the press coverage of Los Angeles mentioned Latinos in any of the articles, there was almost no mention of the fact that most of those arrested were Latinos, let alone a serious discussion of what this fact indicated about race relations in Los Angeles.

Given the impetus for ethnic minority papers to insulate their communities from criticism, that *La Opinión* might overlook the significance of the patterns of arrests is self-explanatory. However, that the *Los Angeles Times* and the Asian American newspapers brought little attention to Latinos is perplexing. One possible explanation may be the tendency for journalists to write about race relations as binary relationships. Most news coverage analyzed in this book presented relations among the groups in terms of links between Blacks and Latinos, Whites and non-Whites, Asian Americans and Latinos, or Asian Americans and Blacks, and almost never as a relationship among the four main ethnic groups. Perhaps we can explain this failure to report more complex interethnic conflict by considering the civic agendas of the papers. For example, the Black papers depicted the Latino and Black communities as bound together by their shared experience of abuse by White institutions. Thus, both Blacks and Latinos were worthy of compassion and concern. Portraying Latinos as troublesome may have undermined the narrative of ethnic minorities as worthy victims of White racism.

The focus of the Asian American papers was on Blacks, so Asian American concerns may have viewed the arrest record of Latinos as irrelevant. The *Los Angeles Times* also appeared more concerned about the role of Blacks than of Latinos, perhaps reasoning that its partner *La Opinión* would cover the Latino angle of the story. In any case, an important part of the story of the disturbances and who was involved was left untold.

News Narratives and Racial Formation

The power of racial hegemony is its ability simultaneously to mask and perpetuate what lies at its core, while at the same time perpetuating it. For this study, that means the operation of White privilege and its conceptual partner racial hierarchy are largely unrecognized even while they are constantly constructed and reconstructed as an important part of racial formation. The general circulation and ethnic minority newspapers—racial projects examined in this book—operate within a single prevailing racial hegemony that structures their representations of race, though each set of newspapers is not identical in the ways they depict interethnic conflict. In this section, we briefly outline the ways in which the newspapers discuss White privilege and racial hierarchy, two important elements of racial hegemony, and the role of these depictions in racial formation.

White Privilege

The literature on the political economy of Miami, Washington, D.C., and Los Angeles indicates long-term control of banking, real estate, media, and other key institutions by Whites, even though the political leadership in these cities at the time of the disturbances involved non-Whites in significant numbers. However, there was almost no discussion of White economic power and control of key resources by the general circulation papers in the three cities examined. In fact, the general circulation press mentioned Whites in relatively few stories even when they were involved in significant ways in the disturbances. In Miami, the coverage mentioned White police racism but not racism by Whites generally. In Washington, D.C., coverage barely mentioned Whites in any of the stories. In Los Angeles, coverage mentioned Whites when they are sympathetic victims such as Reginald

Denny. However, the *Los Angeles Times* more than the other general circulation papers raised issues of White privilege and questioned the idea that "White" is equivalent to "American." The relative absence of discussion of White privilege is indicative of the way hegemony works to absorb or neutralize opposition. To seriously analyze Whiteness and its privileges would be a severe breach of existing racial hegemony. Thus, although the general circulation press occasionally mentioned White privilege, it appears without a critical edge.

By largely ignoring the role of Whites and the impact of White privilege, the general circulation press, as a racial project, participates in the process of racial formation by linking culture and structure in specific ways. The general circulation press avoids discussion of certain structural issues such as power holding and how that affects local distribution of resources and how the three cities historically marginalized ethnic minorities. The general circulation press emptied certain structures of social organization of their race-based power, representing them as neutral and objective arbiters of resource distribution. As a result, the cultural representation of racial bodies (Blacks, Latinos, and Asian Americans) and their associated lifestyles—coded variously in positive and negative terms—become the only explanations for behavior. These explanations of racial strife are typically oversimplified, focusing on direct and immediate causes, which often blame the victims of discrimination and racism themselves because, again, the structures imbued with White privilege have been "de-racialized." Consequently, the general circulation press absolves portions of the majority White community from taking responsibility for their roles in the marginalization of non-White communities. Emphasizing these patterns promotes and reinforces a certain kind of racial ideology—one that posits Whiteness as a norm and non-Whiteness as deviant—as a hegemonic racial formation of ideas and values.

In terms of the ethnic minority press, there is explicit discussion of White power and privilege if we consider the ethnic minority papers as a group. The *Miami Times* made mention of White racism and institutional racism, which in many respects was the same issue in Miami in 1989. *El Nuevo Herald* followed the lead of the general circulation press and downplayed White actors and their actions. In Washington, D.C., the African American papers did not explicitly mention White privilege but referred to it indirectly. *El Tiempo Latino* did not mention White privilege at all. In Los Angeles, the Black press and Asian American press made strong links between economic power and White privilege, whereas *La Opinión* also made linkages, but somewhat less forcefully. Thus, there is more discussion of White privilege in the ethnic minority press, and these discussions are more likely than in the general circulation newspapers to make explicit links between control of economic and symbolic resources by Whites and their relationship to civil unrest. As racial projects, the ethnic minority press, unlike the general circulation press, does not divert attention away from Whites' hold on power and the resulting unequal distribution of resources and interethnic conflict in U.S. cities. Ethnic minority newspapers show the race-based power of social structure and provide cultural representations of the ways these structures affect racial bodies in ways that may lead to unrest. Unlike the general circulation press, the ethnic minority newspapers do not absolve Whites that hold community power of responsibility for creating conditions leading to the disturbances.

But similar to the general circulation press, however, the ethnic minority papers do tend to cast blame on certain minority groups. For example, even while expressing sympathy, *El Nuevo Herald* blames Blacks for the Miami disturbances, and the African American press blames Latinos for the disturbances in Washington, D.C. In Los Angeles, the Black press, although blaming White institutions as the root of the racial tensions, also took to task much of the Black community—rioters, the middle class, and Black businesses. Also similar to the general circulation newspapers, the ethnic minority press did not depict interethnic coalition building as a consistent priority among ethnic groups. For example, the Black press coverage of Los Angeles, although at times noting the need for Blacks to form coalitions with other communities of color, did not encourage linkages with Asian Americans. In fact, the Black papers offered no substantive coverage of how Black communities or institutions had reached out to Asian Americans. Each story about bridge building in the Black press was about projects initiated *by* Asian Americans. *La Opinión* not only sympathized with the Black community but also proposed unity between Blacks and Latinos in fighting police brutality and racism. However, the *La Opinión* did not include Korean Americans in the proposed coalition. The Asian American press emphasized coalitions among Asian American groups and coalitions with Blacks, encouraged government assistance for poor Blacks, and were more likely to spread the blame to (White) politicians, rioters, and even to members of the Asian American community.

Racial Hierarchy

Accompanying the practices of White privilege, as we noted in the introduction, is the creation of racial hierarchy, in which Whites are situated at the top (but rarely discussed, as the empirical results have shown), and non-Whites are arrayed below. This hierarchical organization tends to create homogenized cultural knowledge of non-Whites. For example, both the general circulation press and ethnic minority press frequently failed to consistently distinguish among non-White groups. In Miami, the *Miami Herald* and the *Miami Times* generally did not differentiate between African Americans and West Indians. In Washington, D.C., the *Washington Post, El Tiempo Latino,* and the African American papers made no distinctions among the various Central American immigrant groups. The *Los Angeles Times,* Black press, and *La Opinión* conflated recent Korean immigrants with Korean Americans in Los Angeles. Surprisingly, the Asian American press, although generally describing Blacks as one group, was more likely than Black papers to note ethnic differences among Blacks.

Racial hierarchy also assumes that the cultures, morals, sensibilities, and temperaments of Whites are superior and more desirable than those of Asian Americans, Latinos, African Americans, and other groups considered to be lower in the racial hierarchy. In addition, racial hierarchy in the United States is anchored, in the American cultural imagination, at the top by Whites and at the bottom by Blacks. Asian Americans and Latinos (and other non-White groups) move between these two poles. One dramatic example of ethnic minorities moving between the poles of the racial hierarchy, and a classic example of how the news participates in racial formation, is the depiction of the Korean Americans in Los Angeles. As described in the chapter on the *Los Angeles Times* coverage of Los Angeles, Korean Americans were transformed in news depictions from a "model minority," a position nearer to the top of the racial hierarchy, to vigilantes as many Korean American shop owners began to protect their properties and themselves by shooting at thieves. The latter portrayals of Korean Americans helped undermine the "model minority" image because aggressiveness and lawlessness are typically associated with groups near the bottom of the racial hierarchy. In the section on racial formation and news in Chapter 1, we briefly pointed out that news coverage helps to essentialize racial bodies in ways that makes racial domination an easier task. Whether Korean Americans are depicted as "good" or "bad," these cultural representations may buttress existing social structures of domination. For instance, the image of the "good" Korean American represents a normative model of behavior for Korean Americans as well as other racial minorities. This image can be deployed by Whites to suggest how racial minorities must behave if they are to "fit in" within existing social organization. On the other hand, the "bad" Korean American image can be used to justify structures of domination such as discrimination, excessive policing, segregation, and even racial violence (see Shah, 2003).

In news coverage of racial groups, the representations—general circulation press depiction of ethnic minority groups and ethnic minority newspaper depictions of Whites and ethnic minority groups—often depend on the location of the news and the ethnic affiliation of the newspaper. For example, in Miami, where the city leadership was primarily Latino, the *Miami Herald* and *El Nuevo Herald* presented Blacks primarily as violent and angry rioters. The *Miami Times,* although reporting Blacks' involvement in the disturbances, also depicted Blacks as concerned citizens decrying Black violence. Otherwise, the *Miami Times* emphasized the lack of attention to the Black community's concerns coming from Latino leaders. *El Nuevo Herald,* although expressing some sympathy toward the plight of Miami Blacks, also decried what its writers perceived as Blacks' inadequate work ethic, poor values, and questionable politics.

In Washington, D.C., where the city leadership was primarily Black, the *Washington Post* presented Latinos as violent and angry rioters. The Black press in Washington, D.C., depicted Latinos as "barbaric." *El Tiempo Latino* was more likely to emphasize a wide-ranging victimization of Latinos but infrequently discussed Black leaders and police officers doing the victimizing, much less presented Blacks negatively. The *Washington Post,* however, reported Latino criticism of Black officials and harassment by Black police officers.

In Los Angeles, the *Los Angeles Times* challenged the simple logic of racial hierarchy through stories that revealed and questioned the normalization of Whiteness. *La Opinión* also challenged racial hierarchy through a small number of stories that distinguish between "old" and "new" Latino immigrant populations, asserting that the "new" immigrants are substantially different from the "old" and may not be as fit to be American. In Los Angeles, Latinos are almost absent from the *Los Angeles Times* coverage, and Blacks are cast as the violent and angry rioters. However, the depiction of many Black heroes and only one Latino hero complicated this trend. Further complicating the pattern in Los Angeles as opposed to the coverage revealed in Miami and Washington, D.C., is that *La Opinión,* although depicting Blacks as violent and angry, also clearly depicted them as the victims of systemic oppression from government and from the Los Angeles Police Department (LAPD). In other words, *La Opinión* does not criticize the Black community in Los Angeles as severely as *El Nuevo Herald* criticized Blacks in Miami or as the Black newspapers criticized the Latino community in Washington, D.C.

Muddling the picture even further is the Black and Asian American newspapers' coverage of Los Angeles. The Black papers rarely mentioned Asian Americans, but when they did, it was as culprits in mistreating Black customers. Latinos shared the fate of Blacks as targets of racial and economic oppression. For the Asian American papers, Blacks were often the actors in attacking Asian Americans or their property, but they directed more culpability at Whites. On the other hand, there was also an attempt to illuminate the shared bonds between Blacks and Asian Americans.

Thus, on the one hand, there were the general circulation papers, which saw various ethnic minority groups aligned in a hierarchy, with Whites at the top. There seemed little appreciation that any of the lower-placed groups held much in common. On the other hand, there were several of the Black and the Latino papers (such as those in Miami and Los Angeles), which made some reference to both groups sharing in similar problems, suggesting the possibility of social or political bonds that blur typical racial or ethnic boundaries. For many of the Black papers covering Los Angeles, this link was primarily between Blacks and Latinos. In contrast, the Asian American papers' coverage of Los Angeles noted that Blacks and Asian Americans had much in common and, indeed, that bond meant that they should work together in any future efforts to rebuild.

Implications

What does this teach us about the role of the general circulation press and the ethnic minority press in terms of their roles in racial formation? One conclusion may be that the performance of the press seems related to the local political economy of race relations. Racial formation is a useful theoretical statement about the nature of race relations in the United States. It helps describe conditions and relationships that create a set of structural and cultural parameters within which relations of race emerge and transform. But what our study of news coverage of interethnic conflict in three cities shows is the importance of local political economies in structuring cultural representations of race. In the cities where one ethnic group is clearly dominant in formal politics, the general circulation press, even while solidly embedded in dominant racial ideology, aligns itself with that group. Thus, in Miami, the *Miami Herald* coverage emphasized Latino viewpoints and priorities. In Washington, D.C., the *Washington Post* rarely criticized the Black community or city leaders. In Los Angeles, however, where the city government was more racially mixed, the *Los Angeles Times* was not clearly aligned with any ethnic group and was not necessarily supportive of city officials, though the paper clearly supported conservative financial solutions for recovery. Overall, this pattern is consistent with previous research that suggests that general circulation media "reflect, refract, and amplify the concerns of power groupings in the social system" (Viswanath & Arora, 2000, p. 41).

What our study also shows is that the racial composition of groups in power appears to have little or no impact on the orientation of the general circulation newspapers. In the three cities studied, the general circulation press is more concerned with its proximity to social, economic, and political power than it is with the race of those in power. In other words, in a classic hegemonic move within the process of racial formation, the general circulation press retains its dominant status by aligning itself with the local power brokers no matter their racial status. It matters little that the governing group probably could not have come to power without tacit approval from (e.g., Miami, Washington, D.C.) or strategic alliances with (e.g., Los Angeles) centers of White power and privilege. What seems to matter most to the general circulation newspapers is the competitive edge provided by steady access to government officials, cooperation from city offices, and reliable information subsidies.

In terms of the ethnic minority papers, they often appear to be advocates for the positions of their own group regardless of the racial make-up of city government. In Miami and Washington, D.C., for instance, the Black press views Latinos as a threat. In Miami, the threat is to Black employment, social standing as Americans, and potential political power. In Washington, D.C., the threat is to employment, law and order, and American culture. In both Miami and Washington, D.C., the Spanish-language press appears to buy in to the notion of assimilation into American life and advocates for societal acceptance of Latino groups. In Los Angeles, the picture is, again, more complicated. *La Opinión* advocates for Latinos but also calls for a Latino–Black alliance in demanding social change and protecting minority rights. Calling for alliances is the pattern for the Black and Asian American newspapers also. The Black papers make a point of including Latinos in much of the discussion about who was affected by the riots and by racial and economic oppression. For the Asian American press, ties between Blacks and Asian Americans are important linchpins to economic and social recovery. Whether asserting self-interest, recognizing common interests with other communities of color, exposing White privilege and power, or challenging racial hierarchy, the ethnic minority press seems to be as concerned with power as the general circulation press. Unlike the general circulation press, however, the ethnic minority press appears to channel this concern with power, to some extent, into articulating ideologies that challenge racial hegemony of dominant groups.

In Chapter 1, we argued that "once a racial project makes a choice about how the link between culture and structure will be represented, a narrative chain follows logically and effortlessly." What we argue in addition is that the political economic conditions in the communities in which the newspapers operate influence the choices of representation. Thus, racial formation is best understood when examined as a *structurally and culturally localized process*.

A second conclusion is that the general circulation press seems more thoroughly bound than the ethnic minority press to a model of reporting that seems to result in misunderstanding interethnic conflict. In this study, the general circulation press was more likely than the ethnic minority news-papers to primarily blame individuals as causes of conflict and to propose individual actions as solutions. It was also more likely to de-emphasize the views and voices of community residents in favor of statements from city officials. The general circulation press was less willing than ethnic minority newspapers to openly discuss racism, interethnic tensions, and structural obstacles to resources such as housing and employment that are a daily feature in the lives of U.S. racial and ethnic minority groups.

In general, the differences between the general circulation press and the ethnic minority press may be summarized as the difference between a "tra-ditional" and an "alternative" approach to journalism. The following chart summarizes characteristics of these approaches in terms of several dimen-sions of news stories:

	Approach	
Story Dimension	*Traditional*	*Alternative*
Focus of story	events	process
Primary sources	officials	ordinary people
Writing style	factual	interpretative
Basis of legitimacy	science	grounded knowledge
Purpose	description	explanation/orientation

In the "traditional" model, the emphasis is on providing factual accounts of seemingly disconnected events drawing upon the words of officials and the legitimacy of science (experts, polls, statistics) as evidence to support the account. The primary purpose is to describe the event by recounting the "who, what, when, and where" (less frequently the "why" and "how") of the story. In the "alternative" model, the emphasis is on understanding how apparently discrete events fit into ongoing processes. Journalists interpret the meaning and significance of the facts rather than only letting them speak for themselves. To understand the subject they are reporting, the journalists rely not only on officials and experts but also on ordinary local people and their ground-level knowledge about the situation. The purpose of their work is to provide an explanation of why the news is relevant and a cognitive map that attempts to illuminate the significance of current events (see Shah, 1996).

Despite the obvious shortcomings of the traditional approach to journalism, the conventional wisdom, nevertheless, is that it yields the best reporting and writing and that the general circulation press is its prototypical practitioner. The general circulation press, with its White, male, middle class, and urban biases, has been criticized from many perspectives for its shortcomings, but it remains the conventional benchmark for excellence in many quarters because it is assumed that there is no better model in existence. Based on our examination of general circulation and ethnic minority newspapers and their coverage of relations among ethnic minority groups, we believe that a traditional approach does not adequately work to examine the complexity of the issues involved. The type of news produced by the application of the traditional model of journalism may do little to facilitate deliberation and discussion of pressing social concerns of the day among news consumers.

Within the racial formation process, the traditional approach serves the interests of racial hegemony because it avoids asking questions about the exercise of power, the dispensation of social justice, and the prospects for ethnic and racial survival. Raising these types of issues under the traditional reporting model is relatively difficult because it would force journalists to jettison the notion—artificial though it may be—of detached reporting and writing (See Christians, Ferré, & Fackler, 1993).

For journalism to assume a more meaningful social and civic role, it must do what the traditional model does not allow. It must raise fundamental questions about power, social justice, and culture. It must be willing to articulate racial ideologies that challenge racial hegemony. It must, in the terms of racial formation theory, signify structures of racial organization in ways that do not essentialize race and "work for" a process of racial domination. This effort requires that, whenever appropriate, journalists actively interpret facts, let ordinary people speak about their experiences, and make responsible judgments about the nature of capitalism (and racism, sexism, homophobia, patriarchy, etc.).

The two approaches to journalism are akin to ideal types, and none of the news organizations studied here match either approach perfectly. All newspapers studied in this book, to one extent or another, embody styles of reporting and writing suggested by each journalism approach. For example, newspapers in both categories focused on events *and* processes, used officials *and* community residents as sources, wrote factually *and* interpretively, and made judgments about capitalism. However, the problem, as we see it, is that the general circulation press is ultimately more likely to support the status quo of racial hegemony with White privilege and racial hierarchy at its core. Thus, as important as it might be to employ techniques of an alternative model of journalism, perhaps more important are the uses to which the alternative practices are put. In this light, it is the ethnic minority papers rather than the general circulation press that lean more heavily toward the alternative model of journalistic practice, that more often articulates racial ideologies challenging racial hegemony, and that represents more potential to contribute to progressive racial formation.

Ethnic Minority Newspapers, the Public Sphere, and Competing Visions

The ethnic minority papers are not perfect examples of the alternative model of journalism: The Black newspapers in Washington, D.C., and Los Angeles, for example, produced very few stories about the disturbances in their own cities despite the magnitude and proximity of the events. We can say the same for *El Tiempo Latino* and *El Nuevo Herald* (which reprinted several *Miami Herald* stories) and the extent of their coverage of the disturbances in their respective cities. Nevertheless, many aspects of the ethnic minority newspaper coverage of interethnic relations may be worthy of emulation. As we indicated earlier, the ethnic minority papers seem more frequently to include ordinary citizens as sources, point out structural causes for interethnic conflict, and allow reporters to explicitly interpret the facts from their positions as members of the community. The result is reporting that more accurately conveys the racial and ethnic complexity of interethnic conflict than the coverage in the general circulation press. With this style of reporting, the ethnic minority papers not only represent a guideline for reporting interethnic conflict but also become a logical location for racial projects that may challenge prevailing racial hegemony.

However, among the general circulation press and the general public, the ethnic minority newspapers are not often viewed in these terms. In fact, they are viewed, at best, as a supplement to the general circulation press and, at worst, as the propaganda arm of identity politics. In either case, many deem the journalism of the ethnic minority press to be professionally unaccomplished, self-serving, gossipy, vulgar, corrupt, and a danger to the more accomplished traditional journalism of the general circulation press. However, if we are to have a truly "public" public sphere, we must take seriously the ethnic minority papers because they provide important resources and services to ethnic minority groups in America, and they serve as an important voice for a large segment of the American population. Though not *necessarily* or *always* counterhegemonic, ethnic minority newspapers provide a valid worldview that is significantly different from the general circulation press. For communities of color, the ethnic minority press is an important source of "expert" information of a kind difficult to find in general circulation newspapers. If the public sphere is to be inclusive of multiple worldviews, as opposed to multiple perspectives on a single worldview, then the voices in the ethnic minority newspapers must be heard, taken seriously, and engaged by all public sphere participants.

We are not arguing for a kind of simple pluralism in the public sphere, because that would deny the realities of continuing differences in power and culture among ethnic groups in America. We are not advocating a model of pluralism in the public sphere that erases difference and declares a "color-blind" discursive space. Given the realities of racialized power differences in U.S. cities, such a move would amount to positioning ethnic minority media and publics in a subordinate role to the "main" public sphere and would represent another form of erasure—not only between dominant and oppressed, but also among the various subaltern groups themselves. Rather, we want to urge the cultivation of a general public sphere where differences and priorities among all groups are acknowledged, respected, and taken seriously. We argue for a public sphere that remains contestatory and vibrant but where none of the participants are expected to or feel compelled to conform to normative expectations imposed by the hegemony of dominant groups. We want to see a public sphere in which the most powerful could look to the less powerful for new ideas, new approaches, and new practices in ways that are not hegemonic but complementary, inclusive, and democratic.

But at the same time, we recognize the importance of the ethnic minority press at the heart of ethnic minority public spheres, which are independent of the general public sphere. The relationship may be one of "fluid overlap." In other words, the ethnic minority newspapers can choose the times, places, and intensity of participation in the general public sphere. With this orientation, the ethnic minority press can strengthen its position and the position of the communities it serves and can most effectively challenge racial hegemony of White institutions with alternative racial ideologies.

But it may not be enough for the ethnic minority press to challenge institutions of White privilege. Given demographic trends that suggest a huge ethnic minority presence in the United States within a decade or so, we argue further that White institutions themselves will have to share power if they are to remain credible to all Americans. In terms of what will be required of the general circulation news media, this means that they must participate in exposing White privilege and racial hierarchy and socio-economic differences based on race. They must support and share resources with the ethnic minority press. They must help convince young journalists that working within the ethnic minority press is a legitimate career choice. They must actively participate in "confessional diversity" (Christians, Ferré, & Fackler, 1993, p. 188) that promotes multiple cultures and the "survival of an array of ideologies, philosophies of life, and beliefs." Thus, what we suggest is not only that the general circulation press should emulate certain journalistic practices of the ethnic minority press, but also that it literally relinquish some measure of its hegemonic power (not merely absorb opposition) for the overall health of civil society. The alternative may be a much smaller ethnic minority presence on the news scene along with a general circulation press with little or no credibility among communities of color.

In the current global contexts of increasing corporate control of mass media, decreased state funding for public service media, and a trend toward uniformity in style and substance in general circulation news media, a healthy and vital ethnic minority press is especially crucial. Without ethnic minority newspapers, the range of issues, the diversity of voices, the breadth of explanations, the richness of vision available to the public could all shrink into a numbing narrowness that could benefit primarily those interested in maintaining the racial status quo. Ethnic minority newspapers provide cultural resources that may help us to imagine the nation in ways that challenge important aspects of racial hegemony. The ethnic minority press, to a significant extent more than the general circulation press, identifies and critiques institutions of White power and privilege, reveals the connections between racial and class-based inequities, and historically contextualizes ongoing racial oppression in America. As such, the ethnic minority press represents a vital part of a fractured, contestatory model of the public sphere. As largely counterhegemonic components within the racial formation process, ethnic minority newspapers serve an indispensable role for voicing alternative racial ideology and competing visions of America.

Appendix A

Details on Collecting Source Material

Initially, our intent for this book was to examine how different newspapers explained and described all manner of race relations involving people of color. In our previous research that explored news magazine coverage of these interactions during the 1980s and 1990s, we found that most coverage focused on conflicts; specifically, the coverage centered on "riots" in Miami, Washington, D.C., and Los Angeles (Shah & Thornton, 1994; Thornton & Shah, 1996). We found a similar pattern of coverage when we began examining newspaper articles in preparation for writing this book. We considered and then dropped the idea of examining the Black boycotts of Korean grocers in New York because the case was not comparable to the other three in which riots were the focus of coverage and, more important, the local ethnic minority press in New York gave the boycotts scant coverage.

Reading through each paper looking for the few articles on interactions proved to be extremely time consuming. However, the tendency of the press to focus on conflict when writing about race made the process much more manageable. After some time it became clear that, for the newspapers (especially the general circulation press), interethnic interaction was understood as interethnic conflict. Thus, the focus of our study became press coverage of interethnic conflict rather than interethnic relations generally.

General Circulation Newspapers

We define general circulation newspapers here as those that are owned and staffed primarily by Whites, have no official or explicit orientation toward any one racial or ethnic group in the editorial policies, and produce news they deem to be of interest to a general audience. We examined the general circulation newspapers in all three cities included in the study—*Miami Herald, Washington Post,* and *Los Angeles Times.* The *Post* and *Times* were indexed in Nexis for the time period of interest to us. The *Miami Herald* was not available on Nexis for the time period of interest to us, and we obtained the relevant issues on microfilm through interlibrary loan through the Wisconsin Historical Society library.

For the *Washington Post* and *Los Angeles Times,* we used a keyword search to identify and retrieve articles covering the events and issues relevant for our project. But after further examination, the number of articles relevant to our research dropped after we discovered that most articles, although mentioning the various ethnic groups, did not cover actual interactions among the groups.

Ethnic Minority Newspapers

The ethnic minority newspapers are those that are owned and staffed primarily by ethnic and racial minority groups, have an explicit orientation toward members of that group, and produce news of particular interest to members of that group. In contrast to the relative ease with which we searched for and retrieved articles from the general circulation press, the process for finding articles in the minority presses was much more complex. Nexis does not archive minority newspapers. For this reason, getting access to many of the minority papers was difficult or, at times, impossible. We often found ourselves hunting for them by tapping our professional networks and calling on reference librarians in several cities. Many times, we stumbled onto newspaper collections serendipitously. Because of this unique situation, we describe below the process we followed to uncover, identify, and use the articles for examination.

First we consulted the *Gale Directory of Publications and Broadcast Media* and *African American Newspapers and Periodicals: A National Bibliography* (Danky & Hady, 1998) to identify major ethnic minority newspapers in the cities of interest to our project. Based on circulation and reputation, we tagged major newspapers in Black, Asian American, and Latino communities. From that list, we identified about 34 different publications. Working from this list, we turned to Ethnic Newswatch to search for and obtain the relevant articles.

Ethnic Newswatch compiles online articles from a number of ethnic minority newspapers. Although clearly an improvement over Nexis for locating ethnic minority newspapers, Ethnic Newswatch also was limited for our purposes because some ethnic minority newspapers were not included among its catalogued items for the time periods we needed.

For example, the *New York Amsterdam News* and the *Afro-Times,* Black newspapers with large circulations, were not in the Ethnic Newswatch database for 1992. Ethnic Newswatch was also limited for us in that the database begins in 1992 and thus was not useful for the analysis of Washington, D.C., and Miami. Although Ethnic Newswatch gave us access to most of the major Black and Asian American English-language papers, it did not (again, for the time period we needed) include any Latino papers (we discuss next how we dealt with this shortcoming). We found the following papers in Ethnic Newswatch:

A. Black Newspapers

Bay State Banner

Big Red News

California Voice

Call & Post (Cleveland)

Chicago Citizen

Indianapolis Recorder

L.A. Sentinel

Michigan Citizen

New Pittsburgh Courier

Philadelphia Tribune

Portland Skanner (Oregon)

Sacramento Observer

Seattle Skanner

Sun-Reporter

B. Asian American Newspapers

AsianWeek

India Currents

Even after this effort, several key papers were still missing. To obtain a broader base for which to compare, we needed to find copies of papers not included in Ethnic Newswatch. Given our interest in material that was already quite old, the task of finding hard copies of the papers was increasingly difficult. We attempted to obtain the papers through several sources, most often via interlibrary loan and with assistance of librarians in various locations. Many of the papers did not retain copies of their own publications (due to a lack of space and/or money). Others were poorly indexed or otherwise inaccessible (they went out of business or there was no identifiable place to contact them). Thus, many fewer ethnic minority newspapers than we would have liked were available for analysis. Nonetheless, we still had access to many of the major Black newspapers and major portions of the English-language Asian American press. Least represented are newspapers oriented toward the Spanish-language market, but we have one from each city included in the analysis.

One of the ways in which we found additional ethnic minority newspapers was to tap traditional library resources. The Wisconsin Historical Society library on the grounds of the University of Wisconsin—Madison has one of the most extensive collections of Black (and to a lesser degree, Asian American and Latino) newspapers in the country. For many of the Black papers, such as the *New York Amsterdam News,* we scanned several months' worth of microfilm at the Society to identify articles pertinent for our study. We examined the following papers on microfilm:

Black newspapers: *Afro-Times, Amsterdam News, Chicago Defender, Miami Times* (through interlibrary loan)

Asian American newspapers: *India-West, News India, Pacific Citizen*

Spanish-language newspapers: *La Opinión, El Nuevo Herald*

The Asian American Studies Center library at UCLA was a key source for many of the articles from the Asian American newspapers. There, especially helpful students and staff photocopied articles that we required for analysis. We obtained relevant news articles from *Korea Times* and *KoreAm Journal* from this library.

Two papers in the analysis were available at the Library of Congress: the *Washington Afro-American* and the *Washington Informer,* both Black newspapers published in Washington, D.C. We assumed that several Latino and Black newspapers published in Washington, D.C., would be fully accessible at the Library of Congress. We inquired with the reference librarians there and learned that only two of the Black newspapers were available. Ironically, the Library of Congress, located in the same city as the *Washington Informer* and *Washington Afro-American,* did not have complete holdings for them. Hemant Shah went to Washington, D.C., asked for the specific dates of interest, and proceeded to look through each paper for the pertinent information in the *Washington Informer* and *Washington Afro-American*. In the case of Spanish-language papers, the Library of Congress held none of the titles. In the end, *El Tiempo Latino* was the only Spanish-language Washington, D.C., paper we could access. The editor of the paper, Carlos Caban, sent us the issues we required. Given its reputation as the national library of all Americans, it is troubling that the Library of Congress holdings are incomplete for so many major Black and Latino papers.

The Newspapers

Following is a city-by-city breakdown of the newspapers we ultimately analyzed in the project:

	Miami	*Washington, D.C.*	*Los Angeles*
General Circulation Press	*Miami Herald*	*Washington Post*	*Los Angeles Times*
Black Press	*Miami Times*	*Afro-American Informer*	*L.A. Sentinel* *Afro-Times* *Bay State Banner* *Big Red News* *California Voice* *Call & Post* *Chicago Defender* *Chicago Citizen* *Michigan Citizen* *New Pittsburgh Courier* *Amsterdam News* *Philadelphia Tribune* *Sacramento Observer* *Sun-Reporter*
Latino Press	*El Nuevo Herald*	*El Tiempo Latino*	*La Opinión*
Asian American Press			*AsianWeek* *India-West* *Pacific Citizen* *Korea Times* *KoreAm Journal*

Appendix B

Table 1   Number of Articles in Black Press About Interactions Among Ethnic Minority Groups

Northeast	Midwest	West
Amsterdam News 13	*Chicago Defender* 4	*L.A. Sentinel* 6
Bay State Banner 4	*Call & Post* 3	*California Voice* 1
New Pittsburgh Courier 3	*Chicago Citizen* 2	*Sun-Reporter* 1
Philadelphia Tribune 2	*Michigan Citizen* 1	*Sacramento Observer* 1
Afro-Times 2		
Big Red News 1		

Table 2   Racial/Ethnic Labels Used in Black Newspapers

Papers	Terms Used
Northeast	
New Pittsburgh Courier	Black, African American, Hispanic, White, Asian, people of color, Native American
Philadelphia Tribune	Black, African American, Latino, White, Asian, non-White
Big Red News	African American, Hispanic
Bay State Banner	Black, African American, Hispanic, Cuban, White, Asian, Korean, people of color
Afro-Times	Black, African American, Latin American, Hispanic American, White, Asian American, people of color
Amsterdam News	Black, African American, Hispanic, Latino, Mexican-American, White, Native American, Asian, Asian American, Korean, Oriental, Vietnamese, people of color
Midwest	
Call & Post (Cleveland)	Black, African American, Hispanic, Latino, Mexican, White, Asian, Korean, minorities
Chicago Citizen	Black, African American, White, Korean, rainbow
Michigan Citizen	Black, African American, Arabs, Chaldeans, Koreans, minorities
Chicago Defender	Black, African American, Hispanic, White, Korean, Arab
West	
Sacramento Observer	Black, Hispanic, White, Asian
Sun Reporter	African American, Latino, White, Asian, Korean-American, minorities
California Voice	African American, Asian, Japanese, Korean, minorities
L.A. Sentinel	Black, African American, Hispanic, Latino, White, Jewish, Korean, Asian, minorities, multiracials

Note: Three Black papers, while covering the Los Angeles disturbances, did not mention specific interactions among people of color: *Indianapolis Recorder,* Portland *Skanner,* and Seattle *Skanner.*

Table 3   Actors in Black Newspapers

	Blacks	Latinos	Koreans	Whites	Asian Americans	Ethnic Minority Groups	Police	Government
Midwest								
Call & Post	4	3	1	1	1	2	1	0
Chicago Citizen	1	0	1	0	1	1	2	2
Chicago Defender	1	0	1	2	0	0	0	0
Indianapolis Recorder	0	0	0	0	0	0	0	0
Michigan Citizen	1	0	0	0	0	1	1	1
Total	7	3	3	3	2	4	4	3
East								
Afro-Times	0	0	1	0	0	0	0	0
Amsterdam News	5	5	0	4	3	2	5	4
Bay State Banner	4	1	2	1	1	1	2	1
Big Red News	0	0	0	0	0	0	0	1
New Pittsburgh Courier	1	0	0	1	0	0	1	1
Philadelphia Tribune	0	0	0	0	0	0	0	1
Total	10	6	3	6	4	3	8	8
West								
California Voice	0	0	0	0	0	0	0	0
L.A. Sentinel	2	1	0	0	0	4	3	4
Portland Skanner	0	0	0	0	0	0	0	0
Sacramento Observer	1	0	0	0	0	1	1	0
Seattle Skanner	0	0	0	0	0	0	0	0
Sun Reporter	0	0	2	1	0	0	0	1
Total	3	1	2	1	0	5	4	5
Total	20	10	8	10	6	12	16	16

Appendix C

Table 1   Racial/Ethnic Labels Used in Asian American Newspapers

Labels	Asian Week n = 22	India-West n = 5	Pacific Citizen n = 10	Korean Times n = 72	KoreAm Journal n = 26
African American	9	1	5	50	9
Black	10	2	4	65	17
Asian	12	1	5	10	6
Asian American	7	2	6	15	5
Korean	8	3	4	68	18
Korean American	9	1	3	58	17
White	8	0	3	22	6
Hispanic	4	2	0	10	2
Latino	4	0	3	17	2

(continued)

Table 1 (continued)
Racial/Ethnic Labels Used in Asian American Newspapers

Labels: Others	Asian Week n = 22	India-West n = 5	Pacific Citizen n = 9	Korean Times n = 82	KoreAm Journal n = 26
Japanese American, Nisei	4		6	7	7
Chinese, Chinese American	4		2	7	4
Filipino, Philipino	1			2	2
Cambodian	1				2
Jew, Jewish American	2			8	2
Asian Pacific Am	1		2	4	4
Anglo, Caucasians	1		1	1	2
Indian American, Indian		4		1	
Minority, Multiethnic, Person of Color, Fellow Minority, Red, Yellow, Brown		1	5	11	10
Pakistani		1			
Afro-American, African				4	2
Chicano, Mex Am, Latin				3	3
Irish				2	
Greek				1	
Italian, Italian Americans				2	
Southeast Asian				1	
Black-Hispanic				1	
Iranian				1	
Armenian				1	
Thai					1
Vietnamese					2

Table 2   Actors and Victims in *AsianWeek*

	Actors		Victims	
	Actual	*Potential*	*Actual*	*Potential*
Government	2	0	0	0
Mayor, City Leaders	1	0	0	0
Blacks	8	2	13	0
Whites	2	0	0	3
Asian American	3	1	8	5
Japanese American	0	0	4	1
Chinese American	1	0	2	0
Korean American	7	0	14	2
Latinos	3	1	2	0
Jews	2	0	2	0

Table 3   Actors and Victims in *KoreAm Journal*

	Actors		Victims	
	Actual	*Potential*	*Actual*	*Potential*
Government	3	0	1	0
Mayor, City Leaders	3	0	2	0
Society	2	0	0	0
Blacks	12	0	9	0
Whites	4	0	1	0
Asian American	1	0	1	1
Chinese American	0	0	1	0
Korean American	9	1	17	2
Vietnamese American	0	0	0	0
Latinos	3	0	1	0
Jews	8	0	1	0

Table 4   Actors and Victims in *Korea Times*

	Actors		Victims	
	Actual	*Potential*	*Actual*	*Potential*
Government	18	3	2	4
Mayor, City Leaders	5	1	2	0
Society	7	0	7	0
Blacks	41	2	20	1
Whites	13	0	4	0
Asian American	8	0	6	2
Japanese American	2	0	2	0
Chinese American	3	0	1	0
Korean American	48	2	73	7
Vietnamese American	0	0	1	0
Other Asian American	1	0	0	0
Latinos	14	0	4	0
Jews	1	0	1	0

Table 5   Actors and Victims in *India-West*

	Actors		Victims	
	Actual	*Potential*	*Actual*	*Potential*
Government	1	1	0	0
Mayor, City Leaders	1	0	0	0
Blacks	3	1	3	0
Whites	1	0	0	1
Asian American	0	0	0	1
Korean American	0	0	2	0
Jews	0	0	1	0

Table 6   Actors and Victims in *Pacific Citizen*

	Actors		Victims	
	Actual	*Potential*	*Actual*	*Potential*
Government	1	0	0	0
Police	4	0	0	0
Blacks	2	0	3	1
Whites	0	0	1	0
Asian American	3	1	3	0
Japanese American	2	0	4	0
Chinese American	0	0	1	0
Korean American	0	0	5	0
Vietnamese American	0	0	1	0
Minority	0	0	2	0

Table 7   Detailed Themes for Each Asian American Newspaper

Theme	KoreAm Journal	Korea Times	Pacific Citizen	India-West	Asian Week
Pathology:					
Individual	0	2	0	4	0
Group	0	0	0	2	1
Invasion/	0	4	1	0	4
Immigration					
Fear:					
Indirect	8	9	8	27	5
Direct	5	3	0	3	7
Society	2	0	1	0	0
Racism:					
Individual	0	1	0	7	2
Group	3	0	2	0	1
Cultural Values:					
Individual	0	6	0	0	0
Group	10	0	1	0	3
Violence:					
Verbal	2	11	11	4	12
Person	26	0	7	4	0
Property	0	1	3	10	8
Cause:					
Individual	6	0	7	5	12
Institutional	11	0	0	0	0
Structural	1	0	4	12	0
Discontent	11	17	0	0	7
Conflict	26	57	8	4	26
Cooperation	10	43	5	4	15
Pluralism/Diversity	6	9	3	0	10
Assimilation	2	8	0	0	1
Attitudes:					
Individual	7	0	2	21	2
Group	0	1	0	5	0
Minority	13	25	5	1	14
Intersection					
Role of Race:					
Primary	5	8	13	0	16
Secondary/None	10	11	36	4	3
No Mention	0	3	1	1	1
None	2	9	3	1	9

Notes

1. We do not argue, however, that global trade, diplomatic ties, and cultural exchange only appeared in the current era, for global linkages have been a mark of human societies for centuries. Christianization, in the form of the Crusades and, later, colonial missionary work followed by Westernization and modernization are all labels for processes that could fairly be called forerunners of what is now understood as globalization (see Fair & Shah, 1997).

2. That is, "Western technology, the concentration of capital, the concentration of techniques, the concentration of advanced labor in western societies, and the stories and imagery of western societies remain the driving powerhouse" of globalization (Hall, 1997, p. 179).

3. As we address these questions, we will frequently and somewhat interchangeably use the terms *race* and *ethnicity* (and their variants). In general, we believe ethnicity is an accurate term to describe the assertion of group identity based on shared cultural history. The term *race,* on the other hand, often signals physical differences, assignment to certain categories, differences in worth, and so on. We believe that, in the United States, the most common way that most people view group differences is through racial categories based on physical differences. We want to track a somewhat different course and justify our use of both *race* and *ethnicity* as somewhat interchangeable terms by acknowledging the socially constructed—not natural—existence of race as a descriptive category. As the section on racial formation later in this chapter will show, races could be viewed as ethnic groups in the sense that "race," like ethnicity, is created through social and historical processes. So why should we retain the term *race* at all? The concept should be retained because it continues to inform the public imagination about the way the social world is structured and represented. It also should be retained in order to problematize in public discourse this popular meaning of race as physical difference.

4. We define general circulation newspapers here as those that are owned and staffed primarily by Whites, have no official or explicit orientation toward any one racial or ethnic group in their editorial policies, and produce news they deem to be of interest to a general audience. Ethnic minority newspapers are those that are owned and staffed primarily by ethnic and racial minority groups, have an explicit orientation primarily toward members of that group, and produce news of

particular interest primarily to members of that group. In this context, we do not necessarily employ the term *minority groups* in a numerical sense, not least because the groups to whom the term traditionally has been applied are, in many locations, no longer literally the minority. Instead, we employ the term in a sociopolitical sense that refers to racial and ethnic groups that endure some combination of social discrimination, economic exploitation, political oppression, and cultural marginalization. In this sense, our focus in this book is on the ethnic minority press of three groups—Blacks, Asian Americans, and Latinos—though we fully recognize that other groups can easily fall into our definition.

5. The 2000 census revealed a similar demographic breakdown. Between 1990 and 2000, the total population of Miami had increased slightly from 358,000 to 362,470. During the same time period, there was a slight increase in the White population from 11% of the total in 1990 to 12% of the total population in 2000. The Latino population increased from 63% of the total population in 1990 to 66% of the total population in 2000. The Black population, however, decreased from 25% of the total population in 1990 to about 20% of the total population in 2000. The following table, based on Miami Department of Zoning and Planning (2001) numbers, summarizes these shifts.

	1990	2000
Total Population	358,000	362,470
White	39,380 (11%)	43,496 (12%)
Latino	225,540 (63%)	239,230 (66%)
Black	89,500 (25%)	72,494 (20%)
All others	3,580 (1%)	7,249 (2%)

6. No single ethnic category label can capture the differences among the people to which the labels refer. Indeed, such categories serve to homogenize more than distinguish among people. The U.S. Census category "Hispanic," for example, refers to people from Mexico, Central and South America, as well as from Spanish-speaking Caribbean countries with diverse cultural, social, political, and historical backgrounds (Obler, 1995). In Miami, where in 1989 the ethnic mix was one of the most complex in the nation, labeling the population with convenient categories is difficult. Some Cubans and others from Central America and South America are phenotypically White but refer to themselves by a national label rather than as Hispanic or Latino. Many native White Americans recoil at being identified as "non-Hispanic Whites," and "Anglo" is a problem because a high proportion of the category is Jewish. The term "African American" is problematic because of the large number of Blacks recently immigrated from Central America, Cuba, and other parts of the Caribbean (Grenier & Stepik, 1992, p. 8). Thus, any categorical system describing the population in Miami is bound to be overly simplistic. The debate over the terms "Hispanic" and "Latino" is especially contentious in some regions of the United States (Obler, 1995). In this and subsequent chapters, we have opted to use

the term "Latino" in our writing but use "Hispanic" when the term is used in quotations from the newspaper coverage. In addition, we have chosen to refer to the primary groups in this and subsequent chapters as Blacks or African Americans, Latinos, and Whites. In Part II of this book, we will refer to Asian Americans and Korean Americans.

7. There is a long history of racial violence in Miami. Blacks and Whites have had a tense relationship since the city's founding in 1896. Segregated into a section called "Colored Town" (today know as Overtown), Blacks had to contend with harassment first from U.S. Army soldiers stationed nearby during the Spanish American War, from law enforcement officers, and from White residents generally. Lynchings, beatings, arson, and other well-known forms of discrimination against Blacks were commonplace (Porter & Dunn, 1984).

8. Black leaders' relationship with Cuba has proven to be a particularly complicated issue in Miami. In May 1990, the Cuban leadership of Miami refused to give an official welcome to Nelson Mandela when he arrived to speak to a national conference of the American Federation of State, County and Municipal Employees. A few days before his scheduled speech, Mandela had thanked Castro for his support while Mandela was in prison. The city government refused to give Mandela an official welcome, claiming "this is not a racial matter. Mr. Mandela is a confessed communist" (quoted in Croucher, 1997, p. 152). Much of Miami's Black community was extremely upset, and several leading Black professionals and business people organized a Boycott Miami movement, which urged Black groups to take their conventions and tourism plans elsewhere. The boycott continued for three years with mixed success (Croucher, 1997, pp. 142-171).

9. The 2000 census revealed that the total population of Washington, D.C., dropped between 1990 and 2000. There was slight growth in the proportion of the 2000 total population for all racial categories except Blacks. The following table based on U.S. Census Bureau figures summarizes these changes (see United States Census Bureau, 2001a).

	1990	2000
Total population	606,900	572,178
White	166,131 (27.3%)	159,178 (27.8%)
Black	395,213 (65.1%)	343,312 (60.0%)
Asian American	10,734 (1.8%)	15,189 (2.7%)
Latino	32,710 (5.4%)	44,953 (7.9%)

10. The dramatic increases in Asian American and Latino populations and accompanying decreases in White and Black populations in the city of Los Angeles continued for the last decade of the 20th century, as the 2000 census revealed. The following table shows the figures based on the 2000 census (United States Census Bureau, 2001b).

	1990	2000
Total Population	3,485,398	3,694,820
White	1,305,647 (37.46%)	1,099,188 (29.75%)
Latino	1,370,476 (39.32%)	1,719,073 (46.53%)
Asian American	14,919 (0.43%)	369,254 (9.99%)
Black	485,949 (12.94%)	415,195 (11.24%)

11. But over time, even immigrants with graduate degrees did not always obtain jobs in their field of training. Limited competency with English prevented many from passing or even taking licensing exams. Thus, many professionals suffered downward mobility. For instance, the 1990 census revealed that 43% of Asian immigrants with graduate or professional degrees did not work in managerial or professional jobs (Ong & Azores, 1994, p. 111). In addition, many in Los Angeles were hindered by a glass ceiling and forced to work in low-skilled jobs. As a result, large numbers turned to self-employment. About one in six Asian Americans in 1990 was self-employed or was an unpaid worker in a family business. Generally, these entrepreneurs are likely to be concentrated in less desirable, highly competitive business sectors. Only in manufacturing did Asians and Whites in Los Angeles work in equal proportions (about 9%). As a consequence, average self-employment income for Asians was about 80% that of Whites.

But the reality of educational attainment is that, in 1989, 46% of Koreans of working age had limited ability in English or little formal education (these were the "low-skilled" portions of the Korean population in Los Angeles). In contrast, 28% of Koreans were high skilled (Ong & Azores, 1994, p. 105). Koreans, as well as Southeast Asians, outnumbered their Asian American counterparts in high-skill areas. A majority of Filipinos and South Asians fell in the high-skill category (Ong & Azores, 1994, p. 107). These patterns of educational attainment are reflected in average incomes. In 1989, among White, Black, Southeast Asian, Korean, and Latino males in Los Angeles County, Whites had the highest incomes, followed by Blacks, Koreans, Southeast Asians, and Latinos. Latino males represented the greatest proportion of those making less than $12,000, followed by Korean, Southeast Asian, Black, and White males. About 1 in 5 Korean, 1 in 10 Southeast Asian and Black, and 1 in 16 Latino males had an income of more than $48,000 in the county in 1989. Among women, the patterns are similar. For income, White women had the highest salaries, followed by Blacks, Koreans, Southeast Asians, and Latinas. Forty-two percent of Latinas, 26% of Koreans, 25% of Southeast Asians, 11% of Blacks, and 6% of Whites had incomes of less than $12,000. Those making more than $48,000 were most likely White females (11%), followed by Koreans (9%), Blacks (5%), Southeast Asians (4%), and Latinas (2%; Ong & Azores, 1994, p. 116, Table 4.5).

References

Abelman, N., & Lie, J. (1995). *Blue dreams: Korean Americans and the Los Angeles riots.* Cambridge, MA: Harvard University Press.

Anderson, B. (1991). *Imagined communities.* London: Verso.

Appadurai, A. (1997). *Modernity at large: Cultural dimensions of modernity.* Minneapolis: University of Minnesota Press.

Blank, R. (1994). The employment strategy: Public policies to increase work and earnings. In S. Danziger, G. Sandefur, & D. Weinberg (Eds.), *Confronting poverty: Prescriptions for change* (pp. 168-204). Cambridge, MA: Harvard University Press.

Bobo, L., Zubrinsky, C., Johnson, J., & Oliver, M. (1994). Public opinion before and after a spring of discontent. In M. Balassare (Ed.), *The Los Angeles riot* (pp. 103-133). Boulder, CO: Westview Press.

Booth, W. (1998, March 2). Diversity and division: America's new wave of immigrants is changing its "melting pot" image. *Washington Post National Weekly Edition,* pp. 6-8.

Borjas, G. (1984). The impact of immigrants on the earnings of the native-born. In V. Briggs & M. Tienda (Eds.), *Immigration: Issues and policies* (pp. 83-126). Salt Lake City, UT: Olympus.

Borjas, G. (1986). The demographic determinants of the demand for Black labor. In R. Freeman & H. Holzer (Eds.), *The Black youth employment crisis* (pp. 191-232). Chicago: University of Chicago Press.

Borjas, G., & Tienda, M. (1987). The economic consequences of immigration. *Science, 235,* 645-652.

Bourdieu, P. (1977). *Outline of a theory of practice.* Cambridge, UK: Cambridge University Press.

Branigan, W. (1999, February 15). Signs of the times: Amid influx of Hispanics, some Georgia towns are drawing the line (in English). *Washington Post National Weekly Edition,* p. 29.

Butcher, K., & Card, D. (1991). Immigration and wages: Evidence from the 1980s. *American Economic Association Paper Proceedings, 81,* 292-296.

Cain, B., & Kiewiet, R. (1986, February/March). California's coming minority majority. *Public Opinion, 7,* 50-52.

Center for Immigration Studies. (1997). Five million illegal immigrants: An analysis of new INS numbers. *Immigration Review, 20,* 1-4.

Cheng, L., & Espiritu, Y. (1989). Korean businesses in Black and Hispanic neighborhoods: Study of intergroup relations. *Sociological Perspectives, 32,* 521-534.

Christians, C. G., Ferré, J. P., & Fackler, P. M. (1993). *Good news: Social ethics and the press.* New York: Oxford University Press.

Comaroff, J., & Comaroff, J. (1991). *Of revelation and revolution: Christianity, colonialism, and consciousness in South Africa.* Chicago: University of Chicago Press.

Croucher, S. (1997). *Imagining Miami.* Charlottesville: University Press of Virginia.

Dahlgren, P., & Sparks, C. (1991). *Communication and citizenship: Journalism and the public sphere.* London: Routledge.

Danky, J., & Hady, M. (1998). *African American newspapers and periodicals: A national bibliography.* Cambridge, MA: Harvard University Press.

Davis, M. (1990). *City of quartz.* New York: Vintage.

Davis, M. (1995). The social origins of the referendum. *NACLA Report on the Americas, 29,* 24-28.

Davis, M. (2000). *Magical realism: Latinos reinvent the US city.* London: Verso.

Diamond, E. (1993). *Behind the times: Inside the new* New York Times. New York: Villard Books.

Diamond, J. (1998). African-American attitudes towards United States immigration policy. *International Migration Review, 32,* 451-470.

Donnely, H. (1982). Welcome mat wearing thin? Refugees put growing strain on welfare programs. *Congressional Quarterly Weekly Report, 33,* 963-968.

Dunn, M. (1997). *Black Miami in the twentieth century.* Gainesville: University of Florida Press.

Dunn, M., & Stepick, A. (1992). Blacks in Miami. In G. J. Grenier & A. Stepick III (Eds.), *Miami now!* (pp. 41-56). Gainesville: University of Florida Press.

Dyer, R. (1997). *White.* London: Routledge.

Eade, J. (1997). *Living the global city.* London: Routledge.

Emery, M., & Emery, E. (1996). *The press and America: An interpretive history of the mass media* (8th ed.). Boston: Allyn & Bacon.

Fair, J. E., & Shah, H. (1997). Continuities and discontinuities in communication and development research since 1958. *Journal of International Communication, 4,* 3-23.

Felsenthal, C. (1993). *Power, privilege and the* Post. New York: G. P. Putnam's Sons.

Field Institute. (1988). *Statistical tabulations from the February 1988 survey of the Field Institute on ethnic minorities.* San Francisco: Field Institute.

Fine, M., Weis, L., Powell, L., & Wong, L. M. (1997). *Off white: Readings on race, power and society.* New York: Routledge.

Fiske, J. (1993). *Power plays, power works.* London: Routledge.

Fix, M., & Passel, J. (1994). *Immigration and immigrants: Setting the record straight.* Washington, DC: Urban Institute.

Frankenberg, R. (1993). *White women, race matters: The social construction of Whiteness.* Minneapolis: University of Minnesota Press.

Frankenberg, R. (1997). Local Whitenesses, localizing Whiteness. In R. Frankenberg (Ed.), *Displacing Whiteness: Essays in social and cultural criticism* (pp. 1-33). Durham, NC: Duke University Press.

Freeman, R., & Holzer, H. (1991). *The deterioration of employment and earnings opportunities for less educated young* Americans: A review of evidence. Unpublished manuscript.

Frey, W. (1993). The new urban revival. *Urban Studies, 30,* 741-774.

Frey, W., & Tilove, J. (1995, August 20). Immigrants in, native Whites out. *New York Times,* pp. A44-45.

Fuchs, L. (1983). Immigration, pluralism and public policy: The challenge of pluribus to the unum. In M. M. Kritz (Ed.), *U.S. immigration and refugee policy: Global and domestic issues* (pp. 289-315). Lexington, KY: Lexington Books.

Fuchs, L. (1990). The reactions of Black Americans to immigration. In V. Yans-McLaughlin (Ed.), *Immigration reconsidered: History, sociology and politics* (pp. 293-314). Oxford, UK: Oxford University Press.

Fukurai, H., Krooth, R., & Butler, E. (1994). The Rodney King beating verdicts. In M. Baldassare (Ed.), *The Los Angeles riots: Lessons for the urban future* (pp. 73-102). Boulder, CO: Westview Press.

Gabriel, J. (1998). *Whitewash: Racialized politics and the media.* London: Routledge.

Gallup Poll. (1993). *The Gallup public opinion poll 1992.* Wilmington, DE: Gallup Poll.

Gamson, W. (1989). News as framing: Comments on Graber. *American Behavioral Scientist, 33,* 157-161.

Gandy, O. (1998). *Communication and race: A structural perspective.* London: Arnold.

Gillette, H. (1995). *Between justice and beauty: Race, planning and the failure of urban policy in Washington D.C.* Baltimore, MD: Johns Hopkins University Press.

Giroux, H. (1996). *Fugitive Cultures: Race, Violence and Youth.* London: Routledge.

Gitlin, T. (1980). *The whole world is watching.* Berkeley: University of California Press.

Goldberg, D.T. (1993). *Racist culture: Philosophy and the politics of race.* London: Basil Blackwell.

Gray, H. (1987). Race relations as news. *American Behavioral Scientist, 30,* 381-396.

Grenier, G. J., & Stepick, A. (1992). Introduction. In G. J. Grenier & A. Stepick (Eds.), *Miami now!* (pp. 1-17). Gainesville: University of Florida Press.

Hahn, H., Klingman, D., & Pachon, H. (1976). Cleavages, coalitions and the Black candidates: The Los Angeles mayoralty elections of 1969 and 1973. *Western Political Quarterly, 55,* 507-520.

Hall, S. (1975). Introduction. In A.C.H. Smith (Ed.), *Paper voices: The popular press and social change, 1935-1965* (pp. 11-24). Totowa, NJ: Rowman and Littlefield.

Hall, S. (1982). The whites of their eyes: Racist ideologies in the media. In G. Bridges & R. Brundt (Eds.), *Silver linings: Some strategies for the eighties* (pp. 28-52). London: Lawrence and Wishart.

Hall, S. (1997). The local and the global: Globalization and ethnicity. In A. McClintock, A. Mufti, & E. Shohat (Eds.), *Dangerous liaisons: Gender, nation and postcolonial perspectives* (pp. 173-187). Minneapolis: University of Minnesota Press.

Hamamoto, D. (1994). *Monitored peril: Asian Americans and the politics of TV representation*. Minneapolis: University of Minnesota Press.

Hamamoto, D. Y., & Torres, R. D. (Eds.). (1997). *New American destinies: A reader in contemporary Asian and Latino immigration*. New York: Routledge.

Harris, D. (1994). Generating racial and ethnic conflict in Miami: Impact of American foreign policy and domestic racism. In J. Jennings (Ed.), *Blacks, Latinos and Asians in urban America: Status and prospects for politics and activism* (pp. 79-94). Westport, CT: Praeger Publishers.

Hart, J. (1981). *The information empire: The rise of the* Los Angeles Times *and the* Times Mirror Company. Washington, DC: University Press of America.

Hartly, J. (1996). *Popular reality: Journalism, modernity, and popular culture.* London: Arnold.

Harwood, E. (1986). American public opinion and U.S. immigration policy. *Annals of the American Academy of Political and Social Science, 487,* 201-212.

Heer, D. (1996). *Immigration in America's future: Social science findings and the policy debate.* Boulder, CO: Westview Press.

Henry, W. A. (1990, September 19). Beyond the melting pot. *Time, 146,* 28.

Jacobs, R. (2000). *Race, media, and the crisis of civil society.* Cambridge, UK: Cambridge University Press.

Jennings, K., & Lusane, C. (1994). The state and future of Black/Latino relations in Washington, D.C.: A bridge in need of repair. In J. Jennings (Ed.), *Blacks, Latinos and Asians in urban America: Status and prospects for politics and activism* (pp. 57-77). Westport, CT: Praeger Publishers.

Jesse Jackson Goes to Cuba. (1984, July 9). *Newsweek, 104,* pp. 16-17.

Johnson, J., Farrell, W., & Guinn, C. (1997). Immigration reform and the browning of America: Tensions, conflicts and community instability in metropolitan Los Angeles. *International Migration Review, 31,* 1055-1095.

Johnson, J., & Oliver, M. (1989). Interethnic minority conflict in urban America: The effects of economic and social dislocations. *Urban Geography, 10,* 449-463.

Johnson, J., & Oliver, M. (1992). Economic restructuring and Black male joblessness: A reassessment. In G. Peterson and W. Vrohman (Eds.), *Urban labor market and job opportunity* (pp. 113-147). Washington, DC: Urban Institute.

Johnson, J. H., & Oliver, M. (1994). Interethnic minority conflict in urban America: The effects of economic and social dislocation. In F. L. Pincus & H. J. Ehrlich (Eds.), *Contending views on prejudice, discrimination, and ethnoviolence* (pp. 206-218). Boulder, CO: Westview Press.

Kasarda, J. (1983). Entry-level jobs, mobility and urban minority unemployment: Their impact is obvious. *Urban Affairs Quarterly, 19,* 21-40.

Kirschenman, J., & Neckerman, K. (1991). "We'd love to hire them but . . .": The meaning of race for employers. In C. Jencks & P. Peterson (Eds.), *The Urban Underclass* (pp. 28-100). Washington, DC: Brookings Institute.

LaLonde, R., & Topel, R. (1991). Immigrants in the American labor market: Quality assimilation and distributional effects. *American Economic Association Paper Proceedings, 81,* 297-302.

Luttwick, E. (1992, May 15). The riots: Underclass vs. immigrants. *New York Times,* p. A15.

Martin, J. (1995). Immigration contributes over half of U.S. population growth. *Immigration Review, 23,* 1-4.

McClain, P., & Karnig, A. (1990). Black and Hispanic socioeconomic and political competition. *American Political Science Review, 84,* 535-545.

Merrill, J., & Fischer, H. (1980). *The world's great dailies: Profiles of 50 newspapers.* New York: Hastings House.

Miami Department of Planning and Zoning. (2001). *Miami-Dade County facts.* Miami, FL: Author.

Miles, J. (1992, October). Blacks and browns. *Atlantic Monthly, 270,* 41-68.

Miller, S. (1987). *The ethnic press in the United States: A historical analysis and handbook.* Westport, CT: Greenwood Press.

Moss, P., & Tilly, C. (1991). *Why Black men are doing worse in the labor market: A review of supply-side and demand expectations.* Unpublished manuscript, Social Sciences Research Council Subcommittee on Joblessness and the Underclass, Washington, DC.

Mumford, L. (1991). *The city in history: Its origins, its transformations, and its prospects.* Harmondsworth, UK.

Murray, H. (1990). Paul Robeson: A perspective. *Journal of Ethnic Studies, 18,* 125-142.

Nakayama, T. K. (1988). Model minority and the media: Discourse on Asian America. *Journal of Communication Inquiry, 12,* 65-73.

Obler, S. (1995). *Ethnic labels, Latino lives.* Minneapolis: University of Minnesota Press.

Ojito, M. (2000, June 5). Best of friends, worlds apart. *New York Times.* Retrieved October 3, 2001, from www.nytimes.com/library/national/race/0605000jito-cuba.html

Oliver, M., & Johnson, J. (1984). Inter-ethnic conflict in an urban ghetto: The case of Blacks and Latinos in Los Angeles. *Social Movements, Conflict and Change, 6,* 57-94.

Omi, M., & Winant, H. (1994). *Racial formation in the United States: From the 1960s to the 1990s.* London: Routledge.

Ong, P., & Azores, T. (1994). Asian immigration in Los Angeles: Diversity and divisions. In P. Ong, E. Bonachich, & L. Cheng (Eds.), *The new Asian immigration in Los Angeles and global restructuring* (pp. 100-129). Philadelphia: Temple University Press.

Perez, L. (1992). Cuban Miami. In G. J. Grenier & A. Stepick III (Eds.), *Miami now!* (pp. 83-108). Gainesville: University of Florida Press.

Pieterse, J. N. (1992). *White on Black: Images of Africa and Blacks in Western popular culture.* New Haven, CT: Yale University Press.

Porter, B., & Dunn, M. (1984). *The Miami riots of 1980: Crossing the bounds.* Lexington, MA: D. C. Heath and Company.

Reitz, J. (1998). *Warmth of welcome: The Social causes of economic success for immigrants in different nations and cities.* Boulder, CO: Westview Press.

Report of the National Advisory Commission on Civil Disorders. (1968). New York: Bantam.

Rodriguez, A. (1999). *Making Latino news: Race, language, class.* Newbury Park, CA: Sage.

Rose, H. M. (1989). Blacks and Cubans in metropolitan Miami's changing economy. *Urban Geography, 10,* 464-486.

Saltzstein, A., & Sonenshein, R. (1991). Los Angeles: Transformation of a governing coalition. In H. V. Savitch & J. C. Thomas (Eds.), *Big city politics in transition* (pp. 189-201). Newbury Park, CA: Sage.

Sassen, S. (2001). *The global city: New York, London, Tokyo* (2nd ed.). Princeton, NJ: Princeton University Press.

Scott, A. (1988a). Flexible production systems and regional development: The rise of new industrial spaces in North America and Western Europe. *International Journal of Urban and Regional Research, 12,* 171-186.

Scott, A. (1988b). *Metropolis: From division of labor to urban form.* Berkeley: University of California Press.

Shah, H. (1994). News and the self-production of society: *Times of India* coverage of caste conflict and job reservations in India. *Journalism Monographs, 144,* 1-47.

Shah, H. (1995). Race, nation, and news in the United States. *The Electronic Journal of Communication/La Revue Electronique de Communication, 5.*

Shah, H. (1996). Modernization, marginalization, and emancipation: Toward a normative model for journalism and national development. *Communication Theory, 6,* 143-166.

Shah, H. (1999). Race, nation, and citizenship: Asian Indians and the idea of Whiteness in the US press, 1906-1923. *Howard Journal of Communication, 10,* 249-269.

Shah, H. (2003). "Asian" culture and Asian American identities in US television and films. *SIMILE, Studies in Media & Information Literacy Education, 3(3).* Retrieved August 1, 2003, from www.utpjournals.com/simile/

Shah, H., & Thornton, M. (1994). Racial ideology in U.S. mainstream news magazine coverage of Black–Latino interaction, 1980-1992. *Critical Studies in Mass Communication, 11,* 141-161.

Simon, R. (1993). Old minorities, new immigrants: Aspirations, hopes and fears. *Annals of the American Academy of Political and Social Sciences, 530,* 61-73.

Smiley, N. (1974). *Knights of the fourth estate: The story of the* Miami Herald. Miami, FL: E. A. Seeman.

Sojas, E., Morales, R., & Wolff, G. (1983). Urban restructuring: An analysis of social and spatial change in Los Angeles. *Economic Geography, 58,* 221-235.

Sonenshein, R. (1993). *Politics in Black and White: Race and power in Los Angeles.* Princeton, NJ: Princeton University Press.

Starr, P., & Roberts, A. (1982). Attitudes toward new Americans: Perceptions of Indochinese in nine cities. In C. Marrett & C. Leggon (Eds.), *Research in Race and Ethnic Relations* (Vol. 3, pp. 165-186). Greenwich, CT: JAI Press.

Stepick, A. (1992). The refugees nobody wants: Haitians in Miami. In G. J. Grenier & A. Stepick (Eds.), *Miami now!* (pp. 57-82). Gainesville: University of Florida Press.

Stepick, A., & Grenier, G. J. (1993). Cubans in Miami. In J. Moore & R. Pinderhughes (Eds.), *In the barrios: Latinos and the underclass debate* (pp. 79-100). New York: Russell Sage Foundation.

Sturdevant, S. P., & Stoltzfus, B. (Eds.). (1993). *Let the good times roll: Prostitution and the U.S. military in Asia.* New York: New Press.

Tarver, H. (1994). Language and politics in the 1980s: The story of US English. In F. L. Pincus & H. J. Ehrlich (Eds.), *Contending views on prejudice, discrimination, and ethnoviolence* (pp. 206-218). Boulder, CO: Westview Press.

Thornton, M. (1995). Population dynamics and ethnic attitudes: The context of American education in the twenty-first century. In C. Grant (Ed.), *Education for diversity: An anthology of multicultural voices* (pp. 17-32). Boston: Allyn & Bacon.

Thornton, M., & Mizuno, Y. (1995). Religiosity and Black adult feelings toward Africans, American Indians, West Indians, Hispanics and Asian Americans. *Sociological Focus, 28,* 113-128.

Thornton, M., & Shah, H. (1996). US new magazine images of Black–Asian American relationships, 1980-1992. *The Communication Review, 1,* 497-519.

Thornton, M., & Taylor, R. (1988). Intergroup attitudes: Black American perceptions of Asian Americans. *Ethnic and Racial Studies, 11,* 474-488.

Tienda, M., & Liang, Z. (1994). Poverty and immigration in policy perspective. In S. Danziger, G. Sandefur, & D. Weinberg (Eds.), *Confronting poverty: Prescriptions for change* (pp. 330-364). Cambridge, MA: Harvard University Press.

Tienda, M., & Stier, H. (1996). The wages of race: Color and employment opportunity in Chicago's inner city. In S. Pedraza & R. Rumbaut (Eds.), *Origins and destinies: Immigration, race and ethnicity in America* (pp. 417-431). Belmont, CA: Wadsworth.

United States Census Bureau. (2001a). *Detailed race.* Retrieved May 15, 2002, from factfinder.census.gov

United States Census Bureau. (2001b). *Racial/ethnic composition of cities by numbers, Los Angeles County, 2000 Census.* Retrieved May 15, 2002, from www.losangelesalmanac.com

United States Commission on Civil Rights. (1987). *Recent activities against citizens and residents of Asian descent.* Washington, DC: U.S. Commission on Civil Rights.

United States Commission on Civil Rights. (1993). *Racial and ethnic tensions in American communities: Poverty, inequality, and discrimination: Vol. I. The Mount Pleasant report*. Washington, DC: Author.

Veciana-Suarez, A. (1990). *Hispanic media: Impact and influence*. Washington, DC: Media Institute.

Viswanath, K., & Arora, P. (2000). Ethnic media in the United States: An essay on their role in integration, assimilation, and social control. *Mass Communication & Society 3*, 39-56.

Warren, C. L., Corbett, J. G., & Stack, J. F. (1990). Hispanic ascendancy and tripartite politics in Miami. In R. P. Browning, D. R. Marshall, & D. H. Tabb (Eds.), *Racial politics in American cities* (pp. 155-178). New York: Longman.

Welcome to America: The Immigrant Backlash. (1995, November/December). *NACLA Report on the Americas, 29*(3), 13.

Wilson, W. J. (1987). *The truly disadvantaged: The inner city, the underclass and public policy*. Chicago: University of Chicago Press.

Winant, H. (1994). *Racial conditions: Politics, theory, comparisons*. Minneapolis: University of Minnesota Press.

Wolseley, R. (1990). *The Black press, USA*. Ames: University of Iowa Press.

Wong, M. (1986). Post-1965 Asian immigrants: Where do they come from, where are they now and where are they going? *Annals of the American Academy of Political and Social Science, 487*, 150-168.

Yoon, I-J. (1995). Attitudes, social distance and perceptions of influence and discrimination among minorities. *International Journal of Group Tensions, 25*, 35-56.

Index